An Introduction
to the History of
English Medieval Towns

Detail from the fourteenth-century Gough map
East is at the top, London top left, Gloucester at the foot

An Introduction
to the History of
English Medieval Towns

SUSAN REYNOLDS

Clarendon Press · Oxford
1977

Oxford University Press, Walton Street, Oxford OX2 6DP

OXFORD LONDON GLASGOW NEW YORK
TORONTO MELBOURNE WELLINGTON CAPE TOWN
IBADAN NAIROBI DAR ES SALAAM LUSAKA ADDIS ABABA
KUALA LUMPUR SINGAPORE JAKARTA HONG KONG TOKYO
DELHI BOMBAY CALCUTTA MADRAS KARACHI

© *Oxford University Press 1977*

British Library Cataloguing in Publication Data

Reynolds, Susan
    An introduction to the history of English medieval towns.
    1. Cities and towns — England   2. Cities and towns, Medieval   3. England — Social life and customs.
    I. Title
942′ .00973′2   DA110   77–30146

ISBN 0–19–822455–9

Printed in Great Britain by
William Clowes & Sons Ltd
London, Beccles and Colchester

Preface

Whoso desireth to discourse in a proper manner concerning Corporated Towns and Communities, must take-in a great variety of matter, and should be allowed a great deal of Time and Preparation. The subject is extensive and difficult. In *England* much hath been said by Writers to Puzzle and entangle, little to Clear it . . . It hath been my endeavour to remove or lessen those Doubts as I went along.

Sir Thomas Madox, preface to *Firma Burgi* (1726).

Students of medieval England can find histories of a good many towns, but very little of what would now be called 'urban history'. The tradition of English town histories has not changed much since the seventeenth century, when it was set in two main currents: the loving topographical detail exemplified by John Stow's *Survey of London* (1598) and the collection of legal and constitutional antiquities, closely based on municipal records and sometimes compiled by a municipal official, like Nathaniel Bacon's *Annals of Ipswich* (1654). Since then the stream has been muddied by nineteenth-century polemic about corruption and reform, and, sadly, not as much clarified as it should have been by the efforts of teachers and amateurs to overcome the technicalities and obscurities of town records and bring local history alive to a wide public.

At its worst the traditional town history is what Charles Gross in his pioneering *Bibliography of British Municipal History* (1897) described as 'a farrago of heterogeneous odds and ends thrown together at haphazard', which after 'vague conjectures concerning the antiquity of the borough' plunges 'abruptly into the fifteenth, sixteenth, or seventeenth century'. At its best it is a work of deep learning as well as of civic piety, with much meticulous detail from medieval documents. Yet even so its learning tends to be that of the antiquarian rather than the historian, accumulating facts rather than using them to construct arguments or answer questions of wide historical import. Few historians of medieval English towns have betrayed much interest in themes or problems which concern historians at large, or even the historians of other towns. Working in isolation, they have, not unnaturally, sometimes misunderstood the

difficult and technical evidence they have to use, and have therefore
drawn unjustified inferences from it. An example of the dangers of
parochialism is the attribution of merely local causes to general
phenomena. It is unconvincing to attribute the growth of a town
to a new bridge or castle if towns were growing all over the country
at the same time. Nor is it enough to replace parochialism by in-
sularity: it is equally inadequate to attribute the growth of English
towns to purely English conditions if towns were growing all over
Europe at the same time.

The gap between traditional town histories and the work of
professional historians has become more noticeable with the recent
growth of urban history—that is, the general and comparative study
of towns and urban society. Modern urban history has developed
fast in Britain but much less has been done here than abroad on the
Middle Ages. That is surprising in view of the start made around
the turn of the century by Charles Gross, F. W. Maitland, Mary
Bateson, and James Tait. Most later historians of medieval England
have considered towns almost exclusively in general surveys which,
perhaps inevitably, concentrate more on what is known—or thought
to be known—than on points of ignorance or controversy which
might need further investigation. Masterly writing in these has
sometimes concealed the difference between impressionistic seren-
dipity and the results of detailed research. In the last twenty years
things have slowly begun to change. Both professionals and amateurs
are beginning to look harder at medieval towns, with results that
can be seen from the titles and writers repeatedly cited in the text
and footnotes of this book. As yet, however, there is little in the
way of synthesis to bridge either the gap between amateurs and
professionals or the gulf between British and continental work.

This second gap is even more to be regretted than the first:
whereas most British professionals have given too little thought to
towns to be able to help the amateurs very much, the same cannot
be said of historians in countries like Germany or Belgium where
local history traditionally holds a more honourable place in academic
studies than it does in England. To look at some of the questions
that historians abroad ask about medieval towns, and to consider
whether some of their answers might apply to England, is like eating
meat after an exclusive diet of porridge. Continental urban history
may indeed seem too rich in ideas and theories for the British
palate, some previous work on English towns based on foreign

studies having shown signs of indigestion as a result of swallowing a few theories whole. That is not what is advocated here. Rather we ought to sample continental scholarship critically, so as to profit from all the hard thought, investigation, and mutual criticism which has already gone into the history of medieval towns elsewhere. Foreign studies too might even profit by more comparisons with the variables provided by English conditions. At present most continental urban historians, daunted perhaps by the technicalities of Tait's *Medieval English Borough*, accept the usual English claim to uniqueness and leave English towns more or less alone. Among historians—as opposed to archaeologists—the gap between continental and British work is especially noticeable in the early Middle Ages, so that even Martin and McIntyre's *Bibliography of British and Irish Municipal History* (1972), whose *obiter dicta* on their own constitute a notable contribution to medieval urban history, states: 'Before 1066 there seems to be little common ground between continental and English towns'. If this is as true of towns as it is of their historians, then an investigation of why, how far, and in what ways, would raise a mass of important questions. However tentative the answers they could not fail to reduce the obscurity veiling English towns and might further illuminate those across the Channel.

The object of the present work, therefore, is to open up the subject, to try to distinguish what is known from what is not, and to suggest issues for investigation. It is primarily intended to ask questions rather than to answer them, and such conclusions as it draws are extremely tentative. No one—let alone the present writer—could write a learned and definitive work on the whole subject or most parts of it at present, because not nearly enough detailed work has been done. Yet much of the work which is being done on individual towns is hampered by the difficulty of finding any framework of knowledge and issues into which to fit the evidence from each town. If this book can furnish a framework that is worth testing and even demolishing, so that some or most of its conclusions are falsified, then it will have served a useful purpose. Questions will have been asked and answered.

If English medieval towns are to escape from what F. M. Stenton called 'the atmosphere of legal archaeology' one fundamental need, therefore, is to relate them to each other and to the outside world. Another is to try to use the records, which are often predominantly legal and repellently technical, to tell the story of the living society which produced them. We cannot understand or explain the development of towns and of urban institutions merely by linking references in chronological sequence, as if purposes and functions never changed. Unfortunately many town historians have started from an interest in tracing the origins of what they have found in their own time, and so have not stopped to consider whether words like borough, franchise, or guild might have changed their meaning. The dominance of legal history has moreover fostered a tendency to demand exact definition and consistent use, even of words that may have been loosely used and that certainly changed their meaning both during the Middle Ages and afterwards. Failure to think about meanings explains the anachronisms which have bedevilled and still bedevil much town history.

If we are to understand medieval urban society and make sense of individual towns we need to read and think much more about the assumptions, purposes, and values of medieval townsmen—and therefore of medieval society at large—than most historians of medieval towns have felt is their duty. Without some study of political and social vocabulary and ideas, any account of urban politics or institutions is likely to be as garbled as an account of a town's churches or craftsmen would be if it were written without any knowledge of medieval religion or industry respectively.

Nothing that has been said so far is intended to discourage the amateur. Far from it. Amateurs, that is those who do not earn their livings by studying and teaching history, have done some of the most valuable and learned work in the past and should do even more in future. In the first place anyone who is prepared for the difficulties and tedium of using the records, as many amateurs have shown themselves to be, does not need to be daunted by those of the background reading. Secondly, there are more books available today on relevant aspects of history than ever before, and many of them are intended for a wide and non-professional readership. The footnotes to the following chapters suggest some, giving preference where possible to those which are more easily available and are written in English. Thirdly, while the ideal medieval urban historian would need to deploy an impossible range of skills over a fearsome thousand years or so of history, no one in fact has to tackle all aspects of a town's history. This book, written in the belief that it can sometimes be useful to publish interim and incomplete findings, may illustrate only too well the traps that await any historian who

ranges too widely. It may also, however, suggest how much experience and learning former writers have left to guide the beginner
in urban history.

Most urban historians feel bound to try to say what they mean
by a town. Few have succeeded to each other's satisfaction, but it is
impossible to avoid trying again when writing about medieval towns
for a modern audience. If one does not make the effort one may well
meet with the objection that most of the places talked about were
much too small to be called towns at all. Some of the difficulties of
definition may in any case be avoided by bearing in mind that a
definition is different from a description. It is not intended to include
all characteristics of all towns. Furthermore there is no need to
worry too much about borderline cases when considering a category
which cannot be hard and fast. There must be many settlements
which, either for a short while or for centuries, hovered on the
borderline between village and town, just as some nowadays lie
somewhere between being separate towns and mere parts of a
conurbation or suburb. No amount of learning or exactitude is
going to determine finally on which side of the boundary they belong,
yet if we get our definition reasonably agreed we can all recognize
that there are two sides, that some places fall incontestably on one,
and that they are towns.

The working definition in this book is that a town is a permanent
human settlement with two chief and essential attributes. The first
is that a significant proportion (but not necessarily a majority) of its
population lives off trade, industry, administration, and other non-
agricultural occupations. In order to distinguish it from, say, a
monastery or a barracks or even a mining village, one should add
that the inhabitants live off a variety of occupations. Even a town
which appears to have a single dominant industry will have retailers
and other service trades too. Because of the occupations practised
within it the town is likely to serve as some kind of centre for the
surrounding area—generally in marketing, possibly in administration.

The second essential attribute of the town is that it forms a
social unit more or less distinct from the surrounding countryside.
Its social distinctiveness probably derives partly from the greater
density and size of its population (though some agricultural villages
may be larger than some towns), and partly from the difference of
occupations. The crux, however, is that the difference exists:

townsmen feel themselves to be different from outsiders and to have at least some common interests with each other, while countrymen see them in the same way. The separateness of urban society may find expression in political, administrative, and legal ways, but the forms and degrees of that will vary. In the Middle Ages it characteristically took the institutional form of urban liberties and privileges and the physical form of town walls or ditches. As a result some medieval historians have wanted to define towns by these secondary characteristics and have thereby created difficulties for themselves when the incidence of some of the characteristics looks haphazard.

In fact, once one passes from definition to description there are plenty of other attributes that seem to belong to many medieval towns. Town society was more open to visitors and settlers than village life tended to be; it was generally more mobile, both socially and geographically; and yet, despite the mobility, towns developed very strong corporate lives of their own. As soon as one starts on this sort of thing, however, one passes from defining to describing medieval towns, and thus to writing their history, which is quite another matter.

A book which attempts to survey the present position of studies is bound, in current conditions, to be out of date before it appears. It may be useful to the reader to know that the present work was written between 1972 and 1975, and that though some alterations were made, particularly to the earlier chapters, early in 1976, no attempt has been made to incorporate new material after that. It need hardly be said that the book is heavily dependent on other people's work. All conscious borrowings have, I hope, been acknowledged in the footnotes, but I have probably absorbed many more ideas from other people's books and conversation than I have realized. I owe not only gratitude but apologies to those working on the many aspects of medieval towns of which I know little and whose findings and arguments I may have garbled. I hope that some of my mistakes may be of the sort that provoke others to get nearer the truth. I am particularly grateful to Barbara Harvey, Professor Geoffrey Martin, Charles Phythian-Adams, and Keith Thomas, who all read part or all of the typescript and offered valuable criticism and encouragement. My chief thanks go to my sister, Vickie Macnair, who read it all and did her best to make it less cautious and obscure. The obscurities that remain, like the mistakes, are of course my own.

Contents

NOTE on References

The figures in square brackets [ ] after the titles of the works cited in the notes refer to the numbered entries in the List of Works Cited, pp. 202–23, where further details and a list of abbreviations are given.

List of Maps

I

The Anglo-Saxon Settlement and the Roman Inheritance

THE 'CONTINUITY QUESTION'

The first problem that confronts us in the history of medieval towns is where to begin. How much continuity was there between them and the towns of the Roman empire? A significant number of Anglo-Saxon towns, like London or York, stood on the same sites and bore adapted forms of the same names as Romano-British towns. How should the relationship between them and their predecessors be understood and is a discussion of the Roman towns a necessary preliminary to the study of their successors?

The problem of course concerns much more than towns and more countries than one.[1] The 'continuity question' besets all the successor states of the Roman empire and even the regions around its borders. Only as much need be said here as will provide a setting in which to discuss the connection between Romano-British and Anglo-Saxon towns and will show the point of view from which I see the picture. The peculiarity of Britain is that it retained much less of its Roman inheritance than did most other parts of the empire. France, like England, eventually took its name from its barbarian conquerors but the difference between them is signalized by the way in which France inherited from Gaul both its language and its official religion, the latter in turn helping to preserve much of its internal administrative geography. Early Anglo-Saxon England was Germanic-speaking, pagan, and divided into kingdoms which with one or two significant exceptions owed little to the Roman administration of Britannia. Though we may decide that early medieval France, despite profound differences from Roman Gaul, evolved from it by stages, and though French and other

---

[1] On 'continuity' in general see works of Pirenne and others cited on pp. 17–19 below; Dopsch, *Foundations of European Civilization* [112]; Latouche, *Birth of Western Economy* [170]; Musset, *Germanic Invasions* [201]. On towns see Ennen, *Europäische Stadt* [118]. On the case for continuity in England: Finberg, *Lucerna* [122].

analogies will be helpful and suggestive, the same judgements will not necessarily apply to the transition from Britannia to England.

Traditionally the transition has been presented in cataclysmic terms. The inhabitants of Britain were held to have been massacred or driven westward and the foundations of English society to have been laid not in the *civitates* of Britain but in the Germanic forests of northern Europe. Common-sense scepticism about a clean sweep of the existing population has been corroborated in recent years by the results of more critical use of the written sources, by the study of place-names and languages, and above all by new archaeological evidence. Kenneth Jackson, pointing out how the old view of the settlement involved imagining 'the Saxons as capturing a Briton, demanding of him the name of a neighbouring river or hill, and then slaughtering him on the spot, while being careful to remember the form that he told them', has concluded that the linguistic evidence is compatible with a fair survival of Britons and with areas of fairly peaceful settlement and coexistence.[2] Linguists seem ready to accept the disappearance of the British language except in the extreme west, and its failure to influence Anglo-Saxon, without postulating a general extermination of Britons. The similar disappearance of Latin poses rather different problems, since its prestige might have been expected to attract at least the leaders of the invaders. As it was probably spoken most in the towns, the small Latin element in early Anglo-Saxon suggests that urban contact and continuity were relatively low. Conclusions from the many different forms of archaeological evidence are too complex to be summarized here. The most important findings in our context are perhaps that barbarian soldiers seem to have been brought in and settled by the authorities alongside vulnerable towns and routes before the fifth century; that the invaders were neither unified in their culture and activities nor uniformly isolated from contact with the British, minimal though the cultural exchange was in many places; and that the patterns of settlement were too various for all towns to have suffered similar fates.[3] The archaeologists still have much more to learn and tell us about the transitional period, but it will not necessarily make generalization any easier.

[2] Jackson, *Lang. and Hist. in Early Brit.* [155], 229.
[3] See e.g. Myres, *A. S. Pottery* [203]; Frere, 'End of Towns in Roman Brit.' [126]; Wacher, *Towns of Roman Brit.* [274]. *Britannia* (1970–) contains annual surveys of work on Roman sites.

One preliminary point in the 'continuity question' needs discussion before considering the evidence about late Romano-British towns and Anglo-Saxon dealings with them. That is the traditional belief that the Anglo-Saxon and other German 'races' feared Roman towns and were in some fundamental way unsuited to town life. The theory goes back to Tacitus but in spite of its long list of distinguished exponents it involves a confusion of racial, social, and economic factors. To start with, neither the Anglo-Saxons separately nor the speakers of Germanic languages as a whole are or seem to have been a 'race' in any scientific sense, and the later adaptation of many of them to urban life suggests that they could hardly have had an innate incapacity for town life even if that were genetically possible.[4] If we could agree to use the word 'race' more precisely, and to use 'national character' less readily as an explanation of all social differences, then it would be easier to start disentangling the confusion of culture and heredity which underlies earlier uses of both terms and which hampers rational explanation of social changes. It is true that the German-speaking barbarians on the northern boundaries of the Roman empire had neither the political organization nor the economy to require or support much urban life, but the distinction between an urban empire and rural barbarians is blurred from both sides. After saying that the Germans had no *urbes* Tacitus went on to talk of their *oppida*. Recent study of the towns of Germany suggests that it is very difficult to identify a moment when towns appeared there, or to be sure that the change came because the Germans suddenly acquired a new and foreign knack of urban life.[5] So far as the Anglo-Saxons, as distinct from Tacitus' much earlier Germans, are concerned, it has sometimes been suggested that evidence for their *a priori* dislike of living in built-up areas can be found in Old English poetry. The most striking example is 'The Ruin' which is thought to have been inspired by eighth-century Bath and starts

> Wrǣtlic is þes wealstān,   wyrde gebrǣcon;
> burgstede burston;   brosnað enta geweorc.
> Hrōfas sind gehrorene,   hrēorge torras,

---

[4] See e.g. M. Mead *et al.*, *Science and the Concept of Race* (1968); for an example of the traditional use, J. M. Kemble, *The Saxons in Eng.* (1876 edn.), ii. 262–99.

[5] Jones, *Later Roman Empire* [161], 715–62, 1038–40, and 'Cities of the Roman Empire' [160]; Ennen, *Europäische Stadt* [118], 55–8; Schlesinger, 'Stadt und Burg' [245].

hr[un]geat berofen,   hrīm on līme
scearde scūrbeorge   scorene gedrorene
ældo undereotone.

(Wonderful is this wall of stone, wrecked by fate. / The city buildings
crumble, the bold works of giants decay, / Roofs have caved in, towers
collapsed, / Barred gates are gone, gateways have gaping mouths, hoar
frost clings to mortar. / Ceilings save nothing from the fury of storms,
worn away, tottering, / Undermined by age.)[6]

Together with references in other poems to the 'work of giants' this
confirms what we know: that some Roman cities fell into decay
after the Anglo-Saxon settlement and that Anglo-Saxons were im-
pressed by the mighty works of their predecessors. But, even if one
could deduce a general social attitude from a poet's imagination,
'The Ruin' is thought to date from a period when the English had
been settled in a number of Roman towns for a century at least, and
no other poem seems to supply more convincing evidence for the
settlement period itself. Moreover it reflects less dislike or numinous
fear than an admiring contemplation of past greatness by time's fell
hand defaced. The later lines suggest that the poet imagined the
vanished life in much less alien terms than 'the work of giants'
might suggest. To start from the assumption that the Anglo-Saxons
were bound by their nationality to shun existing towns is to beg the
important questions when and why they began to adapt themselves
and their institutions to urban life, and whether and how their
movement into Britain contributed to the change.

ROMAN TOWNS AND THE ANGLO-SAXON INVASIONS:
A GENERAL VIEW

The towns of Roman Britain seem to have reached their peak of
prosperity and growth in the second century A.D., but there is no
reason to assume that they started to decline in any dramatic or
uniform way with its close. On the contrary, though building in some
places slackened off, in others it went on, and Sheppard Frere
suggests that the fourth century may even have seen some growth of
commerce and prosperity.[7] In Britain, unlike Gaul, most towns were

---

[6] Text from *Three Old Eng. Elegies* [55]; translation by K. Crossley-Holland in *The
Battle of Maldon and Other English Poems*, ed. B. Mitchell (1965).
[7] For the following survey see: Frere, *Britannia* [125] and 'End of Towns in Roman
Brit.' [126]; Biddle, 'Excavations at Winchester' [428]; Myres, *A. S. Pottery* [203];
Morris, 'Dark Ages Dates' [199]. Extracts from Gildas in Bede, *Hist. Eccles.* [14]; full
text and trans. in Gildas, *De Excidio* [33].

walled before the barbarian raids became really damaging, so that in nearly every case the circumference of the walls shows the fullest extent of the town. London with 330 acres was large by the standards of any region north of the Alps, and, though the rest were small, Cirencester, Wroxeter, and Verulamium compare quite favourably with their contemporaries overseas. Town-dwellers were probably few in proportion to countrymen but that was the case in much of the western half of the empire. Administration and political education—the collection of taxes, the keeping of order, and the diffusion of *Romanitas*—were the primary functions of Roman cities, and they seem to have been adequately fulfilled by the towns of Britain. The towns probably became steadily more integrated with the social and economic life of the province as the centuries passed: there is no reason to see them by the fourth century as unassimilated or alien and thus doomed to extinction at the slightest shock. If the economy and polity of which they formed part were to collapse, then, like the cities of the rest of the empire, they would suffer, but they were not intrinsically much more vulnerable than the cities of northern Gaul. Having suffered less in the troubles of the third century they may well in the fourth have seemed better fit to survive.

The end of Roman Britain is traditionally placed at the event known as 'the departure of the Romans' in 408–10, when official contact with the government of the western empire was broken. Archaeological evidence apparently suggests that barbarian garrisons—or garrisons including barbarians—had been settled before then by the Roman authorities near to a number of towns in the east, midlands, and south. The relationship between these barbarian soldiers and the later Anglo-Saxon invaders is still disputed— how far, that is, they paved the way for the more hostile forces that followed them or how far they were themselves assimilated before the later invasions started. In any case it seems fair to postulate that they and the towns they protected may have mutually influenced each other to some degree, so that urban life may have been subtly changed even while it was being protected.

The century and a half after 410 is exceedingly obscure. It is very difficult to work out any framework of events that does not do violence to part of the evidence, and recent authorities are not agreed about either the dates or the interpretation of events. Nevertheless it seems clear that the British aristocracy reacted with vigour to their enforced independence. Until some time about the middle of the fifth century they maintained their defences and way of life quite successfully, both against the Germanic invaders in the east and against Picts and Irish in the north and west. Anglo-Saxon settlement went on in the eastern part of the country, but was made at least in part under British auspices, as in the preceding period. The first settlement in Kent probably took place at this stage, perhaps some time before the traditional date of the *Adventus Saxonum* in 449. There is no reason to disbelieve the story of the written sources that the revolt of the Saxons which ended this first phase of sub-Roman government and co-existence began in Kent. An outburst of fury and devastation followed, according to the Briton Gildas, who wrote about a hundred years later. Gildas says that it reached to the western shores of the island, that cities and churches were destroyed, and that those Britons who were not slaughtered fled to the mountains or overseas. Though his style is highly-coloured his testimony that the cities remained deserted and dismantled in his own day is hard to ignore. Even in his own account the Britons were not really all slaughtered or driven out, however, for he tells how they fought back in the second half of the century until the battle of Mons Badonicus (variously dated *c.* 500 or some fifteen years earlier) introduced another half-century of co-existence. Barbarians were poorly equipped for siege-warfare and it has been suggested that, given the chronology outlined so far, any sub-Roman town which survived until Mons Badonicus 'could continue thereafter in prosperity until 550, as far as the Saxons were concerned'.[8] The Saxons, however, were not the only trouble. As always the towns were the product of division of labour and services between themselves and the country, and this in turn depended on the maintenance of communications and exchange between town and country. Disorder around a town endangered its supplies and also, more insidiously, reduced demand for the particular goods and services that a Roman town provided for Roman citizens. As *Romanitas* wore thin and the British aristocrats became warlords the towns must have served for less and less except fortresses. Significantly, the circulation of money and the commercial manufacture of pottery seem to have ended before the middle of the fifth century. Despite the safety which town walls could afford in moments of crisis, a migration to the country

[8] Frere, 'End of Towns in Roman Brit.' [126], 88.

may have made economic sense for many people both before and after Gildas' period of devastation.

Archaeological evidence suggests that during the second half of the fifth century Anglo-Saxon settlements spread around the Humber, and into the midlands, Essex, Sussex, and parts of the south, though the westward expansion of Kent was checked by British forces round the middle Thames. Their territory, particularly in the midlands and south, may have been slightly reduced after Mons Badonicus, but the advance was resumed in the later sixth century, culminating in the early seventh-century situation depicted by Bede, when English kingdoms effectively occupied the area east of the Pennines, the Severn, and the Bristol Channel.

THE EVIDENCE FROM INDIVIDUAL TOWNS

At least some of the evidence about individual towns can be fitted into this outline, and the temptation is perhaps to make it fit too neatly. Much of the archaeological material can only be dated at all precisely by connecting it more or less arbitrarily to the more or less problematical dates of the written sources. Precise chronology has thus sometimes been assumed just where it most needs to be proved. The finding of unburied bodies or mass graves at the top of Roman occupation layers does not, in the absence of datable coins, show just when disaster struck. It does not even prove that the town was taken by storm, since a severe plague which Gildas mentions can be dated with fair certainty to the mid fifth century, just when the Saxons were getting out of hand, and could have given the deathblow to a suffering town. Street-plans provide another sort of evidence that has sometimes been too simply interpreted on the assumption that coincidence, or near coincidence, of plan between Roman and medieval streets proves continuity of occupation. So long as city walls stood, their gateways might dictate an approximate street-plan even to new squatters among the ruins, and recent excavations suggest that few medieval streets run exactly along Roman ones, though this in turn does not prove that a town was ever totally deserted.[9]

The best we can do here is to look at a few of the towns for which a reasonable amount of information seems to be available, while bearing in mind how hypothetical some of the dates and explanations

[9] Collingwood and Myres, *Roman Brit. and Eng. Settlements* [89], 429–31.

must be.[10] Canterbury looks like a possible example of continuity, lying as it does in an area where, though the period of controlled settlement was probably short, the final conquest was swift and complete, so that there may have been relatively little disruption and slaughter. The discovery of some huts of the mid or late fifth century along the line of the Roman streets suggests that by then Canterbury had become a Saxon town. Other evidence suggests that it underwent a time, though perhaps a very short one, of desertion or decay at the end of the Roman occupation, and the humble nature of the fifth-century huts implies that cultural continuity was limited. Against that must be set the tradition recorded by Bede (d. 735) that the missionary Augustine, arriving in 597, 'restored or built' churches; that he established his cathedral in a church which he was told had been built by the Romans; and, even more significantly, that the Frankish and Christian Queen Bertha of Kent had already been using a church on the east of the city which had been built to the honour of St. Martin while the Romans still inhabited Britain. All this is difficult to understand. One cannot imagine how Queen Bertha knew about the church and its dedication unless there had been some continuing Christian community there, whose existence is implicitly denied by the rest of Bede's account.

Nevertheless it would be rash to dismiss out of hand what Bede says about the churches of Canterbury. Though he wrote about a hundred and fifty years later at the other end of the country he is not a writer whom it is ever safe to ignore. We know that Kent had close contacts with the Franks and it is not impossible that visiting Franks had restored or even re-dedicated a Roman church. The siting of two other medieval churches, besides St. Martin's, in Romano-British cemeteries outside Canterbury gives further support to some continuity of religious tradition. If we allow the possibility of a visiting or resident community of Christian Franks who made little or no impression on the apparently solid paganism of their hosts before 597, we might go on to allow that a British

[10] Works already cited and Jenkins, 'St. Martin's Church at Canterbury' [302]; *Med. Arch.* xvii (1973), 140; Clarke, *East Anglia* [88]; Myres and Green, 'Cemeteries of Caistor and Markshall' [387]; R. Com. Hist. Mon. *York* [443], iv, pp. xxvi–xxix; Finberg, *Glos. Studies* [121], 52–61; Hurst, 'Excavations at Gloucester' [325]; Barker, *Origins of Worcester* [431], 15–19; Biddle, 'Archaeol. and Hist. of Towns' [68]; Fox, *Roman Exeter* [321]; Hoskins, *Devon* [149], 46; Griffiths and Bidwell, *Exeter Cathedral Close Excavations* [322].

community could have survived without propagating its faith either. Bede knew nothing of it but it was not easy for him to know about groups which left no monastery to preserve their memory. It may be that the receptivity of Anglo-Saxon England to Christianity in the seventh century is partly explained by previous knowledge gained from such groups. All this is highly speculative and takes us far beyond the problem of St. Martin's church at Canterbury, but it illustrates the problem of 'continuity' and what we mean by it. It also illustrates the difficulty of generalizing about towns at this stage. Kent looks unusual in many ways and Canterbury, for instance, appears to have been unique in England in the part of its Roman name (Durovernum Cantiacorum) which it preserved. Like Lutetia Parisiorum (Paris) and many other towns in Gaul, it preserved the tribal qualification (Cantiacorum—belonging to the Cantiaci) rather than, like Venta Belgarum (Winchester) and other British towns, the substantive part (Durovernum or Venta). The significance of this is made particularly obscure by the use of the old substantive name in Latin documents well into the eighth century, and it is in any case impossible to be sure in the general dearth of information how exceptional the phenomenon may be. It would be possible to make a case for the *likely* preservation of Christianity and other Roman institutions in Canterbury rather than elsewhere, but we do not know that they were in fact preserved. As good a case could be made for other places, notably Carlisle, which, however, did not pass to the English until after they had themselves already been converted.

Less seems to be known about other towns in the zone of early barbarian settlement and even less can be said here. Venta Icenorum (Caistor, near Norwich) had an early garrison settlement and there is evidence there of a sudden fire, which might be connected with a fifth-century revolt such as Gildas describes. Unlike Canterbury, Caistor did not survive to be the headquarters of an Anglo-Saxon kingdom, while the little walled town further west at Cambridge, despite its ring of early settlements, had become deserted by the late seventh century. We know from the Sutton Hoo treasure that by the seventh century an East Anglian king could be rich and powerful but by then the political geography of the area seems to have changed entirely and its urban links to have been broken. Further north but still in the regions of fifth-century conquest, Lincoln and York, like Canterbury, were the centres of early kingdoms but less

information is available about the first settlement. The prosperity of
York must have suffered greatly from floods which covered part of
the town, including the quays, as well as a wide tract of countryside
to the south. Similar flooding probably affected other areas on and
near the east coast.

Within the area thought to have been retained in British hands
into the sixth century, Verulamium is outstanding for the relative
abundance of information, though, as we shall see, not all of what is
usually cited is equally relevant to the town. Excavation has shown
that Verulamium was occupied well into the fifth century. Substantial building went on late in the fourth and included the laying
of mosaic floors. A little later, one fine room was converted for corn-
drying, but even in the less affluent conditions that this implies
proper plumbing was still being maintained. Corroboration of this
picture of *Romanitas* surviving with difficulty into the mid fifth
century has been sought in the story of St. Germanus' visits to
Britain in 429 and the 440s. He visited St. Alban's grave and
found people who had their own magistrates and took an in-
telligent interest in theology, but were defended only by rustic and
pagan levies who needed the saint's inspiration and leadership to
defeat an attack by Saxons and Picts.[11] John Morris, however, has
recently suggested that this 'Alleluia victory', as it became known,
may have been won as far away as North Wales. In fact only the
visit to St. Alban's grave is at all localized in the *Vita Germani*,
which provides evidence that Romano-British life was still going on
fairly normally, though on a war footing, in parts of Britain access-
ible from Gaul rather than specifically at Verulamium. The absence
of early Saxon finds in the Chilterns suggest that Verulamium—or
London—kept the enemy at bay for a while, but there does not seem
to be any evidence from the town itself after the middle of the fifth
century, and its site was later to be remembered only because of its
association with St. Alban's grave nearby: here an Anglo-Saxon
church in a suburban cemetery is very back-handed evidence of
continuity.

Silchester is another town in the fifth-century British zone which
had an early barbarian garrison, and may have survived into the
fifth or even sixth century, but later died. Dorchester (Oxon.) is one
which survived to the extent of becoming the centre of a Saxon
kingdom for a short time in the seventh century. The region was

[11] Extracts from *Vita* in Bede, *Hist. Eccles.* [14], 54–68.

probably not conquered before the sixth century, and the much changed topography of medieval Dorchester may argue a distinct break in the town's life before then. H. P. R. Finberg, one of the chief exponents of 'continuity', thought it unlikely that Cirencester, Gloucester, or Bath ever became completely derelict or 'quite lost their importance as administrative centres', though he points out that the evidence suggests a far from peaceful transition period. Cirencester seems to have maintained its forum well into the fifth century, though here there is some evidence of a period of desertion following a sack or pestilence: perhaps it shows how seriously we should take Gildas' description of destruction spreading to the west, much further than the contemporary settlement of the invaders. Although the area may well, as Finberg argues, have seen a large British survival with fairly peaceful English penetration in much of the countryside, Ceawlin's warlike career in sixth-century Wessex is likely to have turned the towns into fortresses and little more, both before and after their capture or surrender. 'Administrative centres' were something very different under illiterate Saxon warrior chiefs from what they had been in the bureaucratic Roman empire.

To the south, Winchester, which replaced Dorchester as the capital of Wessex in the seventh century, lay in one of the areas that may have been won or fought over in the late fifth century or the early sixth. The High Street here runs almost along the main Roman road, clearly because the gates preserved its line. The rest of the street plan has been lost. King Cenwalh, in the mid seventh century, may have had his headquarters at Winchester for some time before the cathedral was built there in his reign, and the walls may have sheltered others before he came, but excavations on a scale unrivalled in any other English medieval town have so far revealed little in the way of buildings, apart from the church, from before the tenth century. Further west again Devon was not conquered before the seventh century, but rubbish pits were dug in the forum at Exeter in the fifth century or even a little earlier. The town nevertheless retained some inhabitants, who imported goods from the Mediterranean, throughout that century and perhaps even later. The silence of West Saxon sources about the capture of Exeter may, as W. G. Hoskins suggests, indicate how peacefully it happened— or perhaps it shows how unimportant the town had become.

The most important town of all is as obscure as any of the

others.[12] Virtually all that is known of London in the fifth century is that British forces fled there after a defeat in Kent which the Anglo-Saxon Chronicle places in 457. The scarcity of early finds in the surrounding territory, the various earthworks of the Chilterns and the Cray valley (Kent), and the twelfth-century tradition of the citizens' hunting rights in Middlesex, Surrey, the Chilterns, and to the west of the Cray, have been together held to reflect a time when the British city maintained its sway over the surrounding territory. Its situation on the borders of several kingdoms and its failure, despite the survival of its name, to lend it to any of them, even to the puny and ephemeral Middlesex, all suggest that it came under Saxon control relatively late. It has been argued that London 'could not be destroyed . . . The foreign merchants knew it. The roads radiated from it. Sacked or not, people always returned to do business there.'[13] So long as the road system lasted (and much of its outline is still discernible), London with its bridge and wharfs was the potential centre of the whole country. We have no absolute evidence of a bridge before the tenth century, when a witch was drowned beside it, but a tenth-century bridge is surely likely to have been a survivor—if a battered and patched survivor—from the Roman period. The wharfs may have been partly submerged in the Dark Ages, but with or without them the beleaguered London of the fifth century cannot be envisaged as a very busy trading post. J. N. L. Myres has recently suggested that the poverty of the early settlements downstream implies that little trade went past them.

Archaeological evidence within the city is still scanty: some early Saxon finds in the western half of the city led Mortimer Wheeler in the 1930s to suggest that Saxon settlement started there and even that a British settlement might have lingered on beside it around the old Roman city centre in the east, 'if only as a sub-Roman slum'. That sub-Roman occupation did continue, at least in the area behind the water-front in the eastern half of the city, perhaps even as late as the sixth century, is suggested by finds of Mediterranean wares there. That it co-existed with a distinct Saxon settlement in the west seems less likely. Post-war excavation, however, has so far produced mainly negative evidence. Not only were some of the bastions

---

[12] Wheeler, *London and the Saxons* [371]; Grimes, *Excavation of London* [352]; Myres, *A.S. Pottery* [203], 129n; Biddle, *Future of London's Past* [340]. For the bridge see Sawyer, *A.S. Charters* [11], no. 1377; for water-levels see Steers, *Coastline of Eng. and Wales* [251], 400–1, 496–7.

[13] Lethbridge, 'Anglo-Saxon Settlement' [354], 122.

(formerly thought to have been added to the walls in the fourth century) certainly not built before the thirteenth, but more importantly in this context, no traces have been found of post-Roman buildings before the ninth century. The lack is particularly striking since much of the city's bomb-damage, and consequently many of W. G. Grimes's excavations, have been in the west, where Saxon settlement may have started. Grimes, however, points out that the dearth of material continues in the seventh century, after St. Paul's had been founded, and, one might add, when Bede calls London a market of many peoples and tells a story about a Frisian slave trader there. The value of the negative evidence for the earlier period is thus particularly debatable and Grimes is left asking whether it is possible that early Saxon occupation 'was indeed limited to the immediate area of the western hill [Ludgate Hill] on which King Ethelbert built the first cathedral', and whether 'even the limited expansion which would have carried traces of it to the margins of the hill did not take place until the ninth or tenth century'. Unless more archaeological evidence is forthcoming we are left to guess, if we will, that London may have remained a British fortress, though with few inhabitants, during most of the fifth century; that it passed into Saxon hands in the sixth; and that it may never have been entirely unpopulated. It would clearly be rash to conclude that 'continuity' went much further than that.

CONCLUSION

With the seventh century, when territorial kingdoms had become established and when the return of Christianity brought Roman influences flooding back into England, we move into an age of new problems. Before leaving the age of settlement, however, it may be useful to conclude the discussion with a glance at the picture Bede gives us of seventh- and early eighth-century towns. The *Ecclesiastical History* shows us former Roman towns as the capitals of several kingdoms, though not of all, while the *Life of St. Cuthbert* describes the saint being shown round the wall and waterworks (*fontem*) of Carlisle 'formerly constructed in a wonderful way by the Romans'.[14] By now, if not before, the English were accustomed to Roman towns though still respectful of them. Little is known as yet of how they lived within them. Probably most of their buildings were timber: though the *principia*, or headquarters building, at York remained in

---

[14] *Hist. Eccles.* [14]; *Two Lives of St. Cuthbert* [56], 123.

use until the ninth century, there is no clear evidence of Roman buildings being used for dwelling houses.[15] Churches were increasingly built—or, at Canterbury, perhaps restored—in stone, and the ruins around made good quarries for that. Bede calls Canterbury the *metropolis* of Ethelbert's empire and London the *metropolis* of the East Saxons, while Bamburgh is the *urbs regia* of Bernicia and places like Dorchester, Rochester, or even Tilbury are *civitates*. Such words distinguish them from the apparently less urban places which Bede calls *vici*, and even from *vici regii* or *villae regales*. Too much should not be made of the distinction: Bede's work is inevitably coloured by the Latin in which he wrote so that his *urbes* may sound much more urban than they were. Although, as the next chapter will discuss, there is evidence of trade and perhaps of growing trade at the time, early Anglo-Saxon society had little use for towns of the sort that once flourished in Britain. The towns that survived from the Roman period were transformed by their changed functions in a changed society.

It seems, then, that present evidence does not entitle us to go far in support of the present tendency to stress elements of continuity through the age of settlement. Roman walls made good fortresses and the Roman road system survived in Britain to a degree unusual in the northern part of the empire, so that Roman town sites continued to be useful, both in disturbed times and, as the economy recovered, for trade. Many sites were probably inhabited either continuously or with very short breaks, and individuals of British, English, or mixed descent may well have lived together on some of them. Some town sites had, after all, been occupied before the Romans came: they were what Alan Everitt has called 'primary towns', to which the patterns of routes and settlements gave more or less urban functions very early on. Despite all changes, these patterns, he suggests, may have persisted so that the nodal points within them, the 'primary towns', were likely to weather successive storms and preserve economic, administrative, and even religious functions in successive ages[16]. All this shows little beyond what German historians have called 'Kontinuität der Ruinen'. The evidence for continuity of institutions or culture is as yet lacking. Indications of Roman custom in Anglo-Saxon England that have been noted in the past all come after the seventh-century conversion

---

[15] Though see Ekwall, *Street-Names of London* [351], 37.
[16] 'Banburys of Eng.' [119], 30–6.

and can better be explained as corollaries of that than as genuine survivals. To say all this is not to prejudge the wider issue of continuity which Finberg himself characterized as 'before all else a problem of agrarian history'. Nor is it even to maintain that evidence of urban continuity cannot or will not be found. Together with any information bearing on all the circumstances of the collapse or capture of the Roman towns it must be sought and then examined in the most rigorous way possible.

2

The Origins of Growth

THE NORTH EUROPEAN BACKGROUND

Whatever the fate of the Romano-British towns, there is no doubt that in the first few centuries after the Anglo-Saxon settlement urban life in England was at a low ebb. By 1200 it was flourishing. Though nearly all the twelfth-century towns were very small indeed by modern standards, many of them qualified as urban on several counts: they afforded a variety of non-agricultural occupations to a significant proportion of their inhabitants; they served as markets and administrative centres for the surrounding countryside; and they were more or less distinguished from it both in their local government and social institutions and in the density of their population. The next problem that confronts us therefore is to determine the origins and reasons for the striking change.

Countless textbooks have taken it for granted that urban growth—like almost everything else in English history—started with the Norman Conquest. In the 1930s, however, the Manchester historian James Tait conclusively refuted the scholarly arguments to that effect put forward by the American, Carl Stephenson. Tait showed that the evidence of true, though small-scale, urban life began much earlier, earlier even than the fortification of *burhs* or boroughs by Alfred and his successors to which some historians had attached particular importance.[1] Before looking at the evidence, it is advisable to look at the same period in other parts of northern Europe, where some of the same factors were surely at work. The view of most aspects of medieval history from the twentieth century is illuminated by looking at more than one country. In moments of political conflict medieval Englishmen may have shared the belief of some of their descendants that 'wogs begin at Calais', but one needs to remember that in many ways they had more in common with their contemporaries abroad than they had with us. Expressions like 'the

---

[1] Stephenson, *Borough and Town* [255]; Tait, *Med. Eng. Bor.* [258]; see also, e.g., Maitland, *D.B. and Beyond* [186].

mainstream of European life' to or from which England was at different periods joined or divided can be very misleading. In an age of relatively small units of government, little governmental control, and poor communications, every country and even every district could have its own local customs and peculiarities. There was no single 'mainstream' which did not include England, and any assumption that England was at all unique can only be tested by looking at other countries. It is true that from about the tenth century an increasingly strong monarchy in England tended to obliterate internal regional differences in law and political organization, and that this correspondingly tended to accentuate national peculiarities of law and politics, but at the same time the exchange of goods and ideas on many levels and between many countries was accelerating, so that the growth of national identity was everywhere offset by numerous social and cultural links. Urban life and customs in particular look very international, and it is only by comparing the evidence in several countries that one can appreciate the significance of the evidence for any one country. Differences may be striking at first but it is important to consider how far they are merely differences of vocabulary, which conceal similarities in the institutions which they describe.

Arguments about the rise of medieval town life are only now ceasing to be dominated by ideas put forward late in the last century and early in this, notably by the great Belgian historian, Henri Pirenne (1862–1935).[2] Before Pirenne most historians described the beginnings of medieval towns in essentially political or even legal terms. Pirenne brought social and economic factors to the fore. He suggested that the real break between the classical and medieval worlds came not with the barbarian invasions of the fourth and fifth centuries, which he thought left the fabric of civilization and commerce within the Roman empire essentially unchanged, though weakened, but with the invasion of the Mediterranean lands by the Arabs in the eighth century. This, he thought, cut off north-western Europe from its formerly Mediterranean roots and paved the way for the Frankish empire of Charlemagne (d. 814), which was something fundamentally new and qualitatively different from the

[2] Much of Pirenne's work on towns is collected in *Les villes* [216], including a French version of *Med. Cities* [218]. See also *Mohammed and Charlemagne* [217]. For other works before and after his, see the bibliography in *Cam. Econ. Hist.* [79], iii. 605–8, and survey by F. Vercauteren in *XIIᵉ congrès international des sciences historiques Vienne 1965*, v. 649–73. See also Benton, *Town Origins* [65].

Merovingian kingdom which preceded it. Whereas the Merovingian kingdom was essentially a mere successor state, with a
town-based, secular government, turned towards the Mediterranean
and fiscally dependent on trade and tolls, the Carolingian empire
was based on the barely Romanized Rhineland, was more closely
linked with the Church, and was governed by a peripatetic monarchy
which depended for its revenue not on trade but on land and agriculture. The nadir of the towns in Pirenne's opinion came thus not in
the fifth century but at the end of the ninth, when they served no
economic purpose and were occupied only by garrisons and clergy
with their servants and dependants. As he firmly put it, 'la période
qui s'ouvre avec l'époque carolingienne n'a connu de villes ni au
sens social, ni au sens économique, ni au sens juridique de ce
mot'.[3] Such trade as went on flowed not between the walled *civitates*
or *burgi* but between trading posts, or *portus*, frequented largely by
wandering traders, notably Frisians. The feeble life of these places
was snuffed out by the Viking raids, and it was only after these, in
the tenth century, that real revival began. When it did, it started
not from the 'pre-urban nuclei' of the old walled *burgi* but from
new trading suburbs, also called ports (*portus*), which sprang up
beside them. These were not primarily local markets, for Pirenne
saw local trade as irrelevant to the growth of real towns, but exchange points for the long-distance luxury trade which was brought
from the east to a commercially supine Europe by Venetians and
Scandinavians. At first the new suburbs, like the earlier trading
places, were not places of permanent settlement but were visited by
roving, rootless traders 'sans feu ni lieu, sans foi ni loi'. The key
moment in turning them into towns came in about the eleventh
century, when the traders began to settle down to become the urban
merchants and 'patricians' of the great medieval cities. Many of the
suburbs were walled soon after, and town communities and institutions were developed by the unification of the suburbs and the old
fortified *burgi*.

Pirenne's ideas served the excellent historical purpose of stimulating so much thought and research that few historians would now
maintain almost any of his arguments in the form in which he stated
them. They remain worthy of mention, nevertheless, because even
in a brief and over-simplified summary they stimulate thought
about the nature and origins of medieval towns. Moreover so much

[3] *Les villes* [216], i. 345.

work on the subject since Pirenne's day has been conditioned by what he said that it is almost impossible to set out more recent views without first exploring and explaining their starting point in the controversies which he provoked.

It is now generally agreed that valuable as Pirenne's emphasis on economic factors was, he concentrated on them too exclusively and also defined them too narrowly, ignoring the function of both industry and local markets.[4] Most historians would see the cutting of Mediterranean links—so far as they think that that really happened— as only one item in the economic changes of the Dark Ages, and would see the northward shift of trade as something more permanent and positive than Pirenne implied. Even before the fall of the western empire there was considerable traffic around its northern borders, and right through the Dark Ages the North Sea and Baltic seem to have constituted a lively forum of activity. The early Anglo-Saxons themselves had contacts around most of the coastline of western Europe, and from the eighth century Frisians are mentioned trading in the way that Pirenne described as an ephemeral feature of the ninth and tenth. One indication of the unity of the North Sea trading area is the way the word *wik* seems to have been used to describe the early trading centres all around it. *Wik* (or, in Old English, *wīc*) seems to be connected with the Latin *vicus* and its usage is by no means simple to interpret. In some place-names it seems to be quite unconnected with trade, but even so there is food for thought in its permanent incorporation in the names of places like Schleswig, Brunswick, Ipswich, Norwich, and York (Eoferwic), as well as its temporary use in Lundenwic (London), Hamwih (later absorbed in Southampton), and the lost Quentovic (near Étaples, in France). It would of course be rash to assume that all Dark Age traffic around the North Sea was commercial and that all the imported goods that archaeologists find had got to where they are found by means of what we would now consider legitimate trade: plunder, tribute, and gift-exchange no doubt accounted for much of the movement, but even so that does not affect the conclusion that northern trade and society before the ninth century

---

[4] See, e.g., Havighurst, *Pirenne Thesis*[139]; Duby, *Early Growth of Eur. Econ.*[113]; Ennen, *Europäische Stadt* [118]; Lestocquoy, *Études* [175]. On particular aspects: Levison, *Eng. and Continent* [176]; Grierson, 'Commerce in the Dark Ages' [135]; Dhondt, 'Problèmes de Quentovic' [102]; Jones, *Hist. of Vikings* [162]; Sawyer, *Age of Vikings* [240]; Perroy, 'Les origines urbaines en Flandre' [213].

were not merely parasitic upon the Mediterranean and that northern trading places contributed to later urban growth.

Many towns, however, have always depended less on long-distance trade than on local circumstances, among which more disparate factors than Pirenne allowed for could be influential. The general shift from road to water transport in the post-Roman centuries affected local patterns of settlement as well as great international routes, causing shifts of prosperity between neighbouring towns and between the quarters of individual towns. The establishment of a royal or seigniorial court could provide a stimulus to economic activity and so, even more, could the foundation of a church. With its large stationary community of consumers wanting both food and luxuries—wine and ornaments for altars and shrines, for instance—a great monastery was a splendid market for all sorts of merchants. Another ecclesiastical stimulus came with the growing popularity of pilgrimages, which brought a new tourist trade to places along the pilgrim routes and to the towns which had famous shrines of their own. Large concourses of pilgrims at famous feast-days attracted salesmen so that fairs grew up: 'il n'est pas de grande fête sans foire, ni de foire sans fête: l'une appelle l'autre.'[5] Yearly fairs could not produce towns on their own, but they could stimulate their growth. Pirenne's dichotomy between the 'closed economy' of feudal and ecclesiastical society and the long-distance trade of the wandering merchants, between the *civitates* languishing under the dead hand of Church and lord and the free—and, by implication, almost secular or pagan—*portus*, does not seem to fit here.

Many historians see the development of towns therefore not as 'a kind of spontaneous generation'[6] in the eleventh century, but as one symptom of a general growth of population and prosperity over a long period. True, western society was primarily rural, but there is no real evidence that towns were a 'foreign body' within it. They grew because rural population and wealth were growing and therefore the demand for the goods and services which towns could provide grew too. Even trade with the Mediterranean and beyond did not wax or wane merely because of outside forces, merely because supplies were cut off from without: western demand mattered too. As for local trade, its extent and increase is marked by the wide-

---

[5] Huvelin, *Essai historique sur le droit des marchés et des foires* (1897), 40. Cf. Sumption, *Pilgrimages* [257], 147–67, 211.

[6] Lestocquoy, *Études* [175], 39.

spread establishment of markets from about the tenth century. Some markets of course remained merely weekly gatherings, just as some fairs remained merely annual, while only those which developed into permanent trading centres, with resident traders and craftsmen, can be called towns. Some of the markets first recorded about now, however, did just that. Even the others testify to the growing surplus of produce, and demand for it, and to a quickening of exchange which seems to have been taking place over a large part of Europe. It looks as though the first signs of urban growth are not to be found exclusively in those regions, such as Flanders, the Rhineland or even the Meuse-Moselle district, in which it was later strikingly sustained. Instead the evidence suggests, and there is indeed no prima facie reason why it should not, that the towns which later became particularly famous, and whose history was therefore most lovingly studied and recorded by their patriotic citizens, were not necessarily outstanding in the early stages.

Above all, therefore, Pirenne's hard and fast distinction between the non-urban trading places and settlements of the earlier period and the towns of the eleventh century and later seems to be blurred. To call an old walled city of the Dark Ages a 'pre-urban nucleus' is not a bad idea so long as the expression suggests a potentiality for urban growth and not that there may have been one moment when pre-urban became urban. Nor is it at all sure that the *wiks* or trading posts, whether beside or away from the walled cities, should be denied the title of towns before the tenth or eleventh centuries. Much study and excavation has gone on since Pirenne's time and some of it at least seems to refute his suggestions that the early *wiks* were never places of permanent settlement, that they were outside local structures of government and society, and that the Viking raids caused a significant break either in their life or in that of the old walled *civitates* and *burgi*. Viking destruction may have been rather exaggerated altogether and the positive contribution which the Vikings made to urban development correspondingly underrated.

Not surprisingly, the blurring of Pirenne's clear picture of cause and effect by new strands of evidence and the new factors they suggest leaves a general chronology hard to establish. If one is to see towns developing out of a gradual expansion of settlement and growth of prosperity it is likely that no single moment was decisive. Moreover, though the Viking raids, for instance, were widespread, periods of war and peace which might stunt or encourage economic

growth did not always coincide in all countries. The tenth century
was a dark and disorderly time for France, while in Germany and
England relatively strong monarchies fostered trade and tried to
protect merchants. The great influence of French sources and
French historians may account for the way in which historians have
tended to regard the tenth-century signs of urban growth in Germany
and England as somehow exceptional and even illusory. Yet even in
France archaeologists and historians are now beginning to find evidence of a quickening of urban life before 1000. By the eleventh century, though one must guard against confusing an increase of records
with an increase of what they record, the signs of growth throughout
European society are unmistakable. The urban communities which
began to assert themselves in the later eleventh century had surely
been consolidating themselves for some time before then.

It is not at all hard to fit the English evidence into this pattern.
Indeed it would be odd if it were, considering the looseness of the
pattern and the scarcity of the evidence. That is not to say that we
should expect the evidence from England to look the same, or even
mean the same, as that from, say, Germany or France. Differences
of political conditions at the time and of survivals afterwards have
determined the peculiar and differing forms of the documentary
evidence, while the varying traditions and organization of the Church,
as well as the differences of secular government, subjected urban
societies and economies to different pressures in each area. England
was exceptional in having been Roman and yet in not preserving
Roman Christianity, a Romance language, or other discoverable
Roman institutions. Yet from the sixth century both Roman and
non-Roman territories were subjected to some similar general
pressures as well as to differing local ones. Historians of continental
towns seem able to detect parallels and disentangle local variations,
so it seems reasonable to subject English towns to the same critical
comparisons, if only to see how far similar or different factors
applied. The argument we then construct, however, must go from
the particular to the general, not vice versa.

THE NATURE OF THE ENGLISH EVIDENCE

On turning to England one is struck first of all by the relative
scarcity of work on the period.[7] L. A. Burgess in a pioneering study
of early Southampton rightly remarked in 1964 that 'a vast body of

[7] Useful surveys in Loyn, *A.S. Eng.* [180] and 'Towns in late A.S. Eng.' [181].

detailed local research exists in every north European country except Great Britain'.[8] The situation has not changed greatly since then, except in the archaeological field. Although war damage in most English town centres was relatively small compared for instance to that in Germany, giving less opportunity for excavation, and although some opportunities that there were have been wasted, more towns are now beginning to follow the distinguished lead of Winchester in looking to their archaeological heritage.[9] The combination of expensive sites, technical problems, and a smaller popular appeal than that afforded by Roman discoveries is not encouraging, but perhaps as big a handicap to the full exploitation of archaeological discoveries is the absence both of any adequate framework of history into which archaeologists may fit their findings, and of useful questions to pose about the sites which they investigate. Lacking these, the 'early Saxon' and 'late Saxon' remains they describe exist in a void, and undue importance may be given to the archaeologically rewarding town defences of the tenth century and the blessedly well-known landmark of the Norman Conquest.

It is true that strictly historical evidence for this period is both scarce and difficult to use, but, as Burgess suggested and as others since him have shown for Southampton, or as Martin Biddle and his colleagues continue to show on an impressive scale for Winchester, it can go a long way if the disciplines of archaeology and history are combined and if imaginative and informed questions are asked. Compared to parts of the Frankish area England is short of early monastic chronicles, but Bede gives valuable information about the seventh century, saints' lives occasionally mention towns and ports, and the splendid body of Anglo-Saxon laws casts considerable light on the social structure and trade in general. There are also many charters. A considerable number of them were fabricated or touched up later on and most still await critical editing, but there is now a single list of them all, with references to past editions and evaluations. As is shown below, the evidence begins to improve after the late ninth century, when the Anglo-Saxon Chronicle was started in the form in which we know it and became a contemporary record. The great increase of surviving documents from the following centuries,

[8] *Origins of Southampton* [413].

[9] *Medieval Archaeology* (1957–) contains annual notices of excavations; some are also noted in *Current Archaeology* (1967–). See also M. Biddle, 'Excavations at Winchester' [428] and 'Archaeol. and Hist. of Towns' [68].

with Domesday Book a vast source on its own, partly accounts for the traditional belief that English history only gets under way in 1066, though in fact the approximation of date is very rough. The increase of material starts earlier, while little information about the internal life of urban communities, for example, can be found before the thirteenth century. [10]

A third very important type of evidence is linguistic. The significance of place-names has long been appreciated and much material has been collected in the volumes of the English Place-Name Society. It is, however, a sign of the isolation of work on England from that on other countries, and of the divisions that can persist between disciplines, that the trading connotations of the word *wīc* or *wik* seem to have been first recognized in a work on English place-names only in 1964, and that no reference was made there either to historical or archaeological evidence or to the numerous works dealing with continental *wiks*.[11] All the words connected with towns, and above all the word *burh* (*burg*, *byrig*, etc.), need to be studied more closely in the context and chronology of their use when they occur outside place-names. So far it looks as though the early Anglo-Saxons used *ceaster* for Roman towns and other places they presumably considered similar, and *burh* for fortifications. *Burh* could thus be used at first both for a place that might also be called *ceaster* and for a quite non-urban defended site. Derivatives of the latter usage survive in some rural place-names, but by the twelfth century social and economic change had given new and much more urban connotations to the word when it stood alone as a common noun. More studies like those of Florence Harmer on 'chipping and market' in England or of Walter Schlesinger and others on 'Stadt und Burg' in Germany would help to plot the stages of urban growth as they were reflected in changing usage.[12]

TRADING *WIKS*, c. 600–900

On the analogy of continental evidence it looks as if the places with *wīc* names which lie scattered around the east and south coasts and

[10] Sawyer, *A.S. Charters* [11]; Bede, *Hist. Eccles.* [14]. Good extracts from all sources before 1042 are in *Eng. Hist. Docs.* [29], i.

[11] Ekwall, *Old Eng. wīc* [117], though cf. Burgess, *Origins of Southampton* [413]; Liebermann, *Gesetze* [42], ii. 242; Tait, *Med. Eng. Bor.* [258], 13. On wicham: Gelling, 'Place-Names derived from wīchām [132]. For continental *wiks*: e.g. Ennen, *Europäische Stadt* [118], 46–57.

[12] Blair, *Introd. to A.S. Eng.* [70], 277; Tait, *Med. Eng. Bor.* [258], 34–5; Harmer, [137]; Schlesinger, [245]; Smith, *Place-Name Elements* [248], i. 57–63.

which are known to have later developed into ports (in the modern sense[13]) are a likely group of possible early towns.[14] The forms Lundenwic and Lundenwich for London occur in the later seventh century and again in the eighth, when St. Boniface set sail from there, once for Quentovic and once for Dorstad. In the late ninth and tenth centuries London was also called Lundenburg and Lundenceaster. Bede (d. 735) mentions a Frisian slave-trader there c. 678 and describes London in 604 as a market of many peoples coming to it by land and sea, though that should be taken rather as meaning that it was a place of international trade in Bede's own day than as measuring the activity of its port in any precise way or at any earlier date: following their classical models early medieval writers tended to describe towns in terms of imprecise and conventional grandiloquence.[15] Other *wīc* names with possible trading connotations which occur before 800 are Fordwich and Sandwich (Kent), and Hamwih (Hampshire). York is called Eoferwicceastre in the seventh- and eighth-century annals of the Anglo-Saxon Chronicle, written probably late in the ninth, and Swanawic (Swanage, Dorset) occurs in the late ninth century. Ipswich and Norwich are not mentioned before the tenth century, and Harwich is even later, but all may have been early trading *wiks*. There is archaeological evidence of early traffic and industry at Ipswich despite the lateness of its occurrence in written sources: the first pottery made on the wheel in England since Roman times may have come from there in about the year 700.[16] Fordwich and Sandwich are both specifically described as ports in the first references to them. Sandwich was probably by now replacing the Roman Rutupiae (Richborough), as silting and other changes along the coast, which have been going on in the south-east all through recorded history, made it the better port. It commanded what was still an open channel between Thanet and the mainland, giving sheltered passage to the heart of Kent and to the Thames estuary.[17]

---

[13] See *Oxford Eng. Dict.* and *A.S. Dict.* [73].

[14] Early references are collected in Ekwall, *Old Eng. wic* [117], though those from the Anglo-Saxon Chronicle should be taken to relate to the date of compilation and not all the charter references are equally genuine. See Sawyer, *A.S. Charters* [11]. On Norwich, see Campbell, 'Norwich' [385], 25.

[15] *Laws of Earliest Eng. Kings* [39], 22–3; *Vitae S. Bonifatii* [369], 16, 20; Bede, *Hist. Eccles.* [14], 142; cf. Lestocquoy, 'De l'unité à la pluralité' [174].

[16] Clarke, *East Anglia* [88], 151.

[17] Sawyer, *A.S. Charters* [11], nos. 7, 1612; Eddius, *Life of Wilfrid* [26], 29; Steers, *Coastline of Eng. and Wales* [251], 337.

York, called either Eoferwicceastre or Eoferwic, was the capital of a kingdom, a bishop's see from the seventh century and an archbishop's from the eighth, and the home of a famous school. In the eighth century the Frisian Liudgar came to study here but left, along with his countrymen in the area (*provincia*), after a Frisian merchant killed a local noble's son and they feared reprisals. This is generally taken as showing that there was a Frisian colony in York itself, which is probable, though the permanence and location of the colony are not absolutely established by the text. The caution may seem pedantic but the point is worth making because the light cast on an obscure subject by exaggerating evidence tends to be deceitful. Archaeological examination of York's defences suggests that settlement had already spread from the little Roman fortress towards the water-front, where it is known to have been centred in the tenth and eleventh centuries.[18] At Lincoln a similar shift down to the river from a small Roman fortification on the hill above took place in the early Middle Ages, and it is suggestive that the suburb across the river there was called Wigford, which might be a *wīc* name though it is not recorded before the twelfth century.[19] In both places the riverside suburbs probably grew up because the walled areas were so small and because a shift from road to water transport had left them in the wrong places for trade. As with the extra-mural trading *wiks* on the Continent, there is no need to postulate any fundamental social or political cleavage between the inhabitants inside and outside the walls. London's traders presumably lived inside its walls, which enclosed an ample area and extended to the water-front.

Hamwih, however, has been cited as an example of real 'topographical duality'—a trading *wik* beside an older, agricultural settlement. The port seems to have grown up on the shore of a natural lagoon at the mouth of the Itchen, and it has been suggested that a parent settlement of 'Hamtun' may have lain to the west of it, though the evidence for that is more doubtful. There is no doubt that it flourished from the seventh century, began to decline in the ninth, and lost most of its population in the tenth. During its time of prosperity the settlement housed metal-workers of various kinds and was probably the mint place of Wessex. Danish attacks and the silting of the lagoon have both been blamed for its decay but the

---

[18] *Eng. Hist. Docs.* [29], i, p. 725; R. Com. Hist. Mon. *York* [443], ii. 7–9; cf. Radley, 'Anglo-Danish York' [441].

[19] Hill, *Med. Lincoln* [333], 18–25, 35–6.

causes remain problematical; settlement may simply have shifted westwards, even during the tenth century, to the site further west at the Test mouth where we know that post-Conquest Southampton stood. The name Southampton probably came into use to distinguish it not from a possible older Hamtun to its north but from Northampton.[20]

Altogether the *wiks* along the coast and navigable rivers, despite the paucity of evidence, conform to what one might expect from a comparison with *wiks* across the North Sea and Channel. With the possible exception of Hamwih none of those so far mentioned was extinguished in the Danish invasions, though that could well have happened to some of the less well-known places which also bear *wic* names and which have not been separately mentioned here.[21] The fact that so many *wiks* are known to have become towns supports the argument of some more recent continental scholars that the early *wiks* were urban or proto-urban rather than non-urban in character. Their populations were no doubt always small, though not necessarily so by contemporary standards, but there is no reason to doubt that most if not all had some permanent inhabitants. It is difficult to imagine a frequently used harbour without at least a few suppliers of food, lodging, and ships' stores and some hangers-on. Moreover though some of the English *wiks* were fairly far from the inland centres of their kingdoms none is known to have lain outside the local framework of society and the *wik* and royal capital at York were apparently united in one settlement with one name. York also serves to remind us that though we may think of some places primarily in connection with trade, their prosperity probably rested on that of the country round and on its need for a central place of exchange, government, and worship.[22]

INLAND TOWNS, *c*. 600–900

It would be wrong to look for potential early towns only along the coasts and estuaries. *Wic* names seem to have a different meaning inland, but here we might expect to find trading centres in places suited to local distribution rather than to long-distance trade. Some may have fulfilled similar functions for centuries, and even before

[20] Burgess, *Origins of Southampton* [413]; Addyman and Hill, 'Saxon Southampton' [412]; Dolley, 'Pre-Alfredian Mints' [415].
[21] Ekwall, *Old. Eng. wic* [117].
[22] Everitt, 'Banburys of Eng.' [119]: above, p. 14.

the Romans. Some of the same factors caused change here as on the coast. The shift from road to water traffic may have accounted for the replacement of Venta Icenorum by Norwich, and it almost certainly explains that of Silchester by Reading.[23] Local markets could often be stimulated to an urban or near-urban level by the presence of a royal court or great church. Courts, however, tended to move, as they did from Dorchester on Thames in Wessex or Bamburgh in Northumbria, though we may doubt whether Bamburgh could ever have rivalled York even if the kings of Northumbria had remained at the less naturally favoured site. Churches on the other hand—whether cathedrals or minsters—generally proved more permanent. Their contribution to urban growth is suggested in the rendering of *per cuncta urbana et rustica loca* as *eall þurh mynsterstowe ge þurh folcstowe* in the late ninth-century translation of Bede.

Both king and archbishop were established at Canterbury by 600 and some of the most often cited evidence of early urban development comes from there: one may wonder whether other places developed as much or more though the records are lost. Canterbury was a natural centre for the prosperous kingdom of Kent but it probably never served as more than a regional centre of trade. Though it lay on a main road from London to the coast and was as yet only a dozen miles upriver from the open and busy Wantsum channel, much long-distance traffic went past it along the Thames. Some of the earliest English coins may have been made here but that probably testifies less to Canterbury's commercial importance than to its political and ecclesiastical prestige and the close connections of Kent with Gaul. A market-place at the queen's gate at Canterbury is referred to in the eighth century and Canterbury was called a 'port' in the ninth. Its inhabitants were called either boroughmen or portmen—the first word implying that the place they lived in was fortified and the second that it was a place of trade. In the ninth century a local guild of *cnihtan* is mentioned: what sort of people they were has been much disputed and is not at all clear, nor is it clear how closely connected with the town they were, since they occur in a context that implies that they may have been contrasted with *innan burgware*—'boroughmen within'. What proportion of the inhabitants of Canterbury was engaged in trade or other occupations that would distinguish them from countrymen round about

[23] Slade, 'Reading' [401], 1.

is doubtful: possibly not very many, but at least the people of Canterbury were already seen as a separate kind of group.[24] Both here and at Rochester the word haw (*haga*) was used in the ninth century to describe a parcel of land. By the eleventh century this had definitely urban connotations but it may not have had them earlier on: too much town history is bedevilled and its questions are begged by anachronistic etymology. It is more significant that in the ninth century Canterbury custom required a two-foot gap between houses for eaves-drip, which suggests some density of population. There seems, however, to be no evidence to support the suggestion that both Canterbury and Rochester were by then already over-flowing their walls.[25]

It would be misleading to take either Canterbury or Rochester as a model of urban growth: the general impression given by European evidence about the Dark Ages is of fragmentation and, despite the undoubted significance of the North Sea traffic, of the local scale of much of what passed for commercial activity. In such conditions the market centre of a prosperous area like Kent, particularly if it was the seat of a king and of rich churches, might be as urban a place as one could find, whereas later, as horizons widened, it may have lost ground to London and the coastal ports. In Wessex, on the other hand, archaeological evidence suggests that coastal Hamwih was 'the economic centre of Wessex' until the late ninth century or the tenth, when the growth of royal power increased the functions and attractions of Winchester just when a corresponding decline in Kent diminished those of Canterbury.[26] It seems likely that despite the scarcity of finds in Winchester from before the tenth century the ancient Roman town with its cathedral had already been serving as some kind of market centre—no doubt like others in other parts of the kingdom. Hamwih may have been the place of greatest commercial and industrial activity in Wessex but the economic horizons of most West Saxons lay nearer home. Clearly it is difficult to generalize about the fortunes of different places in these fragmented conditions.

The vicissitudes of the Anglo-Saxon Church before and during

---

[24] See below, p. 92.
[25] William of Malmesbury, *Gesta Pont.* [57], 3; Dolley, *A.S. Coins* [109], 17, 40–1, 122–35; Tait, *Med. Eng. Bor.* [258], 8–12, 121; *Eng. Hist. Docs.* [29], i, pp. 460, 484; Sawyer, *A.S. Charters* [11], nos. 125, 1204; Stenton, *A.S. Eng.* [253], 519; Benton, *Town Origins* [65].
[26] Addyman, 'Saxon Southampton' [412].

the Danish invasions make it difficult to know what happened to the settlements which may have grown up beside early cathedrals and monasteries about which very little is known between their foundation and the tenth century. Some of these churches may have decayed to the point of extinction in the eighth and ninth centuries, so that if their dependent settlements did so too the failure may be of restricted significance for urban life in general. Abingdon, Gloucester, Hereford, and Oxford are all more or less obscure examples of this phenomenon and others could be found.[27] Worcester is rather better attested in the intervening period, for the bishop and his church, as well as owning salt-producing properties in Worcestershire, secured exemption from toll on two ships at London in the eighth century. Exemptions from toll like this are one of the few sources of information about trade and trading places in the period: they are recorded for other English churches, including Rochester for instance. Whether the church of Worcester regularly maintained two ships plying from London may be doubtful, but the bishop was granted trading privileges and property there in the ninth century, and witness-lists to charters are said to show that even then, when church life may have been at a relatively low ebb, his household comprised at least ten clerks. It is difficult to believe that the kind of wealth and activity these documents suggest did not stimulate local producers and traders. Though some new tolls and regulations seem to have been introduced when the rulers of Mercia fortified the place in the late ninth century, there was surely some sort of market on the site before then. Nevertheless very little archaeological evidence for the whole Anglo-Saxon period has yet been found in the town.[28]

ALFREDIAN AND TENTH-CENTURY BOROUGHS

Given the scarcity of evidence, the signs of something that could be described as urban or proto-urban, rather than pre-urban, growth before the tenth century are not negligible. From the tenth century the evidence improves in a manner that is confusing as well as helpful: it positively invites us to beg the question whether the growth of evidence is coincidental with real growth or not. Soon after Alfred the Great came to the throne of Wessex in 871 the invading Danes

[27] Biddle, 'Abingdon' [286]; Hurst, 'Excavations at Gloucester' [325]; Jope, 'Saxon Oxford' [393].

[28] Sawyer, *A.S. Charters* [11], no. 98; *Eng. Hist. Docs.* [29], i, pp. 449–50, 451–3, 498; Loyn, *A.S. Eng.* [180], 84–5, 106–7; Barker, *Origins of Worcester* [433], 27–30. For tolls in Gaul: Ganshof, 'A propos du tonlieu' [130].

overthrew the last of the English kings north of the Thames. In their war of defence and then of conquest Alfred and his successors followed a policy of establishing fortified places to be maintained by the surrounding population and to serve as centres of defence and refuge. A document known as the Burghal Hidage contains a list of these fortresses or 'boroughs' (*burh*, *burha*, *burga*, etc.) in Wessex which was probably drawn up in the 890s or soon after. Some versions go on to set out the system by which the manpower of the countryside was allotted to the defence of each borough. Each hide of land was supposed to supply one man, and each pole of the defences needed four men, so that from the hides assigned to each borough in the list it is possible to make an estimate of their respective sizes. This has helped to identify some doubtful places in the list and to plot or confirm the line of Anglo-Saxon ramparts in others.[29] Another series of 'boroughs', established in the midlands, east, and north during the wars to reconquer Danish territory in the first half of the tenth century, is mentioned in the Anglo-Saxon Chronicle, though there is no particular reason to think that the list is comprehensive.[30]

How far all these 'boroughs' were in fact towns is the first question which must be asked here. The Burghal Hidage and the Chronicle seem to use the word borough to mean nothing more than a fortified area, and F. W. Maitland, writing about the turn of the last century, and drawing an analogy with the *burgi* founded by tenth-century Saxon kings in Germany, suggested that that was indeed the essence of the late Old English boroughs. According to his 'garrison theory', the boroughs continued to exist primarily for defence; those parts of the land and people within them which were described by Domesday Book as being attached in some way to properties outside belonged, he thought, to the rural landowners who shared responsibility for their defence. The garrison theory has not stood up so well to argument as much of Maitland's work: the contribution of tenth-century fortification to urban growth in Germany has been minimized since he wrote, and the pattern of 'contributory burgesses' attached to the English boroughs from outside them looks as likely to reflect the needs of trade as those of defence.[31] Carl Stephenson

[29] For the text: Hill, 'Burghal Hidage' [38]; for the date and other problems: Brooks, 'Unidentified Forts' [76]; Davison, 'Eorpeburnan' [101].

[30] *Eng. Hist. Docs.* [29], i, pp. 181–202.

[31] Maitland, *D.B. and Beyond* [186], 186–96. Tait, *Med. Eng. Bor.* [258] is essential for the whole period and lists works on the controversy, p. 26 n.

in *Borough and Town*, while rejecting the 'garrison theory' as such, believed that the boroughs were merely fortified administrative centres, most of the inhabitants of which were engaged in agriculture, just like the inhabitants of villages. As Stephenson's work suggests that he approached the problem with the *a priori* belief—understandable at the time he wrote, when Pirenne's ideas were less challenged—that only 'European Commerce' could create towns and that this did not revive before the eleventh century, it is not surprising that he concluded that the boroughs were not real towns. Yet the fact that documents concerned with military affairs treat boroughs merely as fortifications does not prove that this was all they were.

Many of the Burghal Hidage and Chronicle 'boroughs' were in fact old settlements, some of which are known or likely to have been market centres already. One of the purposes of fortification could be to protect a market, its traders, and the royal dues it attracted, as is shown by the famous charter of Alfred's time in which a recent decision to fortify Worcester is mentioned and the rulers of Mercia grant part of the dues and tolls payable there to the cathedral.[32] Royal policy moreover encouraged the use of boroughs for peaceful purposes: Edward the Elder ordered that all buying and selling must be conducted inside 'ports' and Athelstan repeated the provision, linking it with orders about the repair of boroughs, restricting minting to ports, and specifying the number of moneyers that were to work in each borough in such a way as to imply that boroughs and ports were in this context synonymous. Fortification in itself could not create a borough that would last: some of the early tenth-century boroughs were quite unsuited to become towns, like the hill-top forts of Pilton (Devon) or Chisbury (Wiltshire), and they did not apparently endure as boroughs either. Before the end of the tenth century Pilton had probably been replaced by Barnstaple, down by the River Taw, which soon acquired a mint and may already have been the chief sea-port and market of north Devon.

If it is agreed that some towns of a sort had existed in England before the late ninth century, that many or most of the boroughs which continued to be fortified and used became towns, and that some of them may have been towns or proto-towns already, then it is reasonable to ask how important the moment of fortification was to them. The question has not always been posed very directly be-

[32] *Eng. Hist. Docs.* [29], i, p. 498.

cause of the tendency of historians to concentrate either on the beginning or the end of Anglo-Saxon history and to leave the ill-documented middle alone, so that discussions of late Anglo-Saxon towns have often started with the borough fortifications. In the case of Worcester the charter evidence for the eighth and ninth centuries, which has already been cited, suggests that the Alfredian fortification may not have been an absolute starting point, while in other cases recently discovered archaeological evidence implies the same thing. At Tamworth (fortified in 913), which was described in 1962 as having furnished a 'rural background' for the Mercian court in the eighth century, archaeologists have since found 'middle Saxon' material, including a water-mill, which they thought might date from the eighth century. If it did, the mill would be as early as any recorded in England, and though there is nothing necessarily urban about water-mills the unexpectedness and context of the discovery are thought-provoking. The tenth-century fortifications at Hereford, also in Mercia, have been found to overlay two earlier sets of defences, perhaps of the eighth and ninth centuries. Perhaps in borough-building, as in other ways, Alfred followed Mercian precedents. The absence of information about Mercian—and other—towns before the tenth century says more about the nature and dearth of evidence than about the scarcity of towns.[33]

Nor should much be made of whether places occur in the Burghal Hidage and Chronicle or not. We do not know why London and the Kentish boroughs—Canterbury and Rochester, to go no further—are not in the Burghal Hidage, while at Doncaster, which is not recorded as an Anglo-Saxon borough at all, ramparts have been unearthed which apparently look very like those of the tenth-century boroughs.[34] It may be that the royal policy of fortification only stimulated, or even only helped to defend, towns which were already growing. At places where we know that there were surviving Roman walls, as at seven of the Burghal Hidage boroughs, or earlier Anglo-Saxon defences, as at Hereford, the stimulus may have been at its slightest. At Winchester, for example, little archaeological evidence of occupation apart from the minster and associated buildings has been found before the tenth century, but it would be difficult to attribute all the development of the tenth century to repairs of the walls as such. During the tenth century an increasingly powerful

[33] *Current Archaeol.* i (1967–8), 242–6; iii (1971), 164; *Med. Archaeol.* xiii (1969), 233.
[34] *Current Archaeol.* iii (1972), 276.

monarchy made its headquarters there, Athelstan ordered that there should be six moneyers in the town, the Old Minster was enlarged, and the New Minster was built beside it: fortification was only one of the factors stimulating urban growth at the time.

THE TENTH AND ELEVENTH CENTURIES

The evidence of coins and Domesday

Among the multiplying sources of the tenth and eleventh centuries coins rank high. The late Old English monarchy's control of moneying, as well as being a remarkable achievement in itself, provides a measure of urban growth. The relative number of moneyers and of coins from each mint which have been identified by numismatists probably provides a more accurate guide to the ranking of towns than would be the case in a country where political authority was more fragmented. Over eighty mints working in the tenth and eleventh centuries have been identified, with London producing perhaps a quarter of the country's coins, York a tenth, Lincoln, Winchester, Chester, Norwich, Exeter, and Thetford smaller but still significant fractions. Problems remain: no mints are recorded north of York, and the concentration in the south-west may owe as much to politics and tradition as to the social and economic realities of urban development, but surviving coins are still one of the best sources of information about towns in this period.[35]

Other information comes from the growing quantity of documentary material, culminating in 1086 with Domesday Book, which casts a valuable but flickering light backwards into the late Anglo-Saxon period.[36] There has been much argument about what Domesday means by a 'borough', some of it too anachronistically legalistic to be helpful to the urban historian. There is no reason to believe that borough was a technical term of consistent meaning in the eleventh century, let alone that it had the particular meaning of a place enjoying privileges of local government and representation which later attached to it. The accumulation of evidence suggests that by the mid eleventh century England was by contemporary standards a rich country with an abundant silver currency:[37] as the

[35] See map opposite and Dolley, *A.S. Coins* [109].

[36] Translations of the respective sections of Domesday appear in *V.C.H.* For past interpretations see Tait, *Med. Eng. Bor.* [258], 43–67; for statistics, see Darby, *Domesday Geog.* [100]; for 'boroughs' in Domesday, see below pp. 96–8.

[37] Sawyer, 'Wealth of Eng.' [241].

Map 1
The more important towns in 1086

economy had grown in the previous centuries the places described
as 'boroughs' and 'ports' must have grown and changed too, so that
the words gained new meanings for those who used them. Over a
hundred places are either described in Domesday Book as *burgi* or
civitates or are said there to have burgesses (*burgenses*) belonging to
them. Not all of them were necessarily towns, for in contemporary
Normandy and west France a *bourg* could be a completely rural
settlement, and, though no absolutely comparable example of this
usage in England has been proved, it could have spread here after
the Conquest.[38] On the other hand, some places which are not explicitly described as boroughs in Domesday, like Coventry, may
have been towns, while the entries for Bristol and Gloucester, for
instance, are very defective, and those for London and Winchester
are altogether missing. Nor do the entries which are there all contain
comparable information, present it in a uniform way, or concentrate
on what is significant for our purposes: markets for instance are
seldom mentioned.

Nevertheless Domesday tells us much that is valuable, and even
on the patchy evidence available most of the Domesday boroughs
seem to have had some urban attributes. Nearly all are known to
have had pre-Conquest mints and a good many were marked off
from the countryside, for instance by having their own courts or
by having their revenues collected separately from the rest of the
shire. In most cases too we may guess, even if we do not know,
that land in the borough was held by what later came to be called
burgage tenure, that is, on terms which often involved a fixed money
rent and freer rights of alienation than were customary in the
country.

All users of Domesday Book feel tempted to use its complex,
obscure, and incomplete data to produce more exact statistics than
they will really bear, and notably to concoct estimates of population.
Much discussion has revolved around the relationship between the
people actually mentioned in the entries and the total population—
for instance between 'burgesses' or owners of *mansiones* and the
inhabitants of a town. Darby and his colleagues in the *Domesday
Geographies* use a multiplier of about five, which produces five
towns (apart from London and Winchester) with populations of over
about four thousand: York (perhaps 9,000 in 1066), Lincoln,
Oxford, Norwich, and Thetford; eleven with between two and four

[38] Musset, 'Bourgs ruraux' [202]; E. Miller in *Northern Hist.* iii (1968), 194–6.

thousand; and fourteen more with over a thousand. By modern standards these, let alone the rest which were even smaller, were barely towns at all, but they were clearly not self-supporting in food: instead they fulfilled urban functions, and the difference between their inhabitants and those of the countryside around seems to be reflected in what we know of their institutions.[39]

The Danish problem

Two questions at least arise about the way in which towns grew between the borough fortifications of Alfred and his successors and the making of the Domesday Book. The first is how far the process was affected by the Danish invasions and settlement and the second is how far it was affected by the Norman Conquest.

Despite contemporary lamentations, the undoubted injuries to churches, and the belief of some modern historians that the Vikings dealt a heavy blow to town life, no English town is known to have been destroyed by the Northmen. Hamwih was plundered in 842 but archaeological evidence suggests that it continued to be inhabited for almost a hundred years afterwards. On the contrary there is a good deal to suggest that the impact of the Danes on town life in England, at least after the first shock, was a stimulating and constructive one. According to Domesday many of the largest towns in the country lay in the Danelaw in 1086, while phenomena like streets described as 'gates', church dedications to St. Olave, and (more doubtfully) the institution of lawmen, point to a considerable Danish influence on many of them.[40]

The Life of St. Oswald, written c. 1000, said that York was enriched with the treasures of merchants from all countries, especially Danes, and estimated its adult population at thirty thousand. The figure is a nice example of the casual medieval attitude to statistics, but archaeologists attribute much growth here to the Danish period. By the early twelfth century, despite the sufferings it had endured after the Norman Conquest, the town as described by William of Malmesbury lay on both sides of the Ouse and was frequented by ships plying to Germany and Ireland. Sir Francis Hill, though lacking archaeological surveys comparable to those available at York, implied that the similar riverside suburb at Lincoln was also

---

[39] See map p. 35; also pp. 92–8, below.
[40] Stenton, *A.S. Eng.* [253], 533; Hill, *Med. Lincoln* [333], 32, 36–7; Sawyer, *Age of Vikings* [240], 156–74; Dickens, 'Cult of St. Olave' [105].

Danish.[41] Other towns like Norwich, Stamford, and Northampton, which ranked high by 1086, are recorded for the first time in the early tenth century, while Grimsby, according to a story current in about 1200, was founded by a Danish fisherman called Grim who sold his catch at Lincoln.[42] Perhaps the most striking example of all is Thetford, where a movement across the River Ouse in the eleventh century left the original site of the town more or less empty until the twentieth, and thus available for archaeological investigations. There appears to have been only a very small settlement on the site before a Danish army wintered there in 869, but thereafter one sprang up rapidly, displaying pronounced urban characteristics from the start. By the eleventh century it stretched for a mile along the south bank of the river, with an earth rampart, several cobbled flint roadways, many scattered houses and a few large halls, pottery kilns, cloth and metal works, and probably a dozen churches. A mint was established *c.* 960–70 and from 1072 to *c.* 1095 Thetford was the see of East Anglia.[43]

It is not surprising that Danish settlement should have promoted commercial and urban development. Both at York and in the east midlands the settlers seem to have been grouped around boroughs which formed the headquarters of their armies, and their habits of sea-faring and skill at navigation must have tended to promote contacts overseas. Nevertheless nagging doubts remain whether the towns of eastern England developed merely with and after the Danish settlement rather than because of it. P. H. Sawyer thinks that the scale and consequently the influence of immigration have been exaggerated, and sees the expansion of settlement in eastern England as part of a wider process of internal colonization. He suggests that the sources of England's eleventh-century wealth were wider too, and that the eastern towns flourished chiefly on trade with Flanders and Germany for which Scandinavian contacts and the highest navigational skills would hardly be necessary. It must also be borne in mind that the dates when the 'Anglo-Danish' towns started to grow are, in the nature of things, hard to prove, and sometimes seem to have been rather easily assumed: even if they were proved to be post-Danish that would not conclusively demonstrate a

[41] *Historians of York* [439], i. 454; William of Malmesbury, *Gesta Pont.* [57], 208; above p. 26, nn. 18–19.

[42] A. Bell ed., *Le Lai d'Haveloc* (1925), 25, lines 123–44.

[43] Clarke, *East Anglia* [88], 166, 169–72; Davison, 'Thetford Excavations' [425].

causal connection. The evidence on a subject like this is almost bound to be uncertain, but the gap in the argument needs to be noted both for the honesty of historical reasoning and to preclude any tendency to ignore other influences.

Moreover there are plenty of signs of urban growth outside the Danelaw. London lay just over the boundary, under the control of Wessex. It underwent some, perhaps considerable, Danish influence, as is suggested by the Scandinavian name of its court of husting (first recorded in the tenth century), by the church of St. Clement Danes, and by several churches dedicated to St. Olave (king of Norway, d. 1030). A list of tolls payable *c.* 1000 at Billingsgate specifies the dues paid by men from Rouen, Flanders, Ponthieu, Normandy, the Isle de France, Huy, Liège, and Nivelles, and notes that subjects of the emperor (probably chiefly from the Rhineland and further west) were entitled to trade more or less as natives. Danes are mentioned later on in the same document as part of the local population. Although we have no Domesday entry and cannot really begin to guess at London's population, it was large enough by *c.* 1100 to support and require a local administration of some complexity. Danes had certainly contributed to the city's rise, but there is no evidence that their contribution was decisive.[44]

Canterbury was still among the larger towns of the kingdom in 1086. It also had a merchant guild at about this time, though William of Malmesbury does not seem to have been much struck by its commerce and described it as medium-sized.[45] The south-east ports were also populous and active by the time of Domesday, carrying on a Channel trade that may have owed little to Scandinavia.[46] In the south-west and south tradition and royal protection between them favoured a network of small markets of which a fair number seem to have had some urban attributes. At the bottom of the scale was somewhere like Bedwyn (Wiltshire), which had a mint, a guild[47], and, in 1086, twenty-five burgesses. Later on most of these little towns were to wither under the competition of bigger centres, but as yet trade seems to have been widely dispersed among them. Coins from Wiltshire mints have been found over a wide enough area to

[44] *Laws from Edmund to Henry I* [40], 71–9; Stenton, 'Norman London' [361]; Reynolds, 'Rulers of London' [359].

[45] *Gesta Pont.* [57], 1; Urry, *Canterbury* [303], 385.

[46] See below, p. 44; Dulley, 'Port of Pevensey' [399] and 'Excavations at Pevensey' [398].

[47] For the guild, see below, pp. 81–3.

suggest that their trade was not merely local.[48] There were of course
some larger towns in the south and south-west as well. Winchester
was in the first rank, developing greatly in the tenth century, while
Oxford and Exeter were not far behind by the eleventh. Oxford,
first mentioned in 912 as a frontier post, seems to have become very
prosperous by the eleventh century, partly through trade along the
Thames. This was promoted by improvements in navigation which
in turn resulted from the construction of water-mills and weirs.[49] It
was one of the half-dozen most populous towns in 1086 if Domesday
statistics are to be trusted. Exeter was said by William of Malmesbury to have been fortified by King Athelstan. By the twelfth century it had a flourishing shipping trade and was claimed to rank high
among English towns.[50]

Bristol and Chester both profited from trade with Ireland and so
might come under the head of towns under Scandinavian influence:
Chester indeed was in an area of both Danish and Norwegian settlement. Its site was apparently deserted, perhaps since Roman times,
when a Danish army seized it in 894. It was restored (*geedneowad*)
by the English in 907 and soon afterwards a mint was established
which continued to be very active throughout the Anglo-Saxon
period, reflecting naval as well as mercantile activity on the Irish
Sea.[51] The account of Chester in Domesday includes some of the
book's rare references to trade, for it talks of ships and of marten
skins, probably from Ireland. Bristol is not mentioned before 1051 in
historical sources though the mint is known to have been established
some decades before. The port was the centre of a slave trade with
Ireland throughout the eleventh century and perhaps later. In the
twelfth century it carried on a prosperous trade with Ireland,
Norway, and elsewhere.[52]

As in the previous age, towns in the tenth and eleventh centuries
could be greatly stimulated by royal or ecclesiastical patronage,
which largely and progressively cut across the Danish boundary.
The royal foundation of 'boroughs' as fortifications and royal efforts

[48] *V.C.H. Wilts.* [273], ii. 15–20; *Eng. Hist. Docs.* [29], i, p. 559; Brooks, 'Unidentified
Forts' [76], 78–9.

[49] Davis, 'The Ford, the River, and the City' [391].

[50] Finberg and Hoskins, *Devon Studies* [123], 222–3; *Gesta Pont.* [57], 200–1; *Gesta
Stephani* [32], 22.

[51] Webster, 'Chester in Dark Ages' [307]; Dolley, 'Mint of Chester' [306].

[52] *Eng. Hist. Docs.* [29], ii, p. 123; *Vita Wulfstani* [297], 42–3, 91; *Gesta Pont.* [57],
292; cf. *Gesta Stephani* [32], 37–9; Lobel and Carus-Wilson, 'Bristol' [294], 3.

to restrict trade and moneying to them have already been discussed. Administrative developments in general—the organization of shires and shire courts, the collection of geld and so forth—must have encouraged recourse to the centres where courts were held and taxes collected. While the Danes may have promoted the growth, or even the foundation, of a town at Norwich, the extension of English government to East Anglia stimulated it yet further. The subjugation of Danish East Anglia was accomplished without the chain of fortifications which helped to disperse urban growth farther west. Thereafter Norwich remained the governmental centre of the whole of East Anglia well into the twelfth century. From about 1095 it was a bishop's see as well, so that both political and ecclesiastical factors fostered its position as the economic centre of a large, rich, and densely populated region.[53] Elsewhere other markets must have been stimulated in the same sort of ways at the expense of their neighbours, so that places which may have been much of a size in earlier centuries become classifiable as regional centres or local markets.

A good example of a Church town is St. Albans. According to later traditions of the abbey Abbot Wulsig (*fl.* before *c.* 968) established a market and provided building materials and other inducements to settlers. He built one church at the far end of the market-place from the abbey and two more at the points where the medieval main road left the old line of Watling Street to pass through St. Albans. His successors continued to promote their little town at the expense of Kingsbury, close by but in royal ownership. Abbot Leofstan (d. 1066) had the road from London improved, bridges built, and woods along it cut down. Other towns grew up where monasteries were founded or refounded.[54] At Bury St. Edmunds 342 houses were built between 1066 and 1086 on land which had formerly been under the plough. By 1086 the population included seventy-five bakers, ale-brewers, tailors, washerwomen, shoemakers, robe-makers, cooks, porters, and *dispensatores* who daily waited upon the saint, the abbot, and the brethren—excellent testimony to the economic stimulus provided by a great religious house.[55] From the eleventh century too come the first references to annual fairs in

[53] Campbell, 'Norwich' [385], 5–8.
[54] *Gesta Abbatum* [405], i. 22–4, 32, 39; cf. *V.C.H. Herts.* [404], ii. 470, 476; iv. 414; Beresford, *New Towns* [67], 326–7.
[55] Darby, *Domesday Geog. of E. Eng.* [100], 198.

England, though none of those mentioned was at a place which developed much as a town; whether or not it is significant that these first recorded fairs were in the Danelaw, it is surely not an accident of the sources that they were connected with monasteries and their feast-days.[56] Some monastic towns do not seem to have come to very much, but then most medieval towns were small and by eleventh-century standards somewhere like Bury was quite big. Only later, when competition became fiercer, did the dead hand of Church control probably begin to hold back towns that had once grown under monastic patronage.

This survey leaves the towns of the Danelaw looking larger and earlier than those of English England. There are several reasons why that conclusion still needs to be weighed very carefully. Danish England occupied much of the east where overseas trade was likely to thrive and to stimulate towns. Much of the earlier evidence concerns fortifications so that places which seem to start late may simply have been of no military significance. H. R. Loyn points out that the preservation of documents connected with the great abbeys may also bias information towards the east—though it does not much affect the sketch given above. Lastly the availability of archaeological evidence is necessarily patchy, though here we can set the material for Winchester and Thetford, for instance, to balance one another.

THE NORMAN CONQUEST

The question whether or how far the Norman Conquest affected urban development can be answered more easily than that about the Danes. That the Conquest had some impact is undeniable, but it was mixed and may on balance have been more destructive than beneficial: the evidence that towns started to grow well before 1066 must rule out any serious argument that it was decisive. The Normans continue to haunt the beginner in English urban history partly because of the undeniable topographical changes imposed by their castles and cathedrals, but partly too because their coincidence in time with the general flowering of urban life in medieval Europe has lulled many writers into confusing the two events in their words if not in their thought. That is particularly noticeable in connection with urban institutions and liberties, which are discussed in a later chapter: though some new Norman customs are discernible it is

---

[56] Harmer, 'Chipping and Market' [137].

difficult to see any significant change in English urban institutions which can be attributed to the Conquest.

One reason why towns and townspeople, like the rest of England, suffered from the Conquest was that it involved war and destruction. York was very badly hit: the rebellion and reprisals of 1069–70 and the demolition of houses to make way for a castle within the walls left the population in 1086 perhaps a half of what it had been in King Edward's day. Other places suffered too. At Lincoln, for instance, 166 houses were pulled down to make way for the castle, and at Norwich 98.[57] In some boroughs a considerable proportion of the houses were returned as 'waste' without further explanation. At Norwich the number of burgesses had dropped by about a half and there were 480 bordars—perhaps former burgesses—who did not pay the dues owed by full burgesses because they were too poor. According to Domesday the royal revenues from many of the greater towns were much higher in 1086 than in 1066. This has been seen as a sign of increased prosperity but in cases like Norwich or York it is more likely to have been simply an increased burden and an extra cause of poverty.

On the other hand new lords out to make fortunes in England may have been as likely to foster new towns as to oppress old ones. Small towns grew up at places, like Tutbury, where castles were built in the countryside, while even in older towns castles, once built, must have stimulated markets. Normans and other Frenchmen are known to have settled in some existing towns and though their arrival could lead to friction it presumably favoured growth. At Norwich, Northampton, and Nottingham, for example, the new-comers formed separate boroughs, the 'French borough' of Notting-ham retaining some features of separate organization for centuries.[58] It was, too, probably only after the Conquest, and apparently at the initiative of the Conqueror, that Jews first came to live in England: it would be hard to say how far the subsequent growth of Jewries in the twelfth century should be seen as a direct result of the first move.[59]

The movement from rural to urban bishops' sees, which was accelerated though not started after 1066, must have contributed to

[57] Darby, *New Hist. Geog.* [99], 71–2.
[58] Stephenson, *Borough and Town* [255], 75; *Rec. of Nottingham* [390], i. 124–6, 175, 189.
[59] See below, p. 74.

the prosperity of the chosen towns and benefited the building trades and the markets which supplied their members, though the lavish scale of Norman churches caused some destruction of houses too. The movement of sees, however, should be seen rather as a consequence than a cause of urban growth. Country sees had been established when towns were less important and when royal or ecclesiastical estates made the best bases for bishops to work from. The chief reasons for associating the change with the Normans are that foreign bishops were unaccustomed to rural sees and were also readier to break with tradition than those brought up to revere the places associated with English saints.

How far the Conquest injured trade, and especially trade with Scandinavia, or promoted it with Normandy and France, is very doubtful. The fact that the new king's protection held good in Normandy may have had some marginal influence on trade routes, but we know that merchants from Rouen were already familiar in London. The kings of England and Denmark were at war a good deal after the Conquest, and relations with Flanders were also disturbed for a while, but there is no evidence how far trade was affected. There can have been few periods in the medieval age of urban growth when commerce was safe from war. What does seem clear is that the Channel ports profited from official comings and goings, and despite some defective entries Domesday records an increase of burgesses or of houses at Southampton, Chichester, Pevensey, and Sandwich.[60] Similar growth at other places, like Bury St. Edmunds or Lincoln, is harder to attribute to the Conquest; once more we are brought back to the need to distinguish *post hoc* from *propter hoc*, and to remember that this was a great age of urban growth in Europe at large.

CONCLUSION

It would be pleasant to be able to conclude by helpfully pointing to a single key moment of growth between the dead or moribund towns of the sixth century and the burgeoning life of the twelfth. Unfortunately the information so far available would not justify it, and it is pointless to make guesses without substantiating them. Clearly the tenth and eleventh centuries saw dramatic growth, but it is impossible to be sure that the simultaneous improvement in the

[60] *Domesday Geog. of S.E. Eng.* [100], 351-2, 463, 469, 552; cf. Beresford, *New Towns* [67], 326-38.

sources does not exaggerate it, or to know when it had started. Until we have clearer evidence about When we cannot be definite about Why. It looks as though international trade stimulated the growth of some English towns from a very early date, but that the needs of local exchange were also, and more often, influential. Where a predominantly local market was stimulated by the demands of a court or great church it could produce genuinely urban growth, particularly when military and administrative developments all concentrated settlement on a single site. The best hope of getting a little nearer to certainty on both When and Why lies in the informed excavation of individual towns and in studying all the material—archaeological, historical, and linguistic—with the closest possible attention to chronology.

3
The Twelfth and Thirteenth Centuries

THE GENERAL PICTURE

It is now more or less agreed that demographic and economic growth continued in western Europe for some two hundred years after 1100. The date and reasons for its arrest are a matter of controversy, which so far as it affects English towns is discussed in chapter seven. Here we must consider the abundant evidence of continued urban growth during the twelfth century and at least most of the thirteenth. The usual problem of how far new evidence means new growth is relatively unimportant here, since the previous chapter has shown, or has contended, that the really significant beginnings came much earlier. The rise of towns was, moreover, one aspect of a much wider movement of which the development of record-keeping institutions was another. By the twelfth century the combined results of both are obvious, and the historian becomes less dependent on the archaeologist and numismatist, though still grateful for help from both.

As in earlier centuries the growth of towns must be set in the wider framework of the whole society and economy.[1] It is generally agreed that by 1300 the population of England was much larger than it had been in 1086. Estimates vary, but between one and two million in 1086 and between three and four in 1300 are possible. At the same time, more land was being cleared and cultivated, and trade, both internal and external, was expanding. It was becoming advisable to seek royal permission to hold markets and fairs, so that we know of more places which had them. Though some markets may

---

[1] For Europe see e.g. *Cam. Econ. Hist.* [79], ii, iii; Duby, *Early Growth of Eur. Econ.* [113]; Lopez, *Commercial Revolution* [179]; Ennen, *Europäische Stadt* [118]; Reinhard, *Hist. de la pop.* [232]. On England see Stenton, *Eng. Soc.* [252]; Poole, *From D.B. to Magna Carta* [222]; Miller, 'Eng. Econ. in 13th Cent.' [195]; Russell, *Brit. Med. Pop.* [238], but see p. 140, n.1. On markets see Martin and McIntyre, *Bibliography of Munic. Hist.* [9], i, p. 365–71; *Regesta Regum A.N.* [48], ii, p. xxiv; on the chief English fairs see *V.C.H. Northants* [384], iii. 23–4; *Rec. of Leicester* [331], i. 33; *Cal. London Letter Book A* [344], 3.

have been much older than their charters some were certainly started in this period. By 1300 most people in many parts of the country must have lived within half a day's walk of one. Some of the markets were very small and their sites did not pretend to rank as towns, since their trade was only a weekly affair and they had few or no full-time traders. Nevertheless they demonstrate the volume of exchange, at the lowest level, from which a real town—or 'permanent market'[2]—might develop. At the highest level, great international fairs become discernible in the twelfth century and by the early thirteenth several in England are known to have been attracting alien merchants. Cloth was bought regularly for Henry III's household at the fairs of Boston, Northampton, St. Ives (Huntingdonshire), Stamford, Winchester, and Bury St. Edmunds, while in London, of course, royal purchases of all sorts were innumerable and aliens were constantly around to do business.

English cloth was still being exported in the later twelfth century, as it was in the eighth, but this trade may have declined soon after. It was apparently in the eleventh century that the weavers of Flanders and Artois began to use foreign wool to supplement their own, and, as the cloth industry of the Low Countries grew, so more and more English wool seems to have gone to supply it. Corn too was being exported to Flanders and probably elsewhere by the late twelfth century. During the thirteenth century Italians and other southerners became increasingly common visitors to England, collecting papal taxes and lending money, as well as buying wool and other goods and selling spices, silks, sweet wine, and more humdrum articles. From the twelfth century an increasing volume of England's wine came from Gascony, to which wool, corn, and cloth were sent back in exchange. The Gascon trade seems to have involved less expertise in credit and money-changing than did Italian business, but it was bulky and widely dispersed. Wine went not only to taverns and the tables of the prosperous but to the altars of every parish church in the country. Trade with the Baltic flourished as the Germans colonized the Slav lands and merchants from the new and growing towns of north Germany travelled to Russia, Scandinavia, and England. As English supplies ran down, such goods as hawks, furs, and ships' stores came in growing volume from Scandinavia and the Baltic. By the early fourteenth century, apart from the

[2] Prou, 'Une ville-marché' [228], 379.

products which flowed steadily along these major lines of trade, other imports and exports went in and out in greater variety and more haphazard directions than are always allowed for in the textbook stereotypes of medieval commerce. Southampton's trade in 1308-9, for instance, included the export of bacon, meat, carpets, blankets, and, of course, wool; the import of fish, liquorice, leather, oil, tin, iron, corn, woad, and Spanish wool; and the re-export of iron, fish-oil, salt, and coal.[3]

Regular statistical evidence of English trade begins in 1275 with the accounts of the wool custom imposed in that year. In 1303 the 'new custom' was imposed on goods imported and exported by aliens, and in 1347 came the cloth custom. The early accounts of the wool custom, together with other records, suggest that aliens were then responsible for much of English overseas trade. Inland and coastal traffic, however easily overlooked by the historian because it finds so little space in the records, comprised a large volume of business in which they were presumably much less involved. There is no doubt that an increasing number of Englishmen were engaged in industry and commerce at some level and that that has a great deal to do with the multiplication and growth of towns that is revealed in the records.[4]

The sources of information about urban growth are manifold, even though for any individual town they may turn out to be disappointing. One of the best known types of evidence is political— the formation of municipalities and the grant of liberties and charters to them which are discussed in chapter five. So striking is this development that it has even been propounded as a principal cause of growth.[5] It is true that liberties could help a town and their absence could cripple it, but a study of individual cases and above all the general chronology suggest that the relation of cause and effect is more complex. Another obvious source of information is topographical: churches and parishes multiplied, harbours were improved, market-places laid out, and bridges and walls built— though the relatively peaceful conditions in most of England made

---

[3] Verhulst, 'La Laine indigène' [269]; Harvey, 'Eng. Inflation of 1180-1208' [138]; Platt, *Med. Southampton* [416], 82-3. See Carus-Wilson, *Med. Merchant Venturers* [81] and 'Towns and Trade' [83]; Ruddock, *Italian Merchants* [417]; James, *Studies in Wine Trade* [158]; Veale, *Eng. Fur Trade* [268]; Bridbury, *Eng. and Salt Trade* [75].

[4] Gras, *Early Eng. Customs System* [134]; Carus-Wilson and Coleman, *England's Export Trade* [22]. On alien and Eng. merchants, see pp. 76-7.

[5] Postan, *Med. Econ.* [224], 212-13.

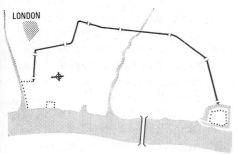

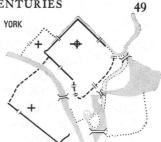

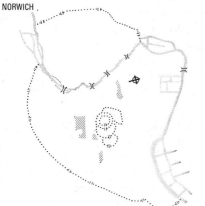

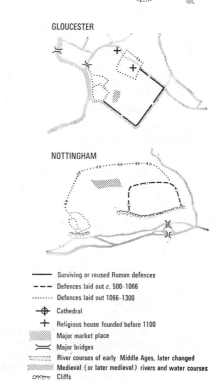

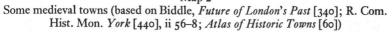

Map 2
Some medieval towns (based on Biddle, *Future of London's Past* [340]; R. Com.
Hist. Mon. *York* [440], ii 56–8; *Atlas of Historic Towns* [60])

walls a much less good guide to growth than they are or were in most of Europe, and the number of churches did not bear any very consistent relation to the size of the population. Literary descriptions and references also multiply and the fact that contemporaries considered that towns had individual characteristics which were worth describing is in itself significant. William of Malmesbury (d. *c.* 1143), for example, described briefly some of the towns with cathedrals or famous monasteries, and Richard of Devizes (*fl.* 1190–1200) in the course of a long, improbable, but lively anecdote gave bad characters to a number of the towns. His own Winchester escaped condemnation except for the mendacity of its citizens. About a hundred or so years later a light-hearted list of over a hundred places, most of them towns, appears to have been in circulation. It gives a reason for the fame of each place, like the sanctuary of Canterbury, the whores of Charing [Cross], the schools of Oxford, the russet [cloth] of Colchester, the knives of Thaxted, the herrings of Yarmouth, and the soap of Coventry. Also from the thirteenth and fourteenth centuries come the first maps of England to show the main routes of the country and the places that lay along them.[6]

For a general view of urban development and the comparative ranking of towns, tax records are useful. We know the fixed lump sums ('farms') paid each year by most of the more important towns, and the occasional taxes ('gifts' or 'aids') which they paid from time to time before 1189 have been tabulated by Carl Stephenson. Thereafter the figures are not so easily available and for the years after 1216 few of the annual government accounts (the Pipe Rolls) in which they are recorded are yet in print. In any case the occasional taxes, which now became known as tallages, were produced by pretty rough and ready bargaining and assessment and tended to become fixed at customary totals. They can only be used for rough comparisons of scale, not to show the real or changing wealth of any particular town. A customs duty of a fifteenth *ad valorem* levied in 1202–4 suggests the relative activity of a number of ports, though it omits most of those in the west, and the sums listed probably represent the wealth passing through the port rather than the wealth of

---

[6] See pp. 102–14, 190–2; walls: Ganshof, *Les Villes entre Loire et Rhin* [131] and Turner, *Town Defences* [266]. William of Malmesbury, *Gesta Pont.* [57]; Richard of Devizes, *Chron.* [49], 64–9; the thirteenth–fourteenth century list: *Eng. Hist. Docs.* [29], iii, pp. 881–4; Matthew Paris, *Four Maps* [44]; *Gough Map* [36].

its inhabitants; in many cases the goods assessed would not have belonged to resident merchants. The regular 'enrolled accounts' of customs after 1275 do not relate to individual ports and do not therefore establish their size or activity.

From 1275 tallage gave way to new parliamentary taxes, which were paid from 1294 at a higher rate in towns than in rural areas—that is, normally a tenth instead of a fifteenth. The list of places paying at the higher rate ('taxation boroughs', as modern historians call them), like that of the 'parliamentary boroughs' (also a modern description), which sent members to parliament, varied for a while. Though the two lists differed slightly both constitute guides to which places contemporary officials thought of as towns. Unfortunately few assessment rolls survive from before 1327, though there are more between then and 1334, when the system of assessment was changed. Some of the extant rolls have been printed, and the lump sums paid in 1334 have been mapped and tabulated by R. E. Glasscock.[7]

In the absence of better taxation records or of any proper records of population two other sources for the relative standing of towns may be mentioned. Although it became much shorter in this period, the list of mints remains useful, provided that the reasons for the disappearance or survival of a mint are not oversimplified.[8] Friaries of the mendicant orders are also a surprisingly good guide, since mendicant houses needed to be in centres of population both for material and intellectual sustenance and in order to fulfil their mission. Arriving in 1221, the Dominicans had houses in more than twenty towns by the middle of the century, while the Franciscans, who had come three years later, had twice as many. A map of friaries is thus a good rough index to the chief towns of the later thirteenth century, when the mendicant orders were at the height of their success.[9]

[7] Tait, *Med. Eng. Bor.* [258], 183–4; Stephenson, *Borough and Town* [255], 222–4 (slightly amended list in Darby, *New Hist. Geog.* [99], 134); Mitchell, *Taxation in Med. Eng.* [197], 313, 339–56. For a tallage roll, see Fuller, 'Tallage of Edward II' [292]. Willard, 'Taxation Boroughs and Parliamentary Boroughs' [279]; Beresford, *Lay Subsidies and Poll Taxes* [2]; Darby, *New Hist. Geog.* [99], 178–85; Glasscock, *Lay Subsidy, 1334* [35]. Veale, 'Craftsmen and London Econ.' [367], 135–7, discusses the difficulties of using tax records.

[8] Oman, *Coinage of Eng.* [205], 131, 135, 137, 141, 145, 160, 163–6, 382–3; *Pipe Roll 7 John* [46], p. xxxi.

[9] See map p. 49, based on Knowles and Hadcock, *Med. Religious Houses* [167], 33–7, 212–50, and map. Cf. Le Goff, 'Ordres mendiants et urbanisation dans la France médiévale' [171].

THE PROBLEM OF CLASSIFICATION

Besides all this general information there is an increasing body of information about individual towns in the records of the central government, of lords of estates, and, towards the end of the period, of some municipalities themselves. Like contemporaries we can now begin to discern the individual characters of towns and can, if we wish, try to classify them. In their more questioning and theoretical approach to urban history continental historians have given more thought to the typology of medieval towns than English historians have done. Here the only real attempt at classification has been made through political institutions and degrees of liberty, and since these have been based on the rather meaningless criteria of 'borough status' and the form of charters[10] they have not been very illuminating. Other possible classifications are by origins—whether Roman or later, whether of 'organic' or 'planted' origin; by size of population and wealth; and, perhaps most influential of all, by economic type, distinguishing towns which lived by long-range trade from industrial centres or regional or local markets. The basic difficulty about all classifications is that medieval towns did not grow in social Galapagos Islands so that species or types could evolve distinctly. Towns were and are complex entities, and constant mutual influence makes them hard to classify by reference to one feature such as origin, constitution, or type of economy. Nevertheless the search for types and classes, if flexibly conducted, helps to disentangle strands of influence and discourages that parochial concentration on individual cases which precludes any real understanding of causes. The following survey of urban fortunes in the twelfth and thirteenth centuries is therefore arranged so as to provide some sort of evaluation of the more likely sorts of classification. It starts with new towns, which have often, though perhaps misleadingly, been treated as a distinct category, and will then deal in turn with the commercial and industrial functions of towns in general, and lastly with their population.

NEW TOWNS

Many new towns appeared between 1100 and 1300 and we know much more about them than we do about those founded earlier. The importance of the phenomenon and the fascination of the enquiry

---

[10] See below, pp. 91–2.

have recently stimulated a great deal of work, notably by M. W. Beresford, whose *New Towns of the Middle Ages* (1967) lists many examples county by county and does much to explain when and why they were founded and how they fared. Thanks to his work, a full discussion here is unnecessary, but some general remarks may be useful. Most of the new towns we know about seem to have been established on the initiative of their lords, who set up markets, laid out market-places fronted by small tenements (burgages) suitable for traders, and offered favourable terms to those who might come and settle there. The expansion of the economy made it worth a landowner's while to forgo some of his normal dues in return for money rents and tolls, provided he had a promising site. Other towns were founded for wholly or partly military ends, like many in Wales or the Marches. In either case we should not forget that the lord's initiative, which has a documentary record, may have been prompted by spontaneous developments, like the holding of unofficial markets, which have not.

Some attempts to found towns by offering attractive terms came to nothing, so that evidence of the offer is not in itself evidence that urban life developed. Many more places which did indeed become towns nevertheless remained relatively small, serving as local market and distribution centres. That was natural since, though the growing volume of production and exchange could evidently support new subsidiary markets, social and economic regions had by now been formed around the old-established centres. Some new towns of this type, like Leeds, were to have a grander future in changed economic circumstances later on. Striking successes, on the other hand, both short-term and long-term, were achieved by ports. Newcastle, Boston, Lynn, and Hull, on the prosperous east coast, all throve quickly into the first rank, though Liverpool and Portsmouth, both established for military purposes, took longer to attract very substantial trade. Shifting coastlines promoted some foundations and accounted for some failures: Ravenserodd (Yorkshire), New Winchelsea, and New Romney are among the more obvious examples.

Beresford's *New Towns* lists 172 new, or in his more vivid phrase, 'planted' towns of medieval England. The decades 1170–1250 produce the largest number recorded, with the pace of foundations slackening rapidly thereafter. It is clear that the multiplication of new towns is as striking a feature of the twelfth and thirteenth centuries as is the growth of older ones. Certain problems however arise. Partly because of a dubious analogy with the officially sponsored 'new towns' of the twentieth century and perhaps partly just because interest in the subject has arisen so quickly, a certain confusion seems to have crept into some discussions of it. Historians speak sometimes of 'new' towns, sometimes of 'planted' or 'planned' towns, as if all three meant the same thing. A planned town is, however, presumably to be understood as a town in which the layout of at least the streets, public places, and public buildings has been planned by a single person or group of people. It can be contrasted with a town of unplanned or 'organic' growth where the layout has evolved as a result of the uncoordinated decisions of many people, whether over a long or short period. Too much concentration on topography and layout, the outward signs of a town's social existence, tends firstly to obscure the distinction between a town which is new and a town with a planned layout, and secondly to turn the distinction between planned and organic layout into a distinction between planned and organic towns. The nature of human behaviour and the tendency of humans to plan their activities make it difficult to postulate a total absence of 'planning', a total spontaneity, in anything so complex as the foundation of a town, though the nature and purposes of the planning may vary a great deal. It is with towns as a whole, and not with topography as such, that this chapter is concerned. The important question how far the layout of new towns was deliberately planned, whether for aesthetic or other reasons, is reserved for chapter nine, together with some discussion of how far topography in itself provides evidence of deliberate planning. Here we may note that while a planned layout, if it can be proved, is good evidence of a new or 'planted' town, not all planted towns necessarily had planned layouts; and that the evidence of planned layout is not always entirely obvious or unambiguous.

Nor, leaving aside 'planned towns', is the expression 'planted town' entirely satisfactory as a synonym for 'new town'. We should remember that every town must have been new once. Beresford, glossing 'new towns' as 'planted towns', then defines them as places 'planted' on sites where no settlement existed before, and, by implication, as places which were deliberately intended from the start to be urban. This is entirely understandable as a delimitation of an otherwise unwieldy subject, but it may have led others to infer misleading distinctions. To start with, the identification of a planted town obviously depends on the survival of evidence. This may account for the scarcity of examples which Beresford cites from the earlier Middle Ages and for the way that they multiply in the thirteenth century. If it is agreed, however, that not every new town had a planned layout, then Thetford was as much a new town in the tenth century, although its layout looks untidy and we do not know who decided to 'found' it, as New Winchelsea, with its documentary record and its chequer-board streets, was in the thirteenth. Moreover, because the boundary between urban and non-urban may be hazy, so that some towns which evolved from villages may never have been new at any particular moment, even among this group the transition to urban life could have come so quickly that it would be reasonable to talk of a 'new town' despite the previous existence of a rural community on the same site. The distinction between such 'organic towns', which grew out of villages, and 'planted towns' on virgin sites, is also difficult to maintain if, like Beresford, one allows a 'planted town' to be tacked on to an existing village but regards the development of a town where such an appendage happens to be unrecorded as 'organic'. Higham Ferrers (Northamptonshire) may have been as much—or more—of a new town in 1250–1 as New Thame (Oxfordshire) was in 1219–21. At Higham the earl of Derby freed his villein tenants, turned their holdings into 'burgages', and started an annual fair, so that the whole community was presumably intended to become more or less urban. At Thame the bishop of Lincoln laid out a street of burgages alongside the existing village and diverted the main road through it. Though the names of New and Old Thame imply a degree of separation, the two communities must have been closely linked. Both Higham and Thame, as it happens, are known to have had earlier markets, which suggests that 'organic' or spontaneous development had in each case stimulated the deliberate action of the lord. There is no reason to doubt that Derby's transactions of 1250–1 promoted urban development at Higham just as much as if he had laid out some new burgages, as indeed he may have done for all we know.[11]

When all qualifications have been made new towns remain a significant feature of the period as well as a fascinating topic for archaeological and historical investigation. They constitute a useful category for the urban historian, provided only that we define and

[11] Above p. 38; *V.C.H. Northants* [384], iii. 266–7; *V.C.H. Oxon.* [397], vii. 178; Beresford, *New Towns* [67], 477–8, 497–8. For burgages, see below, pp. 93, 98.

use it consistently and remember that, since new towns, once started, varied in their privileges, economy, and size, it inevitably cuts across other categories.

TRADE

The most famous and discussed category of medieval towns is that of the great commercial and industrial centres of Flanders and Italy. The only clear candidate for it in England is London, which probably had a population comparable to the greater cities of northern Europe though not those of Italy. By the twelfth century it was constantly visited by foreign ships and merchants and had a sufficiently large and floating population to support public kitchens or restaurants on the water-front, weekly horse and cattle fairs, and a variety of public sports and games. In times of dearth it served as a distribution centre for the whole of the country.[12] Such pre-eminence indeed has always been assured to London, in any period in which trade has not been completely stagnant, by its geographical situation and dominance of the road system. At this time, however, it clearly did not deprive other towns of overseas trade. So widely was that dispersed that the assumptions implied in making 'great trading towns' into a single category may be questioned. In England the towns whose citizens participated somehow in international trade, even if they did not entirely live off it, were numerous and many of them were very small. Chief among them of course were the ports.

The history of shipbuilding and shipping in the Middle Ages is still largely unwritten,[13] but it seems that sea-going ships could still use very small harbours though by now they needed proper quays, rather than flat beaches. The wealth of midland and eastern England, its good river communications, and the trading activity across the North Sea and Channel fostered a mass of ports on the east and south coasts. Ships still came to the old river ports of York, Lincoln, Norwich, Gloucester, and Chester, though goods may increasingly have been trans-shipped at coastal towns like Hull, Boston, and Yarmouth. Oxford, on the other hand, was increasingly dependent on roads and probably lost long-distance trade as the Thames seems to have become less easy to navigate.[14] How far the

---

[12] *Eng. Hist. Docs.* [29], ii, pp. 956–62; William of Malmesbury, *Gesta Pont.* [57], 140.
[13] Though see, e.g., Bass, *Hist. of Seafaring* [62].
[14] Davis, 'The Ford, the River, and the City' [391].

rise of new coastal ports injured inland towns could depend on a variety of factors, only some of which we know about. Exeter's troubles with downstream Topsham were exacerbated by the weirs built by the thirteenth-century countess of Devon and her successors, but the city probably retained a good deal of its trade even when the river was impassable and cargoes were unladen at Topsham. Though by 1334 Yarmouth seems to have become the richer town, Norwich seems to have suffered less from its competition than Lincoln did from Boston, especially when Lincoln's alternative waterway to Torksey (opened or reopened in 1121) later became impracticable again. Boston rivalled London in wool exports by the late thirteenth century and was one of the chief ports for both the import of wine and the export of salt.[15] In the south-east, on the other hand, whatever the activity of places like Sandwich, Dover, or Southampton, London always reigned supreme. All the southern coastal ports acted to some extent as London's outports and did well at least partly because they had good communications with London, though Southampton, for instance, profited from direct roads to the midlands and west too. It is noticeable that some of the little ports with only the Weald as hinterland did less well as time went on. Here again individual local factors—like coastal changes, and the effects of the loss of Normandy and war in general on Channel traffic—must be taken into account in any explanation of varying fortunes.[16]

In the west, ports with international trade seem to have multiplied less dramatically than they did in the east. Bristol, Gloucester, and Chester are in some respects less well recorded than some of the eastern towns. Constitutional factors may be partly accountable, and so may their position to the west both of the great fairs and of routes used by kings preoccupied with France, and their armies, though royal campaigns in Wales and Ireland provide some compensating references. How far the scarcer sources reflect less activity is doubtful. Bristol maintained its old contacts with Ireland and developed new ones with Gascony and the Iberian peninsula. It supplied wine to much of the west country, imported large quantities of salt, and dealt in hides, corn, cloth, and wool, though its export of wool—and therefore its total export trade—did not rival that of the south

---

[15] Jackson, 'Med. Exeter' [323]; Hill, *Med. Lincoln* [333], 173, 308; Carus-Wilson, 'Ports of the Wash' [82].

[16] Steers, *Coastline of Eng. and Wales* [251], 305–37; Pelham 'Sussex Trade' [211]; Dulley, 'Port of Pevensey' [399].

or east coast ports. By the thirteenth century the town's suburbs, and notably Redcliffe, may have surpassed the old borough in population and wealth. Towards the middle of the century the town undertook an extensive programme of public works on its harbour, walls, and bridge.

It is, apart from London, among the coastal ports that we should probably look for the dependence on long-distance trade often associated with the stereotype 'great medieval town'. Boston, Bristol, Southampton, Sandwich, Lynn, and Winchelsea would be possible 'long-distance trading towns' (*Fernhandelsstädte*), though none, with the possible exception of Bristol, could be called 'great towns' in other ways. It is, moreover, important to remember how much unrecorded business the fishing and coastal trades must often have contributed to a port's prosperity. Newcastle was sending coal to London by the thirteenth century, while Grimsby lived throughout the Middle Ages largely on its trade with the north-east and with places up the Humber and its tributaries.[17]

Inland, though the mobility of merchants and the holding of the fairs drew international trade over a wide area, it mattered relatively less to individual towns. Just at the time when Oxford, for instance, was perhaps losing some of its trade down the Thames its population was being swollen by the growth of the university. Though that may not have profited the town's upper class of merchants, and certainly led to the circumscribing of their corporate liberties, the clerks of the university must surely have provided a market for food, lodging, and so forth. Downstream, Wallingford enjoyed its liveliest and most far-reaching trade at the same time as Oxford and then lost it, partly because of the same difficulties of river navigation and partly because of competition from Abingdon. Though the Thames may have made both Wallingford and Oxford into boom-towns for a while, Wallingford's primary function was probably always to be a market for villages within half a dozen miles around.[18]

Some international trade avoided inland towns altogether. In the early fourteenth century, and probably before, wool was sold direct from some producing monasteries to the alien exporters, thus bypassing fairs and towns—apart from the ports of embarcation—entirely. The fairs themselves, although like the growing towns a

---

[17] Sherborne, *Port of Bristol* [295]; Lobel and Carus-Wilson, *Bristol* [294], 6–10; Blake, 'Med. Coal Trade' [380]; Gillett, *Hist. of Grimsby* [326], 31–47.
[18] Herbert, 'Borough of Wallingford' [426], 108–51.

symptom of the growing economy, may not have been particularly beneficial to the places where they were held. The very moderate urban development of St. Ives suggests this, and it may be noted that St. Giles's fair at Winchester was held right outside the town, that all trade in the town and within seven leagues of it had to stop, and that the bishop, not the municipality, took all the tolls and profits of litigation, superseding the town's jurisdiction meanwhile. The fair may thus have done little good to Winchester itself, and may even, by handicapping its traders, have helped New Salisbury to supplant it as a regional centre. Even Southampton suffered from the fair, and had to fight hard against a total embargo on its own trade while the fair was on.[19] The bishop's receipts from the fair dropped in the later thirteenth century and Winchester declined meanwhile, but it is unlikely that the first phenomenon contributed to the second: the town had passed its peak of prosperity before 1200. By 1300 the age of great international fairs was drawing to a close, though inland towns that were sufficiently important as regional markets continued to attract foreign goods and purchasers of their regional products.

What provided the basis of most towns' livelihood was not the cake of overseas commerce but the bread and butter of distribution and marketing for the surrounding region—and that might apply to sea-ports like Newcastle, Chester, and Bristol too. The relative importance of local trade and industry is revealed by the occupations of town inhabitants where they are known. The apparent preponderance everywhere of the victualling trades and of craftsmen-traders in metal, leather, and textiles is striking.[20] So too is the relationship between the size of a town and the size and prosperity of its region, or, in other words, between the size of a town and its distance from its rivals. Not only did a large and prosperous region need the services of a larger town, but as a town grew so its demand for food reached further afield, drawing country people to it both as buyers and sellers and as immigrants. Many of the small towns of the south-west, fostered by the West Saxon monarchy in very different political and economic conditions, were probably already

[19] Pegolotti, *La pratica della mercatura* [45]; Donkin, 'Disposal of Cistercian Wool' [111]; Keene, 'Winchester: the Brooks Area' [430], 63–74; Platt, *Med. Southampton* [416], 58.

[20] See works cited below, p. 68, n.3, and, e.g., *V.C.H. Leics.* [332], iv. 37; *V.C.H. Northants* [384], iii. 28; Rogers, *Making of Stamford* [419], 43–9. See, for even Italian towns, Hyde, *Society and Politics in Med. Italy* [154], 156–8.

suffering from the growth of regional centres like Bristol and the county towns. In the east, towns seem always to have been fewer and larger, and the proportion of new foundations is also comparatively low. James Campbell has drawn attention to the exceptionally rich and densely populated countryside around Norwich, to the scarcity of other inland towns in East Anglia, and to the large area of the medieval city occupied by market-places.[21] Perhaps conditions in the east enabled lords there to hold and attract tenants without offering burgage tenure, while the few big towns had a drawing power which discouraged smaller ones from growing. On present knowledge, however, we can only guess at the reasons for regional variations, remembering that so long as the decline of one town was accompanied by the growth of another, and so long as new towns were being founded, it must be right to look for particular rather than for general causes for any town's decline. How far the contradictory trends towards concentration and dispersal can have been compatible, and how they were related in any particular area and circumstances, are problems which need to be solved before we can claim to understand the urban developments of the period.

The relationship between a town and the countryside around it; the range of its drawing power on food-supplies, labour, and purchasers of its products; and the way that these compared with those of its neighbours: all are therefore fundamental aspects of urban history. Between 1100 and 1300 the sources to elucidate them are still sparse, but they begin to appear: the surnames of townspeople, for instance, tell us something of their places of origin.[22] The ownership of urban land by outsiders, like that of country property by townsmen, demonstrates one sort of link; commercial and industrial regulations and the legal records of commercial cases can be informative; and the account rolls of rural manors sometimes mention the markets they used. It is improbable that any full picture of most towns' regional position can be drawn, but more could probably be sketched in if the right questions were asked of the sources and if more towns were looked at in relation to their neighbours and neighbourhoods.

INDUSTRY

How far English lords and churches in the earlier Middle Ages relied on their own domain workshops for manufactured goods,

---

[21] Campbell, 'Norwich' [385], 5–6, 9–10.   [22] See pp. 69–70.

and how far a subsequent movement of industry into towns contributed to their growth is obscure.[23] Some industry of course always remained rural, though even the extractive industries, for instance, stimulated towns through trade in their products, like Gloucester's handling of charcoal and iron from the Forest of Dean, Newcastle's coal trade, or, more surprisingly, Boston's export of lead from Derbyshire.

The most discussed of urban industries is cloth-making, which was important to a number of towns in this period. Weavers in London, Winchester, Lincoln, Oxford, and Huntingdon were sufficiently numerous and influential to purchase royal protection in 1130 and by the end of the century many towns and villages are known to have been producing cloth. It is sometimes difficult to distinguish references to places where cloth was manufactured from those to places where it was marketed, but Miller suggests Lincoln, York, Newcastle, Beverley, Leicester, Winchester, Northampton, Oxford, and London as the most important centres. In some places, including Winchester, York, Oxford, and Northampton, decline had set in by the thirteenth century, but it seems to have been patchy and the reasons are not obvious. Simple general explanations are ruled out by the continued prosperity or even growth of textile industries at Norwich and Coventry late in the thirteenth century. Elsewhere technical developments in fulling may have been less damaging than the repressive and restrictive policies of town governments, and those in turn less damaging than competition from Flanders and Brabant.[24] Cloth-making employed a large number of people in its various stages, and so the result of its decay must have meant hardship for many townsmen and some for towns as a whole, though that varied a good deal. Northampton's fairs and general trade remained active throughout the Middle Ages; in York the leather trade had perhaps employed more people than cloth even in the twelfth century; while difficulties of navigation may have accounted as much for the troubles of Lincoln and Oxford as did the failure of their cloth trade.

The cloth trade and industry may have attracted undue attention because of their ample records, particularly in the later customs

---

[23] *Eng. Hist. Docs.* [29], i, p. 371 (Ine, c. 63); Cunningham, *Growth of Eng. Industry* [98], i. 575; cf. Duby, *Rural Econ.* [114], 153–4; Ennen, *Europäische Stadt* [118], 78–9.
[24] Carus-Wilson, *Med. Merchant Venturers* [81], 183–238; Miller, 'Eng. Textile Industry' [196]; Lancaster, 'Coventry' [315], 5; Campbell, 'Norwich' [385], 15.

accounts, and their connections with the glamour of long-range trade. Other industries are often neglected before they begin to be recorded in the regulations of crafts and town governments, almost as though they were not practised before they were thus regulated and recorded. Earlier they appear chiefly in the casual references to purchases of manufactured goods by kings and other lords and in the occasional lists of townsmen. These last, however, all show that towns large and small encompassed a wide range of crafts to supply the tools, household goods, and leather goods, as well as the textiles, of the country round about. Many of the craftsmen may have bought their own raw materials, sold their own products, and employed unskilled porters and other workers as well as journeymen and apprentices. Though archaeology and more detailed documentary research may yet produce more information about urban industries before the fourteenth century, much will probably remain unknown or mysterious, like the two thirteenth-century references to Coventry's reputation for soap, which seem to find no echo in the recorded occupations of contemporary townsmen.[25]

CONCLUSION

In attempting to classify English towns in the thirteenth century we have to do without reliable information about the vital element of population. There are really no general estimates of any value after 1086 and before 1377, when the Black Death had already hit western Europe as a whole and, probably, the towns most of all. It has been suggested that London's population doubled in the thirteenth century, reaching 30–40,000 before the plague. To judge from the tax assessments of 1334 no provincial town then had a quarter of the capital's wealth. Bristol, York, Newcastle upon Tyne, Boston, Great Yarmouth, Lincoln, Norwich, Oxford, Shrewsbury, Lynn, Salisbury, and Coventry, in that order, were the next highest assessed. Of these all but Shrewsbury, Salisbury, and Coventry had four mendicant friaries by 1300. Northampton, Winchester, Cambridge, and Stamford all had four too, while Chester, Leicester, Ipswich, Gloucester, Canterbury, and Scarborough had three. It may be that only a handful of English towns had more than 10,000 inhabitants by 1300 and that many had less than 5,000. In spite of that most of them were clearly marked off from the countryside by their lively corporate life and the occupations of their inhabitants.

[25] *Eng. Hist. Docs.* [29], iii, p. 883; Robert of Gloucester, *Chron.* [316], line 143.

Map 3
Mendicant Friaries established by 1300 (based on Knowles and Hadcock,
Med. Religious Houses [167], 212–50 and map)

Though London was the only really great town that could com-
pete in size with the greatest of contemporary European towns, it
should not be concluded that other English towns were smaller than
most towns in northern Europe. The famous towns of Flanders,
Germany, and Italy were exceptions, not types. The wide gap
between London and the rest was more unusual, but it is important
to remember that London was by no means the only centre of long-
range commerce or sizeable industry. Whatever may be the case in
Germany or Italy, in the English context the categories of great
town and long-range trading town are distinct. The evidence here
supports the thesis that though the long-distance and luxury trades
of course stimulated economies out of proportion to their bulk, and
though they have at times rather bedazzled historians, the majority
of medieval towns were sustained and enriched by humbler and more
local activities. Trade as a whole, moreover, cannot be separated
from other urban activities. Though the military, political, and
religious functions of towns may have loomed less large as trade and
industry grew, they still went on. Canterbury and Reading profited
from the pilgrim trade as well as from simply, like Dunstable and
Baldock, being on a main road. The confluence of people attracted
by cathedrals, local courts, the visits of royal justices, or even relics
like Reading's hand of St. James, stimulated markets and crafts in
some towns rather than others. With the increasing pace and volume
of exchange transport facilities were also becoming more important:
it was the building of a new bridge at Salisbury, leading to a drier
route that bypassed Wilton for the main road to the south-west,
which helped the new cathedral city to eclipse the old county town.
Wilton was probably already stagnating, despite its privileges and
ancient prestige, yet it was there that the Dominicans settled when
they came to the area in 1245, only a year after the bridge was built.
They moved to a suburb of Salisbury in 1280.[26]

It seems reasonable to connect the smallness of English towns
with their dispersal, and to attribute this distinctive pattern not
merely to widespread rural prosperity but to the distinctive political
conditions of England.[27] Powerful kings and a relatively highly
organized government maintained relatively good law and order, so
that traders did not have to collect behind the walls of strongly
defensible towns. Nor did the royal government allow the internecine

[26] *V.C.H. Wilts.* [427], vi. 13–15; see p. 190.
[27] Though cf. Ennen, *Europäische Stadt* [118], 202.

struggles by which great towns abroad often subjugated their small neighbours and cut off their trade. Competition there was but it remained peaceful. That it nevertheless increased as the economy developed looks likely though, like other trends, it would be hard to prove: with the fourteenth century come not only better sources but the sort of changes that make the retrospective use of them to show trends peculiarly dangerous.

4
Urban Society Before *c.* 1300

The problems of when and why towns started to grow and what they lived off are not only economic ones. They are also social. What sort of people formed urban communities and what sort of communities did they form? How far did townspeople, their communities, their way of life, and their values, differ from those outside? Medieval records are more or less inadequate to answer such questions, which require accurate and full statistics on the one hand and plenty of personal papers on the other, but unless we make some attempt to consider them our talk of such subjects as urban liberties and the policies of town governments, as well as of townspeople themselves, will sink into a morass of unexplored assumptions about the communities which won the liberties and made the policies.

It is, for instance, often assumed by a facile sort of economic determinism that what gave towns their corporate unity, and made townsmen struggle for independence from rulers outside, was that townsmen were traders and, as such, had intrinsically different interests and values from those who lived and worked in the country. According to this view townsmen wanted to rule themselves simply in order to further their trade and economic prosperity, and when they gained a measure of self-government they used it directly to those ends. There is certainly a good deal of truth in this, as later chapters on the winning of independence and the conduct of town governments may show. But the underlying assumptions about the solidarity and separateness of urban society, as well as about the origins of urban wealth, need some examination. However close the bonds of common economic interest may have been—and it requires to be demonstrated that town communities were always dominated by exclusively commercial or industrial interests—those were not the only factors creating social solidarity. One of the most fundamental, for instance, was the simple fact of physical propinquity. People living close together—literally, geographically close—formed a social group which would tend to accumulate rules and customs of its own, and in so far as its circumstances—the size and density of its population, for example, as well as their occupations—differed from those outside, might accumulate different rules and customs. Whatever the economic interests of a town's leading inhabitants, the conditions in which they and their inferiors lived created both solidarity against outsiders and conflicts within. The conflicts in turn, in the way conflicts may, bound them together as well as divided them. On the other hand English towns were never cut off, politically or socially, any more than they could be economically, from the rest of the country. Their links with the rural world, as well as their differences from it, must be considered. Little as we may be able to find out about all these aspects of urban history, they form a necessary part of any enquiry into medieval town life.

One particular problem which has been much discussed by continental medievalists is that of the origin of urban populations and urban wealth. Were townsmen originally recruited from Pirenne's rootless, wandering traders, the scum of agrarian society? If not, where did they come from and how did the early merchants build up their trading capital? Where records are available and have been studied the results suggest that some at least of the urban 'patricians' of the twelfth century were descended from seigniorial officials or small landowners and that both rural and urban property may have been as important a source of their capital at first as pure trade. It has also been suggested that moneyers, straddling the frontiers between seigniorial service, trade, and industry, may have formed the nucleus of some early town aristocracies. This possibility needs to be examined in the particular context of late Old English minting. The wanderer from outside 'feudal society' who settled down in a trading suburb and founded a patrician merchant family remains elusive in the sources, though the search for him should certainly go on, not least in England, the home of Pirenne's classic wandering trader, Godric of Finchale.[1] To look for evidence, however, is one thing. To apply all the arguments about Italy, Germany, or Flanders wholesale to England would be another. In particular we might start by thinking how applicable to English towns are the words

---

[1] See Pirenne, *Les villes* [216], ii. 104; for Godric, ibid. i. 366–8 and *Dict. Nat. Biog.* viii. 47–9; Lestocquoy, *Études* [175]; Planitz, *Deutsche Stadt* [219]; Hibbert, 'Origins of Medieval Patriciate' [145]; Lopez, 'Aristocracy of Money' [178]; Witt, 'Landlord and Econ. Revival' [280].

'patrician' and 'patriciate', on which some of the past discussions have centred. Jean Lestocquoy, while defining the medieval patriciate as '[la] bourgeoisie riche ayant une part notable dans le gouvernement de la ville', reminds us that the actual words themselves are not found in the sources.[2] Their use must therefore run the risk of appearing to create consistent categories where none existed, even if it is restricted to the context for which they were coined. That context is one of great merchants (or those who are thought to have been great merchants), dominating great towns which depended (or are thought to have depended) on long-distance trade, and whose government was monopolized by a closed and therefore easily definable group of families. In towns which seem sometimes to have lacked a well-defined native and resident merchant class, enjoyed a smaller degree of independence and separation from external society, and do not seem to have been ruled by self-perpetuating oligarchies, the concept of a patriciate would be less appropriate. Continental studies will therefore provide an essential stimulus in this field, but the historians of English towns must do their own work: it is a great help to have the questions raised, but each town must provide its own answers.

There is in any case more to consider about urban society than the origin of the so-called patriciate. That is only part of the whole subject of the nature and structure of medieval urban society. As yet there is too little material in print—and perhaps too little available in the documents—for a proper survey, but this chapter attempts to outline some of the questions that should be asked about urban society and, where possible, suggests some of the answers that have been offered in work published until now. Unfortunately a good deal of published work has leant towards picturesque detail rather than to systematic exploration, while the gaps in the evidence for individual towns have sometimes been filled by assumptions or analogies drawn from others which invalidate any conclusions and make it difficult to ascertain just what we do know.[3] Information

[2] Lestocquoy, *Les Villes de Flandre et d'Italie* [173], 13, 242; *Cam. Ec. Hist.* [79], iii. 30.

[3] For a learned study on the later Middle Ages see Thrupp, *Merchant Class* [364]. Except where otherwise noted information on towns mentioned below is drawn from: Reynolds, 'Rulers of London' [359]; Williams, 'London, 1216–1337' [372] and *Med. London* [373]; Hilton, *A Med. Society* [147], on W. Midlands; Urry, *Canterbury* [303]; *V.C.H. Yorks. E.R.* [329], i (Hull); Martin, 'Church Life in Leicester' [330]; Hill, *Med. Lincoln* [333]; Lobel, 'Med. Oxford' [394]; Pantin, 'Before Wolsey' [395]; Davis, 'An Oxford charter' [392]; Platt, *Med. Southampton* [416]; Carus-Wilson, 'Stratford on Avon' [422]; Herbert, 'Borough of Wallingford' [426]; *V.C.H. Yorks: York* [444].

about urban society can, however, be wrung from most of the sources for towns, if they are looked at in the right way: deeds, whether original or in cartularies, and wills (though few of the latter are preserved before the later Middle Ages) provide most information about individuals. The earliest municipal records come from the very end of the twelfth century with some useful guild rolls among the first survivors. Seigniorial records like surveys, extents, and rentals can be helpful. For the twelfth century the printed Pipe Rolls of the central government record purchases for the king and thus cast occasional sidelights on trade and traders, while from the thirteenth century the records of the chancery and royal courts offer occasional information on various subjects.[4] Since what material there is comes largely from after 1100 and the changes after about 1300 are reserved for a later chapter, most of the tentative conclusions presented here deal with the twelfth and thirteenth centuries.

THE ORIGINS OF ENGLISH TOWNSPEOPLE

The way in which towns grew between the tenth and thirteenth centuries suggests that they must have recruited much of their population from outside. Even after the first stages of growth the likelihood that death-rates were higher in towns than outside implies that immigration would have been necessary in order to maintain, let alone to increase, urban populations. Sylvia Thrupp, studying London merchants of the later Middle Ages, thought that the group could barely have maintained its numbers by natural replacement. Though her figures have been questioned and demographic changes anyway make them less applicable to the period before 1300, the growth of towns in the earlier period suggests that immigration may well have supplied a significant proportion of urban population then too.[5] The size of the proportion is even more problematical than the size of urban populations altogether, but the probable persistence of immigration is confirmed by what is known of a few individual families—particularly if family relationships are not assumed uncritically. Surnames, themselves partly a symptom of urban

⁴ Martin, 'Eng. Borough in 13th Cent.' [189]; Martin and McIntyre, *Bibliog. of Munic. Hist.* [9], pp. 120–2, 124.
⁵ Wrigley, *Population and History* [284], 95–100; Thrupp, *Merchant Class* [364], 191–210 and 'Problem of Replacement Rates' [265]; Williams, *Med. London* [373], 315–17, argues most strongly for a stable 'patrician' population where his evidence is weakest: cf. Reynolds, 'Rulers of London' [359], 345.

conditions, are also helpful. A surname derived from a place-name suggests the place of origin of its bearer, or, as surnames became hereditary, of his forebears, while the bearer of a patronymic surname may generally be assumed to live in a community where his father lived before him. The use of surnames and descriptions at this period is too inconsistent, and the occurrence of names in the sources is too haphazard, for them to be used statistically, but they can give useful impressions.[6]

It seems, on this evidence, that most English towns drew much of their populations from relatively close by: Stratford upon Avon, founded at the very end of the twelfth century, seems in its first fifty years to have attracted people almost entirely from within a sixteen-mile radius, while it has been argued that the great majority of people in all the towns of the west midlands in the late thirteenth century came from within thirty or forty miles. At the other end of the urban scale Londoners came from all over the British Isles and beyond, though even here most of them came from relatively close, and some families survived for several generations in the city. Arguing that the change of London speech from a southern or Saxon dialect to a midland or Anglian one derived from a change in London's population, the philologist Eilert Ekwall used surnames to show that, whereas most Londoners until about the middle of the thirteenth century came from the home counties and the south-east, after that more of them came from the midlands and East Anglia. Although to a historian Ekwall may seem to beg social and economic questions a little, most of his conclusions look convincing and show what can be done by prolonged study of a massive range of this kind of material. The inhabitants of Hull probably came mostly from the East Riding and north Lincolnshire with some from the midlands. York is thought to have had a core of Anglo-Scandinavian citizens in the twelfth century and to have recruited immigrants thereafter primarily from the plain between Doncaster and Thirsk, and secondarily from other parts of the north country. Only a few came from further afield, but they included people from Scotland, Flanders, France, and even apparently Italy.

The social origins of immigrants are very unclear. Whether or

---

[6] See, e.g., Ekwall, *Early London Personal Names* [349], 119–22, *London Subsidy Rolls* [365], 43–71, and *Studies on Pop. of Med. London* [350]; Cam, *Liberties and Communities* [78], 22, 26; Reaney, *Origin of Eng. Surnames* [230], 296–316; Hilton, *A Med. Society* [147], 183, oversimplifies. See also Woodward, 'Freemen's Rolls' [12].

not most of the first townsmen, let alone the richest among them, came from the *pauperes* of agrarian society, as Pirenne thought, many of those who migrated to towns from villages near at hand must always have come from fairly humble circumstances. By the twelfth century entry into full membership of an urban community was a recognized means to freedom from a servile condition. Although many immigrants never achieved such membership it was not impossible for former villeins to rise high in town society. In the twelfth century, when Ralph 'the villein' became bailiff of Lincoln, the word may not have borne such precise connotations of unfreedom as it later acquired, but as late as 1308, when conditions had probably become more restrictive, it was apparently still possible for a man allegedly born as a villein in Norfolk to become an alderman and sheriff of London—though it took him four years to prove his freedom.[7] It should however be remembered that many English towns, including the largest, may have recruited many of their immigrants from the east of the country where freemen were always numerous. It is unlikely that the typical townsman of any class was ever a fugitive villein.

Although most of the surviving information about the social origin of individuals concerns the richer burgesses it is unlikely to tell us whether the first fortunes were based on land, siegniorial service, or trade, since the relevant documents hardly appear before the twelfth century. By that time most of the important towns were well established and the first fortunes must have been made. Twelfth-century Londoners seem to have had fairly diverse origins. Though the citizens claimed to be 'barons' and some of them owned property, even property held by knight-service, in the home counties, few had significant links with the rural landowning classes, and none can be shown to have based his fortune on rural land: some certainly, and many probably, acquired their country property with money made from London rents, industry, money-lending, trade, or administrative office. Their links with the king's court, through service of various kinds, were close. In York two of the small group of dominant thirteenth-century families were descended respectively from a city landowner and a moneyer of the twelfth century. In Oxford 'the prominence of royal minters and other *ministri* among the important citizens in the early eleventh century and the twelfth' has been noted though it is not clear how substantial the evidence may be. At

[7] *Year Book 1 & 2 Ed. II* [375], 11–13; see below, pp. 100–1, 124–6.

Canterbury, not surprisingly, ecclesiastical office and the service of the great monasteries contributed significantly to civic prosperity. More information should be available for the thirteenth century but little work seems to have been done on it as yet. One can think of various *a priori* reasons why the classes from which both upper and lower urban classes were recruited may have changed; whatever material could be extracted from the records, and it may not be very rewarding, will need careful assessment before its significance is plain.

ALIENS AND JEWS

Like London and York, a good many larger towns contained families of alien origins. Apart from a few hints about visiting Frisians in earlier centuries, the first immigrants of whom we know anything were the Scandinavian settlers of the ninth and tenth centuries. Whatever the nature and scale of their contribution to urban growth, there is no doubt that by the eleventh century Danes were an important and assimilated part of town society, not only in the Danelaw but also, most importantly, in London. At that time German, French, and Flemish traders were also familiar there; the Germans ('the emperor's men') were expected to winter in the port.[8] The bulk and scope of Flemish trade in many English towns by the thirteenth century is no doubt reflected in the frequent occurrence of people called *Flandrensis* or *le Fleming*, but it was not only trading interests that brought migrants. Many towns both new and old received an influx of Normans and other north French during and after the Conquest. In London intermarriage between them and the native citizens started very quickly. Everywhere, despite some relics of separate customs and organization, Norman and English freemen were apparently indistinguishable within a century.[9] After the eleventh century trade probably accounted for a larger proportion of settlers, though Alderman Arnold fitz Thedmar (d. *c.* 1274), for instance, was descended from German pilgrims to the shrine of St. Thomas. It has sometimes been said that two prominent twelfth- and thirteenth-century London families were descended from Italian immigrants who settled there after the Conquest. Apart from the fact that there is no prima facie reason to connect the immigration of Italians with the Norman Conquest,

[8] See above, pp. 37–42.
[9] *Eng. Hist. Docs.* [29] ii, p. 523.

there is however no evidence to connect either family with Italy. The first recorded Italian resident in an English town may be Pantaleone of Canterbury (*fl.* 1180).

Foreigners were not always made welcome. By the twelfth century London had a rule which in principle restricted alien merchants to stays of forty days, and which may have spread from there along with other London customs, for it is found in other towns soon after. It was, however, liable to breaches and exceptions: Danes and Norwegians, for instance, were allowed to stay the whole year in London in the twelfth century, and though Lotharingians (despite the earlier privilege of 'the emperor's men') were then normally restricted to forty days, Henry II presumably exempted the men of Cologne from the rule when he gave them and their property in London his protection. During the next hundred years more and more 'Easterlings' (Germans from further east, and especially from the Baltic towns) began to frequent England, and the various German groups in London were eventually (1281) joined in the united German Hanse with permanent headquarters at the Steelyard.[10]

How far these regulations and exemptions were designed to protect trade and how far to restrict immigration as such is hard to say, and it is not at all easy either to say what their effect was. That most of the citizens and burgesses whose names suggest that they were of alien origin lived after 1200 may simply reflect the improved sources. At the same time the pattern of long-distance trade was beginning to change, so that it was conducted less by travelling individuals buying and selling at fairs situated between their respective towns, and more by firms which maintained agents in relatively few important places. Whereas most goods from the Mediterranean may formerly have changed hands before they reached England, Italians might now, therefore, come here more frequently themselves. There were established colonies of Italians and other southerners in London quite early in the thirteenth century. On the other hand aliens may have been less readily assimilated into local society than had been possible earlier on. Their firms maintained control over them and sometimes replaced them, while at the same time a growing nationalism and even xenophobia was besetting English society. Permanent settlement may have been more discouraged just at the same time as the volume of trade was growing. Any suppositions about the

[10] Carus-Wilson, 'Towns and Trade' [83], 234–6; *Brit. Bor. Ch. 1042–1216* [16], 211–14; *Hansisches Urkundenbuch* [37], nos. 13, 14.

changing numbers of aliens and their relationship to local society need therefore to be tested by the evidence from individual towns.

Jews constitute one category of aliens who are known to have settled in some numbers in a good many English towns. The first settlement seems to have been that made in London by Jews who were brought over by William I. During the twelfth century Jewries were established in many towns, though their number dropped again before the final expulsion of Jews from medieval England in 1290. A list of medieval Jewries is not easy to compile, for some Jews moved about and the records of royal tallages levied on them sometimes imply permanent settlements where none existed. Even where there is known to have been a permanent Jewry its significance in economic terms is hard to assess. How far Jews in this country stimulated trade and industry, and how far a Jewry is a sign of a town's commercial importance is uncertain: though some Jews certainly engaged in other occupations, and many probably did so, most surviving records concern their money-lending. Many of their loans were made to landowners so that their economic function may have concerned rural society as much as urban. All the same they certainly constituted a notable feature of town life in the twelfth and thirteenth centuries. Jews and Christians associated together on occasion in business, as when Aaron of Lincoln joined some prominent Londoners in property development late in the twelfth century. One Jew is recorded as having been admitted to the merchant guild of Winchester in the thirteenth century, and a converted Jew became reeve of Worcester. It is probably safe to say that they were exceptions, but the nature of the social boundary between Jew and Christian, and the part played by Jews in town life, remain curiously obscure.[11]

THE CLASS STRUCTURE

Medieval English urban society is generally, if rather hazily, seen as divided into three main classes: merchants, craftsmen, and servants or employees. Divisions existed within each group: some merchants or craftsmen were richer, some crafts ranked higher than others, while the category of employees ranged from casual labourers and domestic servants to apprentices or journeymen who might later become masters themselves. The wage-earning class is particularly

[11] William of Malmesbury, *Gesta Regum* [58], i. 37n; Richardson, *Eng. Jewry* [236]; Mellinkoff, 'Jews in B.M. Cotton Claudius B. iv' [193].

obscure, emerging from time to time in the fitful light of wage regulations or political disputes, as when the town authorities of late thirteenth-century Southampton fixed the rates to be charged by porters for transporting goods from quays to warehouses; when the wages of women wool-wrappers at Leicester were fixed at 1*d.* a day, winter and summer, with food provided; or when a crowd of people, 'the sons of divers mothers, many of them born outside the city and many of servile condition' riotously intervened in the government of London in the 1260s. Many of the dependent workers, as the indignant tone of the aldermanic chronicler implies, were not formal members of the town community at all, since they did not rank as burgesses (or citizens) any more than did visiting aliens or country people.[12] All alike ranked as 'foreigns' in terms of urban customs and rights. One point should however be made: despite the alderman's contempt, only those of the London rioters who actually lived outside the city bounds can have been 'servile' in the usual sense of the common law. Earlier there certainly had been unfree men in towns; there still continued to be a few, mostly in small and unprivileged towns; and urban freedom did indeed stop sharply at the borough boundaries; but the development of urban liberties and of law in the twelfth century left nearly all townsmen technically free in terms of the common law.[13] That is not of course to say that their freedom always meant very much: the living-in apprentice or servant may have had worse prospects and fewer real liberties than many a rural villein living under his own roof.

The basic classification of merchants, craftsmen, and servants is, however, not entirely straightforward. To start with, it raises problems of definition: in the earlier Middle Ages the word merchant (*mercator*) was used very widely to include even retail traders, as in the expression 'merchant guild' (*gilda mercatorum, gilda mercatoria*). Later it was usually restricted to those primarily engaged in wholesale trade, and this is the sense in which it is used in most modern works, including the present. The boundary between wholesale and retail was often blurred in practice and is even more invisible in the records. When Sylvia Thrupp said that merchants formed a distinct category not only economically but politically, through their control of municipal government, and explained that 'the merchants of each

---

[12] *Rec. of Leicester* [331], i. 186; *Liber de Ant. Leg.* [348], 36; *Cal. London P. & M.R. 1364–81* [345], pp. lxi–lxiv; for burgess qualifications, see pp. 123–6.

[13] See pp. 100–1.

town formed a class there, locally, and these local classes may be regarded as linked together to form a more or less uniform segment of the nation', she may have misled those less learned than herself into assuming that in every town, whether in the fourteenth century or earlier, merchants formed a distinct and separate class and that urban élites were by definition mercantile. Both statements need to be proved in individual towns. It is fair to wonder whether occupation, even where the distinction between merchants and craftsmen-retailers was clear, was always the criterion. Eleanora Carus-Wilson asserts that 'rank in the medieval city was determined by wealth',[14] and some people who were at least partly concerned in wholesale trade were poorer than some craftsmen. Records of thirteenth-century urban conflicts sometimes divide the burgesses into the rich, great, or powerful; the middling; and the lesser or poor. This classification of course largely omits the employed.

A society stratified by wealth is different from one stratified by groups defined by their occupations or by their functions in a market economy. Though the social stratification in medieval towns may well have been formed by an unconscious muddle of both principles, we shall not be helped to understand it by using merchant, craftsman, and servant as synonyms of rich, middling, and poor. Other factors too influenced contemporaries' views of the social hierarchy. Long settlement probably conferred prestige on a family and the influence of noble values helped lend weight to descent and land-ownership. What exacerbated class divisions and class consciousness seems to have been less the direct conflict of the differing economic interests of merchants and craftsmen than the control over local taxation and government which municipal independence gave to the dominant men in a town, whether they were craftsmen, merchants, or landowners.[15]

It is sometimes suggested that in the earlier Middle Ages English towns lacked a real merchant class, not because their merchants did not generally form a distinct class, which is probable, but because English trade had not yet progressed from a 'colonial' stage of alien dominance to one of native independence. The underlying assumptions that change was all in one direction, and that English townsmen were a homogeneous group progressing together under foreign instruction towards advancement, do not bear much scrutiny. Though

---

[14] 'Towns and Trade' [83], 251.
[15] *Cam. Econ. Hist.* [79], ii. 30–4; iii. 195–7; see below, pp. 130–9.

the reasons for rejecting this view have often been expressed[16] its implications for urban history are so important that some of them may be worth rehearsing.

Anglo-Saxon merchants seem to have travelled a good deal. In the eleventh century they were familiar visitors in Lombardy and the custom that a merchant who had voyaged three times overseas should have a thegn's wergeld (i.e. should rank as a noble) implies that some native merchants were prosperous, that prosperity went with overseas trade, and that prosperous traders were respected and well-integrated in their society.[17] Undoubtedly there were wandering traders like Godric of Finchale or the earlier Frisians and Vikings but where they fit into the urban scene is not clear. Evidence for the twelfth century is disappointingly scarce, though in its later years Londoners are known to have been living and trading in Genoa. During the thirteenth century, when the records improve, aliens seem to have dominated but did not monopolize overseas trade. They presumably took much less part in internal and coasting trade, easily overlooked because so little recorded, but their share in general may have grown in the past hundred years. The expansion of the Flemish cloth industry; the increasing activity of Italian merchants and financiers, who in the thirteenth century were handling the growing volume of papal taxation along with their own affairs; Henry III and Edward I's use of Italian financiers, and Edward's patronage of Gascons, could all have contributed to it. Even so the Chancery records show a good many Englishmen trading abroad in their own ships. In the middle years of the century, for instance, a Londoner had merchandise plundered in Lübeck. The expansion of trade in the twelfth and thirteenth centuries surely allowed the number of English merchants to grow even though their wealth and operations did not compare with those of the Italians: greater alien participation need not have bereft English towns of their merchants.[18] On the other hand the existence of a distinct merchant class in any particular town and at any date must be proved. We must beware of assuming that because one rich or dominant man was a merchant so were all his peers in his town.

[16] e.g. Power, *Med. Eng. Wool Trade* [225], 57–62; Miller, 'Eng. Econ. in 13th Cent.' [195].
[17] Southern, *Making of Middle Ages* [249], 43–4; *Cam. Econ. Hist.* [79], ii. 239–41; *Eng. Hist. Docs.* [29], i. p. 432; cf. Cam, *Liberties and Communities* [78], 23.
[18] Reynolds, 'Eng. settlers in Genoa' [234]; *Cal. Close R. 1247–51* [18], 289 (indexed as Leipzig); *Liber de Ant. Leg.* [348], 118–19.

As usual the fullest information concerns London, the only English town likely to have developed a 'mercantile patriciate' on the scale of the great towns of Flanders and Italy. The aldermen seem the best candidates as potential 'patricians' or, if we avoid the word as too question-begging, as the dominant group in London. The first (probably incomplete) list of them, which dates from *c.* 1127, includes two probable moneyers and one possible canon of St. Paul's. Later on merchants and other craftsmen appear. Though most twelfth-century aldermen look more concerned with land than with trade, that may well be an illusion created by the bias of the sources. Even so it is likely that landownership, law, and both royal and civic administration provided fortunes for a good many. Mercantile interests become discernible about 1200, when the records improve. Purveyors of goods, and particularly wine, to the court by then formed a recognizably significant category. At least some of them traded overseas and it is probable that their predecessors had done so too. Gwyn Williams suggests that London was dominated in the earlier thirteenth century by a close and interrelated group of 'patrician dynasties' who were displaced in the political troubles of the century by men connected more closely with industrial crafts and the German trade, rather than with wine, thus leaving London with a wider and more open ruling class. The 'patrician dynasties' depend, however, too much on shaky genealogies and unjustifiable assumptions about common interests for the model of simultaneous social, economic, and political change to stand up.

In so far as the balance of classes in London altered during the century it was, as Williams pointed out, primarily the result of growing population and trade: there is no real reason to believe that the actual nature of the classes or the shape of the social pyramid changed. At the end of the period London had a prosperous élite, who were distinguished from their fellow-citizens by wealth, municipal influence, and less measurable elements of social prestige, rather than by their practice of any particular trade. The same may hold good for the twelfth century, and even the eleventh too for all we know, though whether as many members of the élite were then merchants is less likely: at present it cannot be proved either way. Below the élite, master craftsmen, shopkeepers, and householders presumably formed a middle class of many gradations, with the employed— including some who were legally citizens, just as some of the middle category were not—and indeed the unemployed, below them.

Some of the larger provincial towns had the same sort of social pyramid, though it was generally lower and class divisions were slighter in proportion to the smaller opportunities both for the upper classes to amass wealth and exercise power and for the poor to find employment. In some areas the provincial merchants had to contend with the competition of Londoners as well as aliens, but conditions favoured multiple growth. The distribution of wine and luxuries, together with the staple crafts of cloth, leather, and metal-working, and with urban property-owning and in the earlier part of the period minting,[19] supported some sort of élite in many places. Edward Miller says that thirteenth-century York boasted a small and stable élite whose 'core resembles the *viri hereditarii* who ruled the cities of thirteenth-century Flanders'. They owned land in and around the city and included a few merchants trading overseas in wine and wool. York society, however, was predominantly one of fairly humble craftsmen, and according to tallage records of 1204 'men with moderate substance were relatively few, and men with considerable wealth very few indeed'. Lincoln looks rather similar, with many references to visiting alien merchants but some to natives too. Here citizens appear divided into great, middling (*secundarii*), and lesser in 1274–5, and the class of casual labourers is reflected in a thirteenth-century version of the lay of Havelock. It tells how its hero waited for two days among the porters at the bridge before he was hired by the earl's cook to carry food from the market there to the castle—which set him, less credibly, on the road to marrying the princess and confounding his villainous master.

Prima facie one would expect the many towns with less overseas trade and smaller hinterlands to have had an even less distinctively mercantile upper class than did York and Lincoln. To some extent the wide geographical scatter of rich merchants may have diminished the size and cohesion of the class in individual towns. In the late thirteenth century Laurence of Ludlow, *nominatissimus mercatorum*, who negotiated the extra wool custom of 1294 for the king, ap-parently belonged to Shrewsbury. Even the little town of Dunstable had its outstandingly rich wool merchant, who consorted with the local gentry and lent money to the local priory.[20] A small group of richer burgesses, whether or not they were merchants, can be

[19] On mints, see above, pp. 34, 51.

[20] *Ann. Mon.* [13], iii. 275, 294, 302, 313, 358, 389–90, 510, 518; Power, *Med. Eng. Wool Trade* [225], 112–13; *Beds. Taxation, 1297* [318], 90–96.

discerned in a fair number of places, sometimes through complaints of their monopoly and misuse of municipal power, complaints in which middling people occasionally joined the poor.[21] Grievances were expressed for instance at Oxford, where there seem to have been a few men of substantial wealth who have been dignified with the label of 'patricians'. They included one of the two aldermen in office when the town gained control of its fee-farm, who may have been a fishmonger (d. 1204), and his son, the first mayor. Even in small market towns where independent craftsmen formed a large majority of the working population, a few richer inhabitants are sometimes visible: Stratford upon Avon in 1251-2 boasted no luxury traders but some of the tanners and one of the metal-workers held several tenements and may have been relatively rich. Thame (Oxfordshire) by the early fourteenth century apparently had several citizens of higher standing whose wealth came both from land and from trade, including the wool trade. In the cloth-making towns there seems quite often to have been an élite of entrepreneurs, sometimes dyers, who influenced the merchant guilds to exclude the weavers and fullers from the guild and to repress them generally.[22] It should be noted, however, that though the élites generally included merchants, there is no real evidence to see merchants as such or in every trade as entrepreneurs or to see merchant guilds in general as oppressors of craftsmen. Again, it seems that the fundamental differences were those of wealth, aggravated by the way that the rich could control local government in their own interest.

How much mobility there was between classes is difficult to judge, since so little is known about the origins of many of the rich and successful. The known expansion of the twelfth and thirteenth centuries, the constant appearance of new names among burgesses, and the rules for receiving villeins into the urban community, all suggest that towns were places of relative opportunity. The number of hopeful immigrants who found the streets paved with gold may have been larger than in periods when the economy was contracting or when trade and industry required more capital.

GUILDS, CHURCHES, AND SCHOOLS

In spite or because of the uprooted condition of many townspeople urban society was prolific in local associations, some of which cut

---

[21] See below, pp. 130-9.
[22] Carus-Wilson, *Med. Merchant Venturers* [81], 235-8.

across class divisions. The earliest that we know about are the guilds of Anglo-Saxon England, in which both sociability and common interests could find an outlet. Some English historians, following the lead of Charles Gross in *The Gild Merchant* (1890), have drawn a line between Anglo-Saxon religious and social guilds on the one hand and the commercial and industrial guilds of the post-Conquest period on the other. A comparison of English and continental evidence suggests that that is wrong, and that guilds were originally social and religious associations, primarily for drinking and fellowship, and probably of pagan origin, some of which began to acquire purposes connected with trade and urban government as and when their members' interests developed in those directions.[23]

Many guilds, both urban and rural, may have disappeared without trace. Those that we know of are recorded in laws which show guildsmen (*gegildan*—sometimes used in a very general sense of 'associates' or perhaps kinsmen) sharing responsibility or being marshalled in the interests of law and order; in charters and other documents which mention guilds in particular places, like those of Canterbury, Winchester, or Dover; or in guild regulations or membership lists, most of which have been preserved by the churches to which the guildsmen made payments. Of the twenty or thirty places which are known to have had guilds before the twelfth century only about half can fairly be called towns, and there is evidence to suggest that in some of those the guilds themselves were exclusively urban in neither membership nor purpose.[24] These points are worth making because it has been suggested that the 'vague ideas that the origins of guilds should be sought in a purely social context' are wrong and that Anglo-Saxon guilds 'need to be fitted into the general European pattern of urban development'.[25] That is true only in the sense that the needs and opportunities for corporate action in towns sometimes transformed guilds formed in pre-urban circumstances. We should not deduce the existence of a town from an early guild, but we may see the way some guilds developed as responses to urban development.

[23] Coornaert, 'Les ghildes' [93]; Thrupp, 'Med. Gilds' [264]; *Eng. Gilds* [28]; Martin, 'Eng. Borough in 13th Cent.' [189], 126–7; Westlake, *Parish Gilds of Med. Eng.* [278]; *Eng. Hist. Docs.* [29], i, p. 334 (cf. Ine's and Alfred's laws, and *A.S. Dict.* [73]). The modern variant spellings (guild, gild) have no historical significance.

[24] *Eng. Hist. Docs.* [29], i, pp. 347–8; ii, pp. 963, 965; Tait, *Med. Eng. Bor.* [258], 119–20; *V.C.H. Hants.* [429], i. 530–2; *V.C.H. Leics.* [332], iv. 12, 33; Hill, *Med. Lincoln* [333], 185–6; *Brit. Bor. Ch. 1042–1307* [16], i, pp. lxxi–lxxii; Stenton, *Eng. Feudalism* [254], 134–5.

[25] Loyn, 'Towns in Late A.S. Eng.' [181], 123.

Gross's contention that merchant guilds were a Norman innovation was wrong but we should not therefore assume that all earlier guilds had essentially the same purpose and functions as the twelfth-century merchant guilds. The guild of 'knights' (*cniahtan*, *cnihtan*) at Canterbury in the ninth century thus may not have been a genuinely urban association, any more than the rather later thegns' guild of Cambridge. Despite much discussion the social position and functions of the *cnihtan* in the Canterbury guild, and in the guild referred to in the eleventh and twelfth centuries at London, are obscure. That members of Canterbury's merchant guild (*cepmannegilde*) of *c.* 1100 were *cnihtan*, and that a burgesses' guild existed there in 1066 suggest that one association may have evolved over a long period. Such evolution could account for apparent anomalies and uncertainties of status and functions. Although merchant guilds as such are not referred to until after the Conquest—the Canterbury one being one of the earliest—two were then said to have been in existence earlier. That seems quite likely, for such associations are discernible across the Channel from the tenth century.

The relationship between a town and its guild could be close. At Canterbury the burgesses' guild and the merchant guild were the same and the burgesses of Dover had a guildhall by 1066. One of the most obvious fields of corporate activity in a town enjoying expanding trade would be the protection of guildsmen—or townsmen—at home and abroad against extortion, violence, and perhaps outside competition. Consequently the guild—whether or not actually called a guild merchant—could become the body which campaigned for privileges for the town's traders, and its president, or alderman, might become the spokesman for the townspeople at large. Some towns sought or achieved corporate liberties not through their guilds but under the name of a commune, in which a large or small proportion of the townsmen might formally bind themselves by oath. Sometimes, as the social and convivial purposes of a guild were absorbed in the new political purposes of its members, the words guild and commune were used interchangeably.[26] Sometimes guilds were described as hanses; this emphasized their economic side, for though by the twelfth century the two words were sometimes used interchangeably in England, hanses elsewhere had originally been simple associations of merchants who secured corporate exemptions from

[26] See below, pp. 103–4, 107.

tolls and other dues.[27] The haphazard use of the words is illustrated by the way in which the name 'guildhall' was applied to so many town halls. It was apparently used in that sense in London, which is not recorded as ever having a guild merchant, quite early in the twelfth century.

Though they claimed to represent towns as such, merchant guilds were often in fact both wider and narrower. Landowners and traders who were not actually resident in the town might join in order to be able to do their business there toll-free, while some guilds were more or less taken over by merchants and wholesalers, as in the cloth towns, where weavers and fullers were excluded. Many merchant guilds, however, were 'merchant' in the old, wider sense of the word, and included some very modest craftsmen-traders. They should not be seen as invariably representing coherent class interests. Even merchants, after all, wanted guilds for good fellowship as well as for more sinister purposes.

As towns grew and their societies and economies became more complex the impulses towards association produced other sectional associations within them. By the twelfth century lesser guilds and fraternities appear, some of which were linked to particular trades or industries and some of which were not. Presumably some of them, particularly those which had no property, were shortlived: connections between successive guilds with apparently similar names or purposes should be proved rather than assumed. The earliest recorded trade or craft guilds seem to be those of weavers and bakers. Some of the weavers' guilds sought royal protection against the rulers of their towns, but the implied economic conflict may have been the reason for the occurrence of the guilds in the records rather than for their original formation. All guilds and fraternities of the period probably oscillated between official recognition and disapproval, according to whether they seemed subversive or helpful to established authority. As town governments became more powerful they sometimes prohibited sectional guilds or brought them under municipal control.[28] Except in London, where some traders were beginning to organize themselves by the 1260s, the regular and formal organization of separate trades in English towns seems to be

---

[27] Michaud-Quantin, *Universitas* [194], 174–7. On the Flemish 'hanse of London' see Perroy, 'Le Commerce anglo-flamande' [212].

[28] Unwin, *Gilds* [366], 31–54 (but see below, p. 166, n. 13); Urry, *Canterbury* [303], 131; *Rec. of Norwich* [389], i. 16–17; Gross, *Gild Merchant* [136], i. 227.

a phenomenon of the fourteenth and fifteenth centuries, and it is modern, not medieval, usage to use the word guild particularly for this kind of association.[29] In the Middle Ages almost any voluntary association or club might be called a guild, and its members—whether united for trading, political, religious, or any other purposes—would bind themselves together by the characteristic methods of feasting, religious ceremonies, and perhaps oath-taking. Guilds were, in G.H. Martin's excellent phrase, 'a form of association as unself-conscious and ubiquitous as the committee is today'.[30] Within the framework of religious ceremony, brotherly conviviality, and mutual assistance, they provided for multifarious needs in urban life.

Although the Church was closely linked with guilds, especially through burials and commemorative services, it never entirely lost its early distrust of them and their possibly subversive nature.[31] Meanwhile it provided its own framework for local society through parish churches. The parish system in England developed at very much the same time as towns were growing, or a little earlier. Before the tenth century most towns were served by a single mother church, possibly with subordinate church buildings dotted around, but with the clergy working more or less as a group. In some cases, like Hereford and Worcester, this pattern survived for some time, but in others the tenth and eleventh centuries witnessed a multiplication of small churches each with its own priest, to which separate parishes, with their own incomes, were soon attached. As the twelfth century wore on, the hardening of rights to tithes and dues and of canon law in general made it more difficult to divide existing parishes in order to form new ones. The process therefore continued more slowly, and was more often formally recorded, while towns that only started to grow in the new climate often stayed united under a single parish church.[32]

The varying pattern of parishes must have provided a wide variety of local groupings and loyalties. Many urban parishes were minute: Lincoln had forty-three churches, probably most of them parochial, by the mid twelfth century, Canterbury twenty-two, and London an astonishing total of 126 'lesser, parish churches' as well as its thirteen 'greater, conventual churches'. Some town churches, like country ones, were founded by lords for their tenants, but others, like one

[29] See pp. 164–8.
[30] 'Eng. Borough in 13th Cent.' [189], 126.
[31] *Councils and Synods* [23], ii (1), 313.
[32] Addleshaw, *Parochial System* [59]; Keene, 'Winchester: the Brooks Area' [430], 54–60; Platt, *Eng. Med. Town* [220], 148–58; and below, p. 191.

recorded at York and probably a good many at Norwich, were built by groups of citizens for themselves. The income of town parishes could be small and hard to collect: personal, or non-agricultural, tithes were contentious, and other dues may not always have made up much. Colswein of Lincoln (*fl.* 1086) provided two churches for thirty-six new houses, but gave them no endowment. Sir Francis Hill guessed that some of the Lincoln parishes comprised only a 'cluster of houses' each. How long the local enthusiasm that must explain some of these parishes could survive in such circumstances is uncertain. Some urban parishes disappeared later in the Middle Ages when the desire to increase funds by amalgamation may have been strengthened by envious comparison with the large well-staffed parishes of the new towns or with the friars' churches. Elsewhere, however, additional endowments came to the rescue, while even in big parishes there was still room for smaller, cosier associations around parish guilds and chantries. By the later Middle Ages most towns had at least one chantry under the management of the corporation, who might profit both from the chaplain's prayers and from the foundation's endowment.[33] In the same way merchant, craft, or other guilds and fraternities were sometimes linked with particular parish churches so that religious and secular associations were indistinguishable.

Non-parochial churches were part of town life too, and need to be studied by the urban historian from this point of view. In addition to the cathedrals and older Benedictine monasteries which lay at the heart of so many medieval towns and dominated the townsmen's lives in so many—not always harmonious—ways,[34] other houses lent new religious flavours to most towns. Many houses of Augustinian canons appeared in the twelfth century, often in towns and enjoying urban property, whether in rents or the endowments of parish churches.[35] At Leicester the earl, as patron of the town churches, gave the patronage to the Augustinian abbey of St. Mary which he founded in 1143. Since Augustinians were not cloistered monks but secular canons they should have been well suited to exercise an urban 'group ministry', but they do not seem to have been very effective at Leicester. In the thirteenth century the friars superseded them as

[33] Little, 'Personal Tithes' [177]; Wood-Legh, *Perpetual Chantries* [283], 155–81.
[34] See below, pp. 115–16.
[35] Southern, *Western Society and the Church* [250], 241–50; Knowles and Hadcock, *Med. Religious Houses* [167], 20–1.

the new wave of the Church's mission to towns. By 1300 friars were numerous in many towns and their churches and houses were becoming larger and more impressive. Preaching, acting as confessors, conducting burials, and even helping to provide piped water-supplies, the friars played an active part in town life until the Dissolution, as the many bequests they won from townspeople testify. In addition most towns, even the smallest, had a variety of hospitals and almshouses which were often endowed and supported by the burgesses and provided another focus for communal concern and activity.[36] Hermits, or anchorites, and anchoresses are to be found in some towns from time to time but, except for a brief period later on in Norwich, there do not seem to have been any of those quasi-religious communities of women, called béguines, which were found in some towns of northern continental Europe.[37]

Presumably the standard of lay literacy was always higher in towns than in the country. Some time during the later thirteenth century a festival of the Puy was founded in London. Like that at Arras, of which more is known, this was a society, apparently of rich citizens, which held feasts and competitions in song-writing. Its third 'prince', or president, seems to have been a feather-monger and vintner. People like the members of the Puy may have been educated at home, but towns were in any case relatively well provided with schools. By about 1180 London had enough for the pupils to engage in public disputations together. At Bury, Abbot Samson (d. 1211), who had taught in the town before becoming a monk, provided the school with a stone-built building rent-free. By the thirteenth century most of the more important towns are known to have had schools of some sort, though probably most had little institutional framework. Many were as short-lived as their masters and it is usually pointless to try to trace continuity from one casual reference to another. Where there was an endowment the situation was different, but the sources suggest that permanent endowments were rare before the fourteenth century.[38]

---

[36] Martin, 'Church Life in Leicester' [330]. A history of all religious houses appears in *V.C.H.* whether or not the town histories have been covered. For a well-recorded hospital: *V.C.H. Wilts.* [408], iii. 343–56; for water-supplies, e.g. Lobel and Carus-Wilson, *Bristol* [294], 9.

[37] Tanner, 'Popular Religion in Norwich' [259], 116–30.

[38] *Mun. Gild. Lond.* [357], ii. 216–28; *Cal. London Letter Book A* [344], 36, 57; ibid. *C*, 138–9; Ungureanu, *La Bourgeoisie naissante* [267], 75, 78–9; Orme, *Eng. Schools* [206], 167–84.

Meanwhile England developed, earlier than anywhere else in northern Europe except Paris, the most urban of all institutions derived from the medieval Church—namely the university. It would be difficult to explain just why it was the schools at Oxford and Cambridge which became universities in the thirteenth century. For a while students were attracted not only there and to London but to schools at Northampton, Salisbury, and Stamford, which must have looked very like incipient universities. The effect of exceptionally large and highly privileged schools on the life of their parent towns is too big a subject to be considered here, but the impact on social structure and customs of a fluctuating population of students is not to be ignored.[39]

THE SEPARATION OF TOWN AND COUNTRY

When, why, and how far the social structures and social values of town and country began to diverge is a subject of equal importance and obscurity. Fundamentally it must be connected with the distinctive functions—economic, social, and political—which towns performed and with the distinctive range of personal occupations which they provided. In southern Europe a good many people lived in towns although they worked in the country. In England, though no towns entirely lacked agricultural activity, most people lived in them because they worked there, not because urban life was the norm. That is not to say that people disliked it. By the fourteenth century invasions of privacy were the subject of litigation in London, but the rate of immigration shows that town life had at least relative merits for many people. Even if being a domestic servant or labourer in a town offered no more chance to develop particular gifts than one might have in the country, towns still offered a wider range of occupations for more people. They also offered life and spectacle—markets, courts, religious festivals, and so forth. All this affected more than the surface of life and did so in a more general way than the conditions of any single town can explain. The presence of strangers and foreigners, for instance, must have affected social customs in proportion to their integration into local society.

The institutions of kinship and marriage, which lie at the very

[39] Rashdall, *Universities of Europe* [229], iii; Richardson, 'Schools of Northampton' [383]; Rogers, *Making of Stamford* [419], 56n; *V.C.H. Cambs.* [301], iii. 76–86; *V.C.H. Lincs.* [421], ii. 468–72; *V.C.H. Oxon.* [397], iii. 10–11; *V.C.H. Wilts.* [408], iii. 371; Pantin, *Oxford Life* [396], 99–104.

heart of social structure, were modified in towns, at least for the
property-owning classes, by customs of inheritance which varied
more or less from those outside. Freedom to bequeath land; a tendency to partible inheritance; different systems of guardianship for
orphans, with wardship by near kin increasingly supervised by the
municipal authorities; varying, but often fairly generous, provision
for widows, who might even be allowed to carry on their husbands'
businesses, all seem characteristic of towns and must have conditioned the structure and mobility of urban society, though the
sources have not yet been much exploited with these issues in
mind.[40] Urban social relations were further conditioned by the
structure of trade and industry. Since the household often doubled
as a place of work the bonds of its owner's conjugal family might be
strengthened. Burgess families, largely free of the countervailing
pressures of lordship, may have been particularly close units in some
ways. Living-in apprentices and journeymen could also become
closely integrated in their masters' households, though it is difficult
to substantiate this until very late in the Middle Ages. Among those
of the poor who had their own households the only close and lasting
relationship may have been that of husband and wife, since they
might be separated from parents and siblings in the country and
might put out their children to work very young.[41] The age structure
of town populations may well have also differed from that of society
at large. Though the records for this period are inadequate to prove
it, young unmarried servants and apprentices were perhaps particularly numerous, while the numbers of the aged may have been
reduced both by higher death-rates and by the retirement to the
country of those who could afford it.

Obvious differences between the lives of merchants and country
landowners, for instance, should, nevertheless, not lead us to assume
wide differences in their attitudes and values. How soon the landed
upper class began to see townsmen as a distinct and inferior group
is uncertain. The thegnly wergeld of the merchant who had travelled
thrice across the sea may suggest that distinctions were less clear in
the eleventh century than they had become by the twelfth, when
Richard fitz Neal referred in his *Dialogue of the Exchequer* to a knight
or other freeman so far demeaning himself (which God forbid) as to

---

[40] *Borough Customs* [15], ii. pp. lxxxv–cxv, cxxvii–cxxxv, 102–57; Hemmeon, *Burgage
Tenure* [143], 15–18, 108–53.
[41] Hughes, 'Family Structure in Med. Genoa' [153].

acquire money by engaging in trade. Even at that time and later, despite our lack of sources to tell us about townspeople's social ideals and characteristic reference figures, we should not assume that chivalric stories and feudal values were alien to them. Later in the Middle Ages, when the formal institutions of towns were far more developed, townspeople still shared many of the values of the countryside. Earlier they may well have shared more. As Daniel Waley says of Italy at the same time: 'The ethos of the knight permeated the citizen population.'[42] One obvious reason for that is that a good many town-dwellers had spent their childhood or, if they were apprenticed young, at least their early childhood in the country. Burgesses often maintained links with their birthplaces and sometimes retired to the country, while outsiders of all classes of course constantly visited the towns. Moreover many of the richer townsmen pursued extraordinarily diverse activities: leading citizens often owned land in the country, acted as local or royal administrators and judges, and carried arms for their own protection if for no other reason. The medieval merchant was not deskbound. Consequently there were many pressures to reconcile differences of customs and attitudes between town and country even while their characteristic occupations and interests seem to have been becoming more specialized and diverse. Even while borough courts in general were developing their independence, the twelfth-century custom that a burgess's son proved his majority by counting money and measuring cloth was superseded in some towns by the proof of age familiar to the common law of England.[43]

London should never be taken as a paradigm of English towns: while London closed its husting for Boston fair, Wallingford closed its portmoot for harvest and many another small town may have done the same. Nevertheless London is the best—or least badly—recorded, and so may serve to illustrate the emergence of a distinct urban society. By the early twelfth century it was already a political and administrative unit with its own customs and privileges and its own legal, if not yet political, élite in the aldermen. Yet the 'Londoners' of the period, despite the readiness of historians to generalize about them, are not an easily defined group. London and

[42] *Italian city republics* [275], 165; cf. Hyde, *Society and Politics in Med. Italy* [154], 7, 167–73; Bloch, *Feudal Society* [72], 293, 296; Reynolds, 'In Search of a Business Class' [233]; Dhondt, 'Les Solidarités Médiévales' [103]; Le Goff, 'The Town as an Agent of Civilisation' [172].

[43] *Borough Customs* [15], ii. 157–60; Hemmeon, *Burgage tenure* [143], 18n.

Westminster were the scene of much government activity and many great men had houses there, so that one cannot be sure which of the city's householders and property-owners were reckoned to be members of the London community and what were the interests represented by such members. By the mid twelfth century, however, contemporary chroniclers could speak of 'the Londoners' in terms which excluded the feudal lords who had castles in the city, and William fitz Stephen's famous description of the city, though too long to be included here, demonstrates delightfully the heights to which twelfth-century civic patriotism could rise.[44] In the next hundred years an increasingly well defined, independent, and powerful local administration progressively divided inhabitants from outsiders and the ruling class within from those they ruled. The peculiarity of civic custom and the exacerbation of class divisions thus went hand in hand. Yet at the same time leading citizens were active in royal business; the city as a whole was continually embroiled in national politics; and kings periodically abrogated its liberties and pruned its odder legal customs. To some extent the very diversity of immigrants' origins may have enabled the city to impose its own ways upon them, but even so their numbers, together with the steady loss of leading families by extinction or by absorption into the landed gentry, must, one would think, have diluted the flavour of its social peculiarities.

[44] *Eng. Hist. Docs.* [29], ii, pp. 956–62.

5
The Growth of Independence

BOROUGHS AND LIBERTIES

One of the best known signs and results of the urban growth of the earlier Middle Ages is the way in which the greater towns of Europe, and even some quite small ones, gained a measure of self-government. Despite wide differences in economic and political circumstances they began to do this almost everywhere at very much the same time, namely the later eleventh and the twelfth centuries.[1] The degree of independence which they won varied greatly, yet so much have the great cities of Flanders, Italy, and north Germany dominated historical writing that medieval towns have sometimes been described almost entirely in terms of their liberties, and some historians have only grudgingly admitted the urban status of the less privileged towns of England or France. Without going as far as that one may admit that one of the distinctive marks of medieval towns as opposed to those of the classical world was their political and juridical separation from the countryside—though paradoxically the most independent towns of Italy and Germany extended their rule over the territory around and so partially obliterated the distinction again.

In England the emphasis on the legal and constitutional status of towns has taken the form of talking of 'boroughs' rather than of towns, and of seeing the 'chartered borough' as the type of the medieval town. That is misleading in several ways. To start with, town liberties are only part of town history, and to go on with, the tendency to pass, as if the words were consistently synonymous, from town to borough, from borough to 'free borough', and from 'free borough' to chartered borough can only create confusion. In chapter two something was said about early meanings of the word borough.[2] More will be said here about how its meaning changed.

---

[1] See e.g. Mundy and Riesenberg, *Med. Town* [43]; Waley, *Italian City Republics* [275]; *Libertés urbaines* [84].

[2] See above, pp. 24, 31–2, 34–6.

To understand how it acquired a series of new meanings connected with urban liberties, and to understand the origin and importance of urban liberties themselves, it is necessary to go back to consider how towns were ruled before the drive for liberties began and how and why urban communities began to assert themselves and look for independence.

TOWNS AS UNITS OF GOVERNMENT AND CUSTOM TO c. 1100

It has been suggested that in Gaul the disintegration of the Roman *civitates* into separate *pagi* left the towns which had once been the capitals of the *civitates* alone as separate units, in which by the ninth century the bishops had more or less exclusive rights of government. In Germany many bishops acquired similar powers over their episcopal cities by royal grants in the tenth century.[3] In both countries the urban government which resulted is likely in itself to have promoted the internal solidarity of the urban population, often against its ruler. The structure of local government in England developed rather differently, for the framework of *civitates* had disappeared and kings did not devolve their power to the Church on the scale that they did in Germany. Even so, separate town courts and customs seem to have evolved at very much the same period.

One of the common functions of a town—or of a fortified place which may become a town—is to act as a centre of government. It is therefore difficult to know, for instance, whether the early *praefecti* of Lincoln or Canterbury,[4] or the *burhgemot* mentioned in King Edgar's laws, were urban or proto-urban officials and courts, or merely officials and courts in charge of districts centred upon the towns. The titles *portgerefa* and *wicgerefa* (port-reeve and *wik*-reeve) however are more suggestive, while the use of words like *burgware*, *portware*, and *portmenn* implies that even before the tenth century the inhabitants of towns (or of places which we know were towns later) could be seen as distinct social groups. By the working of Anglo-Saxon custom such groups were quite likely to develop some sort of legal entity. By the eleventh century many towns probably formed

---

[3] Schlesinger, *Beiträge* [244], 42–67.

[4] Bede, *Hist. Eccles.* [14], 192; Urry, *Canterbury* [303], 82–7; for sources before 1100, see notes to chapter 2. The material is very fully discussed in Tait, *Med. Eng. Bor.* [258]. For Domesday material, see Darby, *Domesday geog.* [100], and discussion in e.g. Loyn, *A.S. Eng.* [180], 368–84.

separate 'hundreds' with courts parallel to the courts of rural hundreds,[5] and, though some references to borough courts suggest that their jurisdiction was not exclusively urban, they seem to have derived a particular status and authority from being held in important and populous places. One eleventh-century text makes a general distinction between town law and country law (*burhriht* and *landriht*). Some of the differences certainly lay in the rules of land tenure and others probably derived from the activity of town courts in commercial matters.

Most of the evidence about urban land tenure, 'burgage tenure' as it later came to be called, comes from after the Norman Conquest. However, Domesday Book's enumeration of customs (sometimes explicitly those of King Edward's time), post-Conquest confirmations of existing customs, and the English names of many of the dues owed by townsmen, together show that the elements of a distinctive urban tenure already existed before 1066.[6] The burdens of urban land tenure did not yet always exclude agricultural or other labour services, but people occupying property in boroughs—that is, by and large, the burgesses—more often owed money rents alone, and could dispose of their tenements more freely than was usual for small-holders elsewhere. The landgable or hawgable (a sort of ground-rent) paid by burgesses seems often to have been fixed at a standard figure and was generally paid to the king, who also received other customary dues, including the tolls on transactions and commodities attracted to the town's market. Sometimes his profits were shared with the earl of the shire, or in smaller places all the dues could go to a local lord, but the general principle of more or less uniform money payments seems fairly clear.

It is, however, rash to assume that anything in Domesday Book is clear. The difficulty of knowing for a start what it means by a 'borough' has been discussed in chapter two. Other problems arise in the context of urban land tenure. Firstly, it appears that some householders in some towns in 1086 were not burgesses, and therefore presumably held their houses on different terms from the rest. In Norwich, for example, there were 'bordars' who did not pay dues like the burgesses because they were too poor. How readily men—or

---

[5] i.e. subdivisions of the shire. For 'ports' see above, pp. 18–20, 25, 32. For A.S. courts and law in general see e.g. Stenton, *A.S. Eng.* [253]; Blair, *Introd. to Anglo-Saxon Eng.* [70].

[6] Hemmeon, *Burgage Tenure* [143], 158–66.

tenements—moved from one category to the other is obscure. Secondly, burgesses attached to some boroughs in 1086 were entered in Domesday under the heads of manors scattered through the countryside around. Various explanations have been offered for these 'contributory burgesses', as they have been called. One possibility is that they used their borough holdings for trade, either on their own account or for the lords of their manors, but still owed dues and services in those manors.[7] In spite of these problems, and although it is never safe to make sense of Domesday by ignoring anomalies, it still seems fair to say that a reasonably uniform system of urban landholding was in existence by 1086.

The development of mercantile custom is harder to detect, though it is reasonable to assume that commercial cases would arise most often where markets and fairs were held and that customs concerning them would develop *pari passu* with trade. King Edgar ordained uniform weights and measures in conformity with those of London and Winchester, and the inference that such matters might be adjudicated in urban courts is confirmed by the tenth-century charter which describes two silver cups as containing twelve marks of silver according to the standard of the London husting. By the twelfth century the court of husting, whose name is of Scandinavian derivation, is known to have met weekly and had probably usurped most of the functions of the more unwieldy folkmoot of London. It must have been in a London court, perhaps the husting, that cases were decided about the tolls and penalties listed in the set of regulations known as IV Ethelred 1–4. No other town is likely to have had to deal with commercial disputes on anything like the same scale as London, but there is no reason to doubt that courts in many trading towns were adjudicating, with increasing frequency and hardening custom, on humbler versions of the same kind of thing.

Obscure as all this remains it seems clear that by the time the Normans arrived most towns were legally and administratively marked off to some degree from the surrounding countryside. The organization of London, where folkmoot, husting, and subordinate wardmotes (ward courts) under aldermen, almost certainly originated before the Conquest, was exceptionally complex, for London was exceptional among English towns. Nevertheless at least four other towns (Cambridge, Huntingdon, Stamford, York) were divided into

[7] See e.g. Lobel, 'Medieval Oxford' [394]; Turner, *Town Defences* [266], 28–30; above p. 36.

wards, and five (Cambridge, Chester, Lincoln, Stamford, York) are known to have had lawmen or *judices* who may imply an organized legal hierarchy. It is probably unprofitable to try to penetrate the organization of most Anglo-Saxon towns any further. The existing evidence has been exhaustively—even exhaustingly—thumbed, and too much of it comes from a later date and has to be used retrospectively. That is especially dangerous when we know that the period through which we try to push the evidence back was one of rapid urban growth and therefore probably of institutional change. It is tempting, for instance, to equate lawmen, *judices*, and aldermen together as legal élites of judgement finders, to guess that lawmen and *judices*, like the London aldermen, may have sometimes had charge of quarters of their towns, and to generalize these institutions over all the larger towns—or all the Danelaw towns. That, however, would be pure speculation. It would be wiser to accept that the courts and other institutions of English towns before the twelfth century must remain, at least on present evidence, largely unknown.

Two general points about urban institutions at this stage must, nevertheless, be made. The first is that towns were not yet officially places of particular individual or corporate liberty. Above the level of chattel slavery, which still existed, the degrees of personal freedom all over the country were less clearly and uniformly distinguished than they later became. Though the larger towns must have provided better hiding-places for the fugitive slave or heavily burdened peasant than he might find elsewhere, living in a town did not formally confer any particular liberty. Nor did towns—even London —have any recognized privileges or independence in local government. The reeves who presided over their courts and collected their revenues were officials of the king—or in a few cases of other lords—and were responsible to him and not to the townsmen. The revenues of the more important towns were, it is true, collected apart from those of the shires in which they lay. Like the shire revenues they became fixed in the twelfth century at traditional lump sums known as the 'farm' (*firma*) of the borough or shire. How much they varied before then is uncertain: they certainly seem to have been put up by the Conqueror, who also in a good many cases retained for the Crown the third traditionally allowed to the earl of each county from its revenues. Nevertheless, though the revenues of towns included rather different items, like tolls and landgable, they belonged with rare exceptions as much to the king and earl as did those of the shire at large.[8]

Some of the exceptions look highly significant for the future: some penalties imposed under the London toll-regulations apparently went to the Londoners themselves, and the profits of the courts of Dover and others of what were later known as the Cinque Ports were surrendered by Edward the Confessor in exchange for naval services. The Londoners' own claim to be free of toll throughout the kingdom may also go back some time before it was recorded in the twelfth century: the toll-list of *c.* 1000 shows London was then accustomed to the idea of different rates of toll for people from different places. All who paid the king's customs (i.e. landgable etc.) in Dover were similarly free of toll by 1066, and it was probably in order to free the people of Coventry from local tolls that Godiva, according to a legend that may well have its foundation in fact, undertook her famous—and successful—ride.[9] All this suggests that urban solidarity was developing to the point of corporate bargaining with superior authority. We know that it was also beginning to express itself through the merchant or burgesses' guilds whose development is sketched in chapter four and which sometimes negotiated for exemptions from toll and so forth on behalf of their towns. Though some towns, and notably London, did not have merchant guilds *eo nomine* at all, the guild was a useful forum of corporate activity in a town whose courts might be dominated by royal or seigniorial officials. The same impression of corporate solidarity and nascent ambitions is confirmed by other hints in Domesday Book. Exeter, it says, 'did not pay geld except when London and York paid geld', and it defines the financial and military obligations of other towns in terms which could imply past negotiations. The formal surrender of authority, however, as distinct from the grant of fiscal or military privileges, in England as in most parts of Europe did not start until the twelfth century.

The second point about urban institutions at the end of the eleventh century derives from the first and is one which has already been mentioned. After the acquisition of urban liberties the word borough acquired a technical meaning which historians have tended

[8] The constitutional significance of the earl's 'third penny' from boroughs seems to have been exaggerated. Tait's places not paying it (*Med. Eng. Bor.* [258], 148) seem to be places where Domesday does not mention it.

[9] *Domesday Book* [25], i. 1; *V.C.H. Warwicks.* [317], viii. 242–7; Cazel [311], 135–6.

to extend backwards, talking of towns having 'borough status' in the tenth and eleventh centuries. That implies that the word had a legal or constitutional meaning which can be understood by finding some common denominator among places described as boroughs in Domesday Book or earlier sources. Among the 'marks of the borough', for example, Maitland listed 'tenurial heterogeneity', by which he meant that many Domesday boroughs contained houses held from a number of different lords as well as others held from the king.[10] This surely was a natural consequence of urban prosperity and trade, which made town properties and tenants valuable to lords, rather than a mark of a definable 'borough status'. The clerks who wrote Domesday Book seem to have described as boroughs (*burgi*) those places which they thought of as what we should call towns. Sometimes they used the word *civitas* instead, particularly for ancient and cathedral towns, and sometimes they withheld both from very new agglomerations which had not yet established themselves as urban in public opinion. The places they called boroughs were likely to have markets, mints, their own courts and legal customs, and 'tenurial heterogeneity', just as they were likely to have rich citizens, several churches, and even paved roads. None of these characteristics seems to have been regarded as conferring 'borough status', because it seems that contemporaries were not yet thinking in those terms. They used the word borough to describe, not to define.

The processes that were to change the meaning of the word were, however, getting under way. 'Burgess' seems to have had the relatively precise meaning in 1086 of one who paid his share of the borough dues. Because of the special conditions of tenure in boroughs it was important to know the boundaries of the borough, within which the special conditions in principle applied, even though not all inhabitants were necessarily burgesses. Borough therefore could have a precise *geographical* meaning, though in some cases where Domesday Book uses both *civitas* and *burgus* about the same town, *burgus* seems to have its older and narrower meaning of the fortified area, while *civitas* was used for the whole area contributing to the town's payments and presumably enjoying its privileges.[11] It is possible therefore to say that the similarity of legal conditions within towns (that is, in contemporary terms, within *burgi* or *civitates*)

[10] *D.B. and Beyond* [187], 178.
[11] *V.C.H. Essex* [272], i. 415; *V.C.H. Yorks: York* [444], 19–20.

was beginning to give a similar legal meaning to both words. As yet
however town-dwellers were not likely to campaign for 'borough
status' as such, even if they were beginning to campaign for the
privileges that other towns—or boroughs—enjoyed.

THE TWELFTH CENTURY

Burgage tenure, customs, and guilds

It seems then that by the late eleventh century towns in England
had achieved a combination of corporate solidarity and administrative separation from the country which could form the basis of a
campaign for independence. The campaign becomes discernible in
the twelfth century and it bears a notable resemblance in nature and
chronology to those waged by townsmen abroad. It is unlikely to
have been more than marginally affected by the coming of the Normans. The Normans brought with them local variations of custom
which affected some towns, but their own towns were not more
'advanced' than English ones nor significantly different from them.[12]
Tait's suggestion that 'municipal growth and even aspirations we
should scarcely expect to find among the slow-moving Anglo-
Saxons' is contradicted by the whole tenor of his book. Borough
liberties would surely have developed and Anglo-Saxon kings would
surely have granted borough charters if there had been no Norman
Conquest. Moreover since the gains most widely achieved were
those—burgage tenure, other legal privileges, and freedom from
toll—which some towns had already won, it is plain that, though the
movement gathered force now, it was not essentially new. Part of the
reason why we know more about townsmen's efforts to secure
liberties after 1100 is that the records improve.

The first recorded use of the term 'burgage' comes in a charter by
which Henry I confirmed the archbishop of York's grant to his men
of Beverley of free burgage 'according to the laws and customs of the
burgesses of York, and also their guild merchant with its pleas and
toll, and with all its free customs and liberties'.[13] At about the same
time various towns secured grants of 'customs' which included the
usual features of burgage tenure. The charters in which such grants

---

[12] Bateson, 'Laws of Breteuil' [63]; Ballard, 'Laws of Breteuil' [61]; Hemmeon,
Burgage Tenure [143], 154–83. See pp. 42–4.
[13] Eng. Hist. Docs. [29], ii, pp. 962–3; cf. Tait, Med. Eng. Bor. [258], 213–14. For
charters: Brit. Bor. Ch. [16].

were recorded frequently refer to conditions obtaining elsewhere, as in the Beverley reference to York. The little Norman town of Breteuil (Eure) spawned a family of towns in the Welsh marches and Ireland which enjoyed customs imitated from its own, and Newcastle upon Tyne another in the north-east and Scotland. The most widespread influence, not surprisingly, was that of London, whose customs were at first sometimes bracketed with those of Winchester. Oxford and Northampton, whose charters referred to London, had followers of their own in their turn.

The customs in force in any town were often more eclectic than the charters suggest, but that only emphasizes the extent of interaction and even solidarity between towns, which in turn indicates the forces to which lords were subject. Across the Channel the years after 1127 saw the cities of Flanders, with which the ports of eastern England had many contacts, use the opportunities of civil war to win notable liberties. Longer wars in Germany had already produced moves in the same direction, while towns in north and west France were restive under the local disorders prevalent there. There is no need to postulate deep ideological conflicts between townsmen and feudal lords to explain this: often townsmen were anxious at first only to protect themselves from extortion, oppression, and disorder. Piecemeal successes thereafter produced not only the confidence to make further demands but also rationalizations of the demands which could in time amount to a new ideal of civic government. Not in any case that the town's gain was necessarily the lord's loss, at least in conditions like those in England, where a strong monarchy prevented any sensational victories, partly by ensuring a relatively high degree of peace and order, and thus removing many of the incentives to urban rebellion. Thanks to the financial profits to be derived from a prosperous town, lords other than the king were also willing to encourage trade and settlement by granting reasonably favourable conditions. Even ecclesiastical lords might be willing to allow their urban tenants burgage tenure and some limitations of other dues in the hope not only of avoiding trouble but also of making up on the roundabout what they lost on the swings.[14]

Henry I's charter to Beverley gave 'free burgage' (*liberum burgagium*). Later charters use the same expression, which was superseded during the thirteenth century by 'free borough' (*liber burgus*), which, as James Tait showed, meant very much the same: that is,

---

[14] See pp. 115–16; Beresford, *New Towns* [67], 319–38.

the normal conditions of borough or burgage tenure.[15] It was granted to towns both by the king and by lesser lords who, in the latter case, might then get their grant confirmed by the king, as was the archbishop of York's charter to Beverley. The king could then add such privileges as only he could give: in the case of Beverley he granted freedom of toll throughout Yorkshire. Because of the way towns were securing similar privileges as 'free boroughs' we have now reached a point where the word borough is beginning to have a technical meaning in some contexts, though probably in most colloquial usage it meant nothing more precise than we mean by 'town'. A town's or borough's privileges might or might not amount to much more than burgage tenure, while some towns had burgage tenure although they never had a charter for that or for anything else.

Despite the narrow meaning attached to 'free borough' in official circles, the linking of the word *liberum* to *burgagium* early in the twelfth century indicates the wind of change that was already blowing: mention of freedom no doubt stimulated townsmen, consciously or unconsciously, to increase its content. The idea of the intrinsic freedom of town air—*Stadtluft macht frei*—is in fact an historians' creation of the nineteenth century and, as usually interpreted, implies a generalized theory of individual liberty which is foreign to the earlier Middle Ages.[16] Nevertheless urban communities in the twelfth century were aiming at a corporate freedom from external interference which also involved the freedom of individual townsmen from servitude to external lords. The ruling that a villein's unchallenged residence in a town as a burgess for a year and a day precluded any claim on him by a former lord appears in the customs of Newcastle upon Tyne as early as the reign of Henry I. In Glanvill's lawbook of the 1180s it applied to anyone 'received as a citizen into the commune, that is to say, the guild' of 'any privileged town'. Moreover, although labour services in some boroughs survived to the very end of the twelfth century, the standard acceptation of borough tenure excluded them. That had particular significance at a period when personal freedom was becoming more precisely defined and when labour services were becoming incompatible with it. Though not everyone living in a borough held a burgage or belonged to its commune or guild, legal—as distinct from economic—un-

[15] *Med. Eng. Bor.* [258], 194–220.
[16] H. Strahm, 'Stadtluft macht frei' [256].

freedom was by now, to judge from borough charters, regarded as an anomaly in urban conditions.[17]

The 'customs' frequently granted by analogy with other towns were largely of a juridical nature, including not only those strictly pertaining to burgage tenure but others which would be applied in the procedures of the borough court. They did not, as some towns later claimed and some historians have believed, necessarily imply that the town obtaining the grant had the same constitution of courts and officials, let alone the same degree of independence, as did its model. In contemporary terms, however, the kind of legal procedures which were covered by these grants of customs were in themselves valuable. The townsman's right to defend himself against a criminal charge by oath rather than by battle can be traced back in England to a charter granted by Henry I to London (or perhaps fabricated later in the twelfth century) and was widely copied. It was not a triumph of English conservatism over the new Norman procedure of battle, for the same privilege was valued by towns abroad; Ypres had won it from the count of Flanders in 1116. Other customs shared by towns enjoying the customs of London included rules limiting money penalties (amercements, *misericordie*) and regulating the collection of debts and procedures in cases of debt, and that right of burgesses not to plead outside the bounds of the borough which was the bastion of borough jurisdiction but created awkward conflicts of liberties between equally privileged towns whose burgesses might go to law with each other. In practice, though a good many towns secured a fair degree of autonomy in civil cases, royal power limited the right to have serious criminal charges against burgesses tried only within the walls to a relatively small number of places.[18]

Much more could be said about variations in urban legal custom. Some of the details are of rather technical legal interest but properly understood they can illuminate many aspects of urban society. More work is needed, however, for instance on the stages of their development in different places. The great pioneer collection by Mary Bateson in *Borough Customs* needs to be used with care if chronology and variation are to be appreciated. The most important

[17] *Eng. Hist. Docs.* [29], ii, p. 971; *Glanvill* [34], 58; Jocelin of Brakelond, *Chron.* [299], 99–101; Tait, *Med. Eng. Bor.* [258], 206.

[18] *Brit. Bor. Ch.* [16] *1042–1216*, 132–4; ibid. *1216–1307*, pp. lix–lx; *Borough Customs* [15]; Martin and McIntyre, *Bibliog. of Munic. Hist.* [9], i, pp. 336–41; *Elenchus* [27], i. 309; for the London charter, see below.

general point to notice here may be the wide diffusion from the twelfth century both of more or less independent jurisdiction and of the characteristically urban procedures. Historians have sometimes stressed local and national peculiarities rather too much: both local patriotism and the training and preoccupations of the English common law have made national and international similarities of custom less noticeable to some local historians than they are to a social historian—let alone, perhaps, to a social anthropologist.

The right to form a guild merchant was often associated with the grant of burgage tenure, legal customs, and freedom from toll, for the grantors of charters often regarded such a guild as representing the town as a whole. At Lincoln the members of the guild seem to be defined *c.* 1155 as those paying the king's geld—the similarity of words, with their possibilities of confusion, reflecting a confusing social fact. The earliest guild whose recognition by charter is recorded is that of Burford, whose lord between 1088 and 1107 gave them 'the guild and customs which the burgesses of Oxford have in the guild merchant'.[19] The Beverley charter illustrates the same thing, though the archbishop's charter which the king confirmed referred to the burgesses' hanse rather than their guild. It granted 'their hanse house with all free customs . . . in order that they may there administer their statutes to the honour of God and St. John, and of the canons, and to the good government of the whole town, with the same law of liberty as the men of York have in their hanse house'.[20] The recognition of a guild or hanse implies that local tolls and other dues from the members of the guild were remitted or commuted; the remissions are specified in detail in the Beverley charter. Charters could also enforce guild regulations and monopolies, like those (*c.* 1120–1204) of Cambridge, Lincoln, Nottingham, and Derby, and could give the town a trading monopoly in its county.

The beginning of autonomous local government

Real progress in urban liberty came when towns secured the right to appoint their own officials and thus to control their own internal affairs. In England this came generally through grants of the 'farm of the borough' (*firma burgi*), so that the townsmen became corporately responsible for paying over the annual royal dues and, by

[19] *Eng. Hist. Docs.* [29], ii, p. 965; *Cal. Chart. R.* [17] iii. 7; *Cartae Antiquae* [21], 119.
[20] See above, pp. 80–3.

consequence, for appointing the reeve who accounted for them yearly at the Exchequer.[21] The advantages of such a system are obvious, for it allowed the town some autonomy in raising its farm and running its affairs in general. It must be remembered nevertheless that the king did not give up all his interests in the town when he granted the farm. An elected reeve still had to carry out many orders from the central government, and where a town already paid its farm separately from the rest of the county, as some did, its corporate existence was to some degree already recognized even before it had elected its own officers to pay over the farm. If in practice the central government itself chose reeves from among the inhabitants, as happened during most of the twelfth century in London, then the townsmen might hope that the reeves would represent their interests faithfully anyway. The relatively rich sources for London illustrate the difficulty of taking the official records at their face value as mirrors of civic politics and civic solidarity.[22] All the same there is no doubt that towns liked to hold their own farms. Most important places had secured the right to do so by the fourteenth century, while some towns under the authority of lords other than the king ('mesne boroughs' or 'seigniorial boroughs') gained comparable rights to pay over their lords' revenues in similar lump sums.

The method of achieving a measure of local independence through grants of the borough farm has sometimes been represented as a triumph of law-abiding English moderation, to be contrasted with the violent methods of urban 'communes' abroad. It has even been said that there is no evidence of any aspirations towards independence in English towns. That is certainly untrue. While the monarchy maintained its control throughout, except in a few exciting years during civil wars, and indeed combined a moderate devolution of powers with the steady development of central supervision and of new forms of taxation, it seems impossible that royal grants were prompted by royal grace and generosity alone. English kings were at times confronted with demands which could seem revolutionary. London formed a 'commune' twice in the twelfth century, at moments when the citizens reckoned that they could protect their interests best by strong corporate action.

The word *communitas* and its derivatives were widely used in the Middle Ages to express some of the concepts of affective and

[21] Tait, *Med. Eng. Bor.* [258], 139–93.
[22] For twelfth-century London, see below. Also Reynolds, 'Rulers of London' [359].

institutional community in which the period was so rich. The forms *communio, communia, communa* became particularly attached in the twelfth century to sworn associations of townspeople, often under the leadership of an elected mayor, and then, by natural association of ideas, to some of the more or less independent urban administrations which they set up. The earliest French communes or *conjurationes* were often formed to protect the town and keep the peace in circumstances where self-help seemed the only hope. The communal armies and administrations they formed could nevertheless appear revolutionary to their ecclesiastical and feudal lords, some of whom—and those in the most publicized cases—recognized them only with reluctance.[23] The kind of resonance the word thus acquired in conservative church circles is indicated by a comment on the London commune of 1191 by the English monk, Richard of Devizes, when he explained that neither Henry II nor Richard I would have recognized it for a million marks: 'Communia est tumor plebis, timor regni, tepor sacerdotii'.[24]

There is no evidence of unrest in English towns in the first part of the twelfth century, during the reign of Henry I, despite the troubles which were then raging just across the Channel. Henry's harsh and effective government no doubt protected towns to some degree from all oppression but his own, but the absence of open revolts may have been due as much to lack of opportunity as to contentment, for we know that some towns already had a basis of corporate solidarity from which they were shortly to demand greater autonomy. For whatever reasons, Henry is known to have made concessions to two towns, London and Lincoln. The first surviving Pipe Roll, or annual Exchequer account, which comes from 1130, shows that both had for a fee obtained control of their own farms and officers.[25] Lincoln offered more for its privilege but the grant to London was more valuable, for the Londoners secured the right to elect not merely a town reeve but a full sheriff, and thus took over the little county of Middlesex as well. The reason may be

[23] Vermeesch, *Les Origines de la commune* [271]; Petit-Dutaillis, *Les Communes françaises* [214] and cf. Packard [208]; Michaud-Quantin, *Universitas* [194], 129–66; *Med. Eng. Bor.* [258], 221.

[24] *Chron.* [49], 49; *tepor sacerdotii*, however glossed, seems at best anticlimactic. A scribal error for *terror*, plausible in a twelfth-century hand, is tempting but apparently ruled out by the reading in what appears to be the author's MS.: Cambridge, Corpus Christi College, MS. 339, fol. 36ᵛ.

[25] *Pipe Roll 31 Henry I* [46], 114, 149. For the Exchequer system as applied to London and for reference to other works, see Reynolds, 'Farm and Taxes of London' [358].

that London was more worth conciliating, and the very generous charter which the Londoners apparently obtained from the king a little later could be taken as corroboration. It not only confirms a collection of customs of varying but probably considerable value, but formally grants the citizens the right to appoint a sheriff and a local justice for London and Middlesex, at a farm notably lower than they had owed in 1130. Whether or not the charter in its present form is genuine, Henry's concessions to other towns seem to have been strictly limited. Only four of his surviving charters can be said to confer anything on town communities, and only London and Lincoln got anything more from him than toll-freedom and the recognition of a guild and customs.[26] It is, however, to be remembered that if we had earlier Pipe Rolls, or others between 1130 and 1155, we might know of other early grants of borough farms.

Support from London helped Stephen to secure the Crown in 1135 and explains why he made a pact with the Londoners which looks like the transactions by which rulers abroad recognized communes: it may even have been at this stage that London got the charter which purports to have been granted by Henry I. The Londoners certainly had a commune by 1141. Curiously enough, however, that did not protect them from losing their privileges later in the reign, nor is there any evidence of self-protective communes in other towns during the troubles of the times. Stephen and the magnates of the realm seem to have got away with treating towns as prizes rather than as communities worth conciliating.[27] There are puzzles here which the surviving records seem unlikely to solve. We can only guess that the habits of orderly government and obedience were as yet powerful in English towns.

In the second half of the twelfth century we get hints of urban aspirations as well as more information about the policy and working of the central government. Nearly fifty royal charters to English towns survive from Henry II's reign, many of them confirming what the towns concerned claimed to have enjoyed under Henry I, and most of the rest just conferring the same sort of privileges—toll-freedom, guild-merchant, burgage tenure, and borough customs. Only two charters contained grants of borough farms, but eight

---

[26] *Regesta Regum A.N.* [48], ii, nos. 644, 1137, 1275, 1729, though cf. confirmations by Henry II and customs of Newcastle (*Eng. Hist. Docs.* [29], ii, pp. 970–1); Brooke, 'Henry I's charter for London' [342].
[27] Stenton, *Eng. Feudalism* [254], 234–42.

towns in practice answered for their own farms for longer or shorter periods of the reign. On the evidence of his charters, of his quashing of two English communes, of Richard of Devizes's remark about his disapproval of communes in general, and of his refusal to allow London to have back its farm, Henry II has generally been seen as a more thorough-going opponent of civic liberties than his grandfather. The evidence does not support this. Although the practice of recording concessions by charter was becoming more common it was not yet invariable. Despite Tait's arguments, little can be inferred from the facts that only two grants of borough farms were recorded in that way and that neither they nor those recorded in the Pipe Rolls were explicitly intended to be permanent. Even after charters became a matter of course kings could and did revoke them: political realities mattered more than legal niceties, and neither twelfth-century charters nor the laconic phrases of the Pipe Rolls should be interpreted to conform with anachronistic ideas about legal precision of language or the supposed rules of 'feudalism'. Moreover, although town charters already had a good deal of common form, like the standard £10 penalty for infringement, neither similarities nor differences between them need be very significant: the Canterbury charter of 1155–8 (probably 1155) was copied from that of London, and included a reference to the London suburb of Portsoken which is obviously nonsense for Canterbury; the rest of the document may be an equally poor guide to real conditions in Canterbury.

Henry II's hostility to communes in England was shown in 1170 and 1176, when royal justices imposed amercements (financial penalties) on people who had formed or tried to form communes at Gloucester and York respectively.[28] The episodes prove that English townsmen had aspirations which the government disliked and also illustrate the nature of communes as symbolizing burgess solidarity rather than embodying any particular degree of independence or form of government: at the relevant times Gloucester was already empowered to collect its own farm while York was not. Henry's dislike of communes was nevertheless not so doctrinaire as Richard of Devizes and some later historians have thought, for he sanctioned them in his French lands where he needed the fiscal and political support that they could give him. In England they were

[28] *Pipe Roll 16 Henry II* [46], 79, *22 Henry II*, 106; Tait, *Med. Eng. Bor.* [258], 176–7; Packard, 'The Norman Communes' [207].

unnecessary to him and therefore not worth tolerating. Moreover the word commune did not invariably carry revolutionary impli- cations. When the citizens of Oxford described themselves in 1147 and 1191 as *cives Oxenefordie de communi civitatis et de gilda mercatoria* (or *mercatorum*) they may not have meant anything very different from *communitas* or *universitas*. Glanvill used *communa* and *gilda* as alternative descriptions of lawful town communities.[29] Henry II's treatment of London looks pragmatic: though he did not explicitly allow the city to elect its own officers, he recognized the citizens' corporate responsibility for extraordinary taxes, so that the steady development of such taxes (then known as 'aids' and 'gifts', later subsumed under the name of tallage) seems paradoxically to have stimulated corporate activity. Henry certainly did not like giving up power, as his treatment of his sons demonstrates, but the tenor of his government was such as to encourage communal responsibility in the towns, and he must surely have been more accustomed to treating with urban communities than his grandfather had been.

Richard I and John both needed money and were willing to grant borough farms and election of officials in return. Grants con- sequently multiplied between 1189 and 1216, embodied in in- creasingly standardized charters. The parallel development of royal taxation and of the general eyre (visitations by royal justices) made it possible for many of these grants to be made without serious political or financial damage to the king, and most new urban privileges, like the right to appoint coroners, were only such as to keep pace with administrative changes outside the towns. The latent dangers of urban unrest were however revealed in the 1190s. In 1191, a year after they had secured a grant of their farm from Richard I, the Londoners seized the opportunity of national dis- order during his absence to secure recognition of a commune from his brother John and the other magnates of the realm. Their mayor is first mentioned a little later, but both mayor and commune may have been created even before 1191: communes obviously did not depend on official recognition for their existence though they needed it for success. The London commune did not effect any noticeable change in the city's relations with the central government or in its internal politics, but in 1194 a Londoner was accused of saying, 'Come what may, London will never have any king but the mayor of London'. The accusation may have been false or exaggerated, but it

[29] Davis, 'An Oxford Charter' [392]; above, p. 100.

shows that Richard of Devizes did not invent revolutionary ideas where none existed. When Richard I returned to England briefly in 1194 he apparently avoided recognizing the commune but did not extinguish the mayoralty or withdraw the farm. John, after his accession in 1199, seems to have been unhampered by the memory of 1191, for he intervened in London politics on occasion, and it was not until he had his back to the wall in 1215 that he formally conceded the mayoralty, in the hope of keeping London's support against his rebellious barons.

AUTONOMOUS LOCAL GOVERNMENT, 1216–1500

During the thirteenth century the terrors of communes appear to have receded. In northern France, as in Italy, they had already become legitimized as one sort of privileged town. In England the form *communa, communia* etc. seems to have fallen out of use to describe urban communities in favour of the more general and neutral *communitas*. In London it continued to be used for a while but may have lost favour with the city's rulers after rebels against them used it as a battle-cry in the 1260s. Thirteenth-century urban groups elsewhere seem more often to have expressed their corporate identities (at least in the Latin documents we have about them) as guilds or *communitates*, which, though historians have translated or glossed them as communes, may, even in their English forms, have had less revolutionary overtones.[30] *Communitas* was a word of many respectable uses: any town was in some sense a *communitas*—a social and affective community—and it would only ask to be recognized as such in exceptionally repressive circumstances. More work on the changing implications and uses of the words is needed, and meanwhile their use should probably be more carefully distinguished;[31] it may be that some of the talk of 'communal movements' in English towns in the later Middle Ages, by seeming to assimilate all the efforts to gain official recognition for corporate liberties to the most revolutionary movements of the twelfth century, creates a single movement where none existed.

The twelfth-century communes did, however, leave a legacy on the English scene in the form of mayors, who are found in a number

[30] For some thirteenth-century uses see below, pp. 131–2, 133; for cases where 'commune' does not seem to be in the sources: Davis, 'Commune of Bury' [298]; Lobel, *Bury St. Edmunds* [300], 78–82, 126–31, 175–6; *V.C.H. Leics.* [332], iv. 19; Rogers, *Making of Stamford* [419], 42.

[31] For other, possibly misleading translations, see pp. 114, 136.

of towns, large and small, from the early thirteenth century. Unlike reeves and bailiffs who had financial and administrative responsibilities to the king even if they were appointed by their fellow townsmen, and so were bound to face two ways, the English mayor was from the start a purely urban official who symbolized the town's unity. Just as there were communes which were never recognized, so there were mayors even in towns which never acquired any significant degree of independence. Formal permission to have a mayor was rare before the later thirteenth century, but from John's reign on the government quite often acknowledged the existence and authority of mayors in other ways.[32]

Despite John's last-minute concession of the mayoralty, London lent vital support to the barons in 1215, and Magna Carta not only confirmed the liberties and free customs of cities, boroughs, towns (*ville*) and ports (*portus*), but, by its reference to the aids (*auxilia*) of London, implied that London—though not the other towns—was exempt from tallage. All references to aids and tallages of towns were omitted from the reissues of the charter in 1216, 1217, and 1225, which alone remained valid, but the Londoners fought a long dispute with Henry III's government about their subjection to tallage, hoping to negotiate lower obligations under the guise of aids. Aids were traditionally regarded as freely granted and subject to bargaining, whereas tallages were not. The Londoners failed, however, and the royal recovery after 1216 is exemplified in the way that Henry III repeatedly suspended the city's liberties altogether, appointing officials of his own choice, though generally for very short periods.[33] Most of Henry's charters to other towns were merely confirmations, for the practice was now becoming established whereby towns felt it necessary to purchase charters in each reign even if they gained very little that was new from them. There were some novelties: many towns received grants for a few years at a time of murage, pavage, or pontage, which enabled them to levy tolls from outsiders to build or repair walls and bridges and to pave their streets. Few towns got corresponding exemptions for their burgesses from such tolls.[34] Between 1227 and 1259 eleven more towns

[32] Tait, *Med. Eng. Bor.* [258], 291; *Brit. Bor. Ch. 1216–1307* [16], pp. lvii, 360–6; Hill, *Med. Lincoln* [333], 199–201; Urry, *Canterbury* [303], 87–8; cf. Finberg, *Glos. Studies* [121], 72.

[33] Williams, *Med. London* [373], 204–9.

[34] Nielson, *Customary Rents* [204], 137–41; Turner, *Town Defences* [266], 227–43 *et passim*.

received grants of their farms, but Henry's high view of the monarchy's rights, demonstrated in his treatment of London, was
underlined when he warned towns that failure to pay their farms
promptly could entail forfeiture of liberties. He also began the investigations into the exercise and possible usurpation of local
government duties known as 'Quo Warranto', and made towns
which had by custom received copies of the royal writs from the
sheriff, so that their own officials could execute them within the
borough boundaries, purchase new charters to authorize the
practice. What appears in the charters as a new kind of liberty was
thus, as M. T. Clanchy has shown, just an expensive confirmation
or even restriction of an old practice.[35]

The national conflicts of 1258–67 once more revealed rebellious
tendencies within the towns. The ruling citizens of London at first
gave cautious support to the baronial opposition but were soon over-
thrown by a popular *communa* which was totally committed to it.
Other towns took the same side, which accounts for the famous
decision of the rebel leader, Simon de Montfort, to summon
representative burgesses to his parliament in 1265. After his defeat
and death the *status quo* seems to have been restored in most places
fairly easily, though the Cinque Ports held out for some time
against the royalist forces. Heavy penalties fell on London, which
had to endure several years with its liberties suspended and only got
them back, somewhat amended, at an increased farm.[36]

Edward I followed his father's lead. Many of his charters to towns
simply recited and confirmed those of his predecessors, while
Ipswich, Lincoln, Norwich, Nottingham, Northampton, and
Southampton, for instance, as well as London, suffered suspensions
of their liberties, sometimes for quite long periods.[37] Only one new
borough farm was granted, to Chester in 1300, bringing the total to
fifty by Edward's death. In 1283 Bristol besought the king that

Since none can know so well as those whose work is concerned with
merchandise, and who earn their living by it, how to regulate the affairs
of merchants properly and honestly, the community (*communitas*) of

[35] Clanchy, 'Return of Writs' [85] and 'Henry III' [86].
[36] Williams, *Med. London* [373], 234–42; Jacob, *Studies in Baronial Reform* [157], 281–
9; Hill, *Med. Lincoln* [333], 210.
[37] *Rec. of Norwich* [389], i. p. xxxi; Hill, *Med. Lincoln* [333], 210; *Brit. Bor. Ch.
1216–1307* [16], ii, p. 345–6; Platt, *Med. Southampton* [416], 59. For reasons for interference, see pp. 131–5.

Bristol entreats the lord king that, if he should wish to grant his town at farm to anyone, he should concede it to them, since they would be prepared to give as much for it as any outsider.[38]

They did not get the farm permanently and formally until 1462, though their acquisition of other privileges meanwhile suggests that the deprivation was not very serious. Though the old style of farm-grants continued to be repeated in confirmations and some new examples occurred, they were in fact becoming obsolete. New charters, like that to Chester, take a different form, specifying the officials to be appointed and courts to be held where earlier ones would have been silent.[39] Most of the new grants of Edward I's reign, like those of Henry III, may in fact only have regularized existing situations or extended borough jurisdiction *pari passu* with developments outside. Grants which did not substantially reduce the king's power could nevertheless sometimes help to consolidate the authority and dignity of a town's government. The new privileges conferred on the Cinque Ports in return for increased naval services may be a case in point. By fostering the unity and authority of the confederation Edward I no doubt facilitated his control of the ports through their warden.[40]

One change took place in Edward I's reign which was of great importance in the long run. That was the replacement of the old royal tallage of towns by new parliamentary taxes and the regular summoning of borough representatives to parliaments. This is not the place to consider the constitutional effects for the country at large; it may be enough to say here that, though burgesses for long played a subordinate role in parliament and though there is little evidence of their combining to promote their common interests, their repeated contact with each other and with others present at parliaments must have simultaneously favoured uniformity of ambitions among them and given opportunities for promoting individual borough interests. By the fifteenth century non-burgesses were anxious to get into parliament as borough-members, which enabled some towns to secure influential representatives at no expense to themselves.[41] When in the fifteenth century the

[38] *Bristol Charters, 1378–1499* [291], ii. 42–3.
[39] *Cal. Charter R.* [17], ii. 486–8; *Chester County Court Rolls* [305], pp. xxvii–xxix; *Cheshire in Pipe Rolls* [304], 190–2.
[40] Murray, *Const. Hist. of Cinque Ports* [200], 28–9.
[41] McKisack, *Parl. Repres. of Eng. Boroughs* [184].

unprivileged town of Barnstaple decided to procure itself liberties by getting confirmation of some charters which the townspeople had fabricated, one of their members of parliament seems
to have helped to negotiate the affair for them.[42] The list of towns
which returned members to parliament was extremely variable
at first and only settled down during the fourteenth century,
while, as the example of Barnstaple shows, some 'parliamentary
boroughs' throughout the Middle Ages were without other liberties.

'Parliamentary boroughs', however, are a modern concept. The
variations in the list of boroughs represented in parliament should
remind us that the sheriffs who passed on summonses to towns were
not deciding 'which were the boroughs'[43] in their counties, that is,
which places had 'borough status'. Their categories were less tidy:
they were simply choosing the places they thought suitable to be
represented in parliament. Nevertheless the importance attached to
parliamentary representation came to make it seem a mark of
'borough status' and thus, together with the wide gulf by now divid-
ing the towns with a real measure of local autonomy from those with
only burgage tenure, brought about another change in the meanings
attached to the word borough. By the late thirteenth century
expressions like *villa* or *villa mercatoria* in Latin, *ville* in French, or
town (*tun, toune* etc.) in English were often used to describe towns
in general, less constitutional, contexts, while 'borough' was increasingly, though by no means always, restricted to the more
privileged places. The people of Barnstaple were victims of an irony
of history when they felt that their town, always described as a
borough and regularly represented in parliament, did not possess
the liberties a borough *ought* to have and were tempted to remedy
the defect with illicit success.

Kings continued to interfere in town government on occasion
after the thirteenth century, and Richard II confiscated London's
liberties in a way very reminiscent of Edward I. On the whole, however, methods of control became less crude. Edward III put
Southampton under keepers after a French raid on the town in
1338, but the elected officials were soon reinstated and the keepers,
who were kept on to look after defence here and in other coastal
areas, had to work alongside them. Most of the earlier confiscations

[42] Reynolds, 'Forged Charters of Barnstaple' [289], 709.
[43] Platt, *Eng. Med. Town* [220], 125.

had been at least ostensibly designed to remedy abuses by the town authorities, and such drastic action probably seemed less fitting as autonomous government became more established. Instead, an act of parliament of 1354 laid down a procedure for redressing grievances against municipal governments, while throughout the later Middle Ages townsmen were finding ways of making their own political controls more effective.[44]

The structure of urban liberties was in fact more or less complete by the fourteenth century, for though some towns were still catching up with the more fortunate, only three new sorts of privilege seem to have been bestowed: being an independent county, incorporation, and the commission of the peace. Neither of the first two was entirely new, and the third, keeping pace with parallel developments in the country at large, integrated under a single head many of the untidy and piecemeal jurisdictions of the borough courts as they had hitherto developed.[45] London, with Middlesex as its appendage, had in effect been a county probably since the early twelfth century. Bristol was the next town to have a comparable privilege: in 1373 it was given its own sheriff and made a county on its own. That was of practical value, since Bristol lay on the borders of Somerset and Gloucestershire so that its officers and inhabitants were constrained to deal with two sets of county officials and courts some way away. The same reasons cannot have applied to most of the other large towns, especially several county towns, which followed Bristol's lead during the next hundred years.

Becoming a county was quite often associated, as it was at Bristol, with a stage in the process of formal incorporation. Incorporations provide a striking example of charters which appear to mark a more important epoch in municipal development than they did at the time. By the later fifteenth century a charter which would now be considered a charter of incorporation made a town a fictitious person in the eyes of the law by bestowing on it the so-called five points, namely the rights to have perpetual succession and a common seal, to sue and be sued, to hold lands, and to issue bye-laws. In practice many towns had exercised some or all of these rights long before, and it was only gradually that developing legal theory made their

[44] Barron, 'Richard II and London' [336]; Platt, *Med. Southampton* [416], 112–16, 122–30; Hewitt, *Organization of War* [144], 5–21; *Statutes of the Realm* [54], i. 346–7; see pp. 171–7.

[45] For the London commission of the peace: *Cal. London. P. & M.R. 1323–64* [345], pp. xi–xxxiii.

formal expression useful.[46] London's corporate capacity was so
taken for granted that the city did not receive formal incorporation
until 1608, while the fact that incorporation elsewhere did not at
first seem to constitute an innovation is illustrated by the use of the
traditional word *communitas* to express it. Coventry's charter of
1345, which is sometimes described as the first grant of incorporation, was valuable and notable just because the right to act as a
communitas under a mayor was enjoyed by other towns though it was
a novelty for Coventry. The cathedral priory had succeeded in
restraining urban liberty there until now and indeed tried to do so
for another ten years afterwards.[47] The little town of Woodstock
similarly acquired its first formal liberties in a 'charter of incorporation' in 1453, while Norwich, already one of the first cities of the
kingdom, was 'incorporated' at the same time as a mayor was added
to its civic hierarchy in 1404. By the later fifteenth century the
standard form of incorporation charter gave a town a mayor and
aldermen, made the mayor and others justices of the peace, and laid
down rules for election. Clearly the most important features of incorporation were not the 'five points' of perpetual succession etc.,
whose significance is largely the creation of later lawyers and historians, but the grants of new jurisdictions like the commission of the
peace and, even more, the giving of royal authority to a particular
constitution within the town government, which falls outside the
scope of this chapter. Here it may be noted that, little as incorporation as such might mean at first, it gradually became common
form, so that by the sixteenth and seventeenth centuries even the
smallest towns with any pretensions to local independence were
becoming incorporated, thus giving another gloss to the word
borough, as a legally 'corporate town'.

TOWNS WITHOUT AUTONOMY

So far this chapter has concentrated on towns which attained a
measure of independence. Some quite important places, as well as
many small market towns, did not do so. In many cases they were
those which had another lord than the king ('mesne boroughs'), for
though it was open to such a lord to have any grants of liberties to

---

[46] *Eng. Hist. Docs.* [29], iv, pp. 560, 570–3; Weinbaum, *Incorporation of Boroughs*
[277]; Jacob, *Fifteenth Century* [156], 392–4; Maitland, *Township and Borough* [187],
11–23; Gross, *Gild Merchant* [136], i. 93–6; Tait, *Med. Eng. Bor.* [258], 234–40.

[47] Coss, 'Coventry before Incorporation' [312]; Davis, 'An Unknown Coventry
Charter' [314].

his borough confirmed and enlarged by royal charter, a mesne borough was less likely to receive generous grants than was a royal one. Authority within any one town would mean more, financially and in prestige, to a mesne lord than it would to the king, and the political profit to be derived from making concessions was less available to him. Leicester is perhaps the most obvious example of a large and important town which seems to have suffered in this way. A guild merchant there received the earl's sanction in the twelfth century. Thereafter, though it was not entirely free from his supervision, the guild remained for long the most independent forum of corporate consultation and activity within the town. In practice a good deal of freedom was generally allowed to the portmanmoot, or borough court, but it was under closer seigniorial control and its profits went to the earl. From the mid thirteenth century a mayor, who may sometimes or often have been elected, presided over the portmanmoot and seems to have taken over the duties of alderman of the guild as well. In 1375 the mayor and burgesses for the first time got a lease of the town jurisdiction from their lord, but it was not until after the duchy of Lancaster had passed to the Crown that Leicester's liberties really caught up with those of comparable towns.[48] At the other end of the scale, Barnstaple's humbler communal forum was also a guild under a mayor. When the lordship of Barnstaple passed to greater lords whose officials probably took a less close interest in the town than earlier lords had done, the mayor began to usurp some minor functions of local government. Eventually in the fifteenth century the townspeople forged themselves charters from past kings which in fact could never have been granted to them without infringement of the former lords' rights. It was only after the lords' rights had come to the Crown that the town's position was finally legitimated by a grant of incorporation.

The most restrictive lord of all tended to be the Church, and any religious house that owned rights in the town in which it lay was likely to be very repressive to urban aspirations. A number of reasons could be adduced, from the traditional teaching of the medieval Church about authority, or the duties of bishops and abbots as trustees for their saint, to the high value, in both financial and more general terms, which a monastery would put on the town at its gates. At Abingdon and Bury St. Edmunds, for instance, the respective

[48] *V.C.H. Leics.* [332], iv. 9–23.

abbeys seem to have granted burgage tenure and allowed guilds when that seemed safe and profitable, but fought long and ultimately successful battles in the thirteenth and fourteenth centuries to stop their burgesses from gaining any real corporate independence. It was in conflicts with ecclesiastical lords at this period that towns sought that recognition as *communitates* or *burgi* which has allowed later historians to endow both terms with a significance that they only bore in the eyes of repressive churchmen. Examples could be multiplied, and so could instances of towns, particularly the cathedral cities, where islands of ecclesiastical authority remained outside the control of municipal governments. York, for instance, has been described as 'honeycombed with other franchises'.[49] Not that all setbacks for the towns should be attributed to the Church: royal castles could be tiresome enclaves in municipal jurisdiction too.[50] It is nevertheless notable how largely towns subject to ecclesiastical lords figured in the disturbances of periods like the 1260s, 1326–7 and 1381.

CONCLUSION

Urban liberties have received more attention than most aspects of medieval urban history, and the main stages at which towns achieved a measure of independence are well established. Some problems of interpretation and understanding remain. Charters have sometimes been taken too much at their face-value and, as the most prized documents of a borough, have been assumed to mark a regular progress to greater liberty which either never took place or took place in reality at a rather different pace. In order to understand boroughs, communes, and guilds, more attention should be directed to the social and political structures they embodied and less to the attempts of later historians to attach precise definitions to these words of once colloquial usage. Some of the arguments about the precise relationship of guilds and boroughs, or the precise definition of a commune, seem more suited to academic lawyers' discussions about fictitious persons than to the realities of urban politics in the Middle Ages. Attempts to define boroughs, communes, and so forth,

---

[49] *Eng. Hist. Docs.* [29], ii, p. 966; Slade, 'Reading' [401], 3–4; Lambrick, 'Impeachment of the Abbot of Abingdon' [287]; Lobel, *Bury St. Edmunds* [300]; *V.C.H. Beds.* [319], iii. 349–50; Finberg, *Glos. Studies* [121]; *V.C.H. Yorks: York* [444], 38–40; for a survey of monastic boroughs see Knowles, *Religious Orders* [166], i. 263–9.

[50] e.g. Fuller, 'Tallage of Edward II' [292].

have repeatedly foundered on anachronisms. Though the definitions suggested here are tentative, it may be asserted confidently that better ones will only be found if early uses of the word are not assumed to have been influenced by later ones. This bit of history, at least, must be written forwards, not backwards.

6

Town Government and Politics in the Twelfth and Thirteenth Centuries

THE SOURCES

As towns grew in size and independence their governments became more highly organized and also, like other administrations at that time, better recorded. Even towns which did not secure much corporate freedom could sustain a considerable degree of corporate life, and might even be stimulated to do so by conflicts with seigniorial officials. The earliest records made and preserved by townsmen for their own communal purposes are guild rolls of the late twelfth century. The first town court rolls start soon after, with ´custumals, taxation records, enrolled deeds and similar material, in addition, of course, to the many carefully preserved series of royal charters.[1] All these, with later copies or mentions of other town records which are now lost, and with the multiplying records of the central government, make it possible to sketch the internal administration of some towns in the thirteenth century.

Two features seem to stand out: firstly, the strength of corporate life in many towns, however torn they might be by internal conflicts. It appears most obviously in town governments themselves, but guilds and other unofficial associations bear witness to the same thing. It was also characteristically expressed in physical symbols like the common seals and guildhalls which have sometimes survived, or the town bells and horns used to summon burgesses to meetings, which generally have not.[2] Secondly, despite many local variations, urban political and administrative arrangements show strong family likenesses to each other—and, despite wider variations in vocabulary and political circumstances, to those of towns in other European

[1] Martin, 'Origins of Borough Records' [8] and 'Eng. Borough in 13th cent.' [189].
[2] Michaud-Quantin, *Universitas* [194], 285–304; e.g. Tait, *Med. Eng. Bor.* [258], 235–9; Martin and McIntyre, *Bibliog. of Munic. Hist.* [9], i, pp. 319 ff.; Bateson, 'London Munic. Collection' [339], 502–3; Urry, *Canterbury* [303], 90; Fuller, 'Tallage of Edward II' [292], 180.

countries. Though information gained from elsewhere can be used only with explicit acknowledgement and caution to fill gaps in the history of any one town, no town's institutions can be understood in isolation from others.[3]

THE STRUCTURE OF GOVERNMENT

In towns, as in the rest of medieval society, government and administration were inextricably connected with legal jurisdiction, and much of the self-government that towns won was exercised through their courts. When a town gained some autonomy it generally took over the courts as they stood, so far as its liberties allowed, so that the central institution of government and justice was often the old borough moot or portmanmoot. As liberties multiplied and population and commerce grew, town affairs became more complex and contested, and subordinate courts developed. In London the old folkmoot decayed probably because it was too cumbrous for decision-making, while the court of husting became the centre of political and judicial authority, producing a number of offshoots, notably in this period the sheriffs' court and the mayor's (or mayor's and aldermen's) court, which dealt among other matters with the growing volume of commercial cases. As yet the deliberative and administrative functions of the mayor and aldermen, which were exercised by the sixteenth century in what was by then known as the Court of Aldermen, seem to have been carried out in the husting and mayor's courts indiscriminately with judicial business. London also retained subordinate courts in the wardmotes, under the presidency of their respective aldermen. They seem to have been chiefly concerned with policing, defence, public health, and so forth, rather like hundred courts or manor courts with frankpledge jurisdiction elsewhere. Some landowners' courts for their tenants (soke courts) survived too for a time, though with declining activities. In Ipswich the portmanmoot had been divided by the end of the thirteenth century into great and petty courts and further divisions occurred soon after. In towns like Leicester, where the borough court remained under seigniorial control, the townspeople often exercised what freedom of action they had through the more limited but more independent

---

[3] For useful analogies from town governments abroad see Ennen, *Europäische Stadt* [118]; Lestocquoy, *Les Villes de Flandre et d'Italie* [173]; Pirenne, *Les Villes* [216]; Wolff, 'Les Luttes sociales' [281]; Planitz, *Deutsche Stadt* [219]; Waley, *Italian City Republics* [275]; Hyde, *Society and Politics in Med. Italy* [154].

jurisdiction of the courts (sometimes called morning-speeches) of their merchant guilds.[4]

Just as they took over the existing courts so towns often started their independent histories with the same officials as they had had before, now under their own control and nomination. Their first chief officials would thus be the reeves or bailiffs who were responsible for paying the royal or seigniorial dues, but mayors were frequently superimposed on the civic hierarchy from the late twelfth century onwards.[5] The significance of the mayoralty as the symbol of a town's autonomy is emphasized in cases where his office became merged with that of the alderman (sometimes steward) of the merchant guild, the body which had formerly embodied the townspeople's aspirations towards independence. Sometimes, however, the two offices continued side by side, and the surviving records suggest a range of intermediate situations, reflecting the impact of personalities or the common untidiness of medieval arrangements perhaps as much as recognized differences of interest between town and guild. In any event urban liberties produced a new and developing nomenclature of offices, so that titles like bailiff, reeve (or portreeve), portman or chief portman, mayor, and alderman were not used consistently between or even within towns.

In addition other officials accumulated. Many towns had chamberlains, who often ranked high in the civic hierarchy, to look after money, though recorders—professional law officers—begin to appear only with the fourteenth century. We have a detailed account of how municipal government was established at Ipswich in 1200 after the king had granted the borough farm. Two beadles were then appointed to work under the bailiffs and coroners. Their duties were to make attachments (arrests), distraints, and so forth, and one of them also had charge of the prison. Ipswich had a common clerk by 1272, when he absconded with the records, but no chamberlains apparently before 1320. Lincoln had two city clerks, as well as four beadles, by 1202. The common clerk of London is first mentioned

---

[4] *Cal. London E.M.C.R.* [343], pp. ix–xxvii; *Cal. London P. & M.R.* [345], *1323–64*, pp. vii–xxxiii; *1364–81*, pp. xv–xviii; *1413–37*, pp. xxiv–xli; Martin, *Early Court Rolls of Ipswich* [328], 15; above p. 101.

[5] See above, pp. 102–3, 107, 108–9. For officials and councils, Tait, *Med. Eng. Bor.* [258], 250, 263–301; Gross, *Gild Merchant* [136], i. 25–8, ii. 114–23 (the Ipswich account); Martin, 'Borough of Ipswich' [327]; Hill, *Med. Lincoln* [333], 196, 293–301; Williams, *Med. London* [373], 38–43, 93–6; *V.C.H. Northants* [384], iii. 6–7; Herbert, 'Borough of Wallingford' [426], 46–66; Wilkinson, *Med. Council of Exeter* [324], pp. xvi–xxxiv.

in the thirteenth century and sheriffs' clerks even earlier. By *c.* 1300 the city's staff of clerks is said to have numbered at least thirty-five. Scavengers, toll-collectors, and serjeants or servants of various sorts were also employed everywhere. To modern English eyes the boundary between elected and paid, voluntary and professional, officers looks very unclear. Though clerks, for instance, may often have been career officials, many of them probably lived as much off fees as stipends, and the execution of many orders fell to unpaid burgesses, often serving compulsorily under threat of a fine.

Some town officials are known to have had councils to advise or supervise them: the exact relationships are obscure and were probably ill-defined. In 1200 the congregation of the whole town of Ipswich elected two bailiffs and four coroners to manage its affairs. Twelve chief portmen 'as there are in other free boroughs of England' were then chosen to govern and maintain the borough and its liberties, render judgements, and ordain and do what was useful to the town and its burgesses, 'and this by the advice of their peers'. They swore to obey, advise, and help the bailiffs and portmen, but their exact relationship with them was not at issue: the two bailiffs were also coroners and all four coroners were also portmen. One of the portmen, further, was alderman of the guild merchant which was simultaneously established to look after the town's trade, and four other portmen (one a coroner) were associated with him in the task. By the thirteenth century other towns are known to have had similar sworn councils, generally of twelve or twenty-four members, sometimes called *jurati* (jurats, jurates), to work with their chief officers.

The origin of these councils has been debated. James Tait argued that they should be seen as part of the wave of influence from the foreign 'communal movement' of the twelfth century, rather than as evolving from the traditional élites of the older borough courts. He admitted however that the aldermen of London did thus evolve and that in contrasting English and foreign elements he was in danger of 'underestimating the power of like circumstances'—and he might have added 'like traditions'—'to produce like institutions'. His argument involves other distinctions that are surely anachronistic—between judicial and administrative, and between new and traditional elements. Ipswich may not before 1200 have had a formally defined élite ready to shoulder political power when a measure of independence produced it, but the portmen of 1200 were no doubt already leading townsmen; their authority was linked with justice and exercised through courts; and twelves were traditional units to think in. The allusion in the Ipswich record to councils of portmen in other free boroughs does not prove that all boroughs (not in any case a definable category at this date) had councils, let alone councils identical with their own, nor can it be discredited by showing that some did not. It reflected a contemporary belief that any town with claims to self-government normally had some sort of corporate governing body.

The methods by which officials and councillors were chosen are usually obscure and cannot be deduced from formal phrases like *per commune consilium burgensium* or *per communitatem civitatis*. Though a 'congregation of the whole town' elected the first officials at Ipswich, and though the most important of them, the bailiffs, were to serve for one year, no term was set to the other offices and no provision was made for future electoral meetings. A genuine consensus was possible in a fairly small town, especially in the euphoric moment of liberation, but there is no reason whatever to expect that the votes of the townspeople were considered equal and counted, or that the process was intended to be democratic. The portmen were elected in another full assembly soon after, and this time we know how. The newly elected bailiffs and coroners chose four lawful men from each of the town parishes and these in turn chose the portmen. Somewhat similar indirect elections are known to have been held again in Ipswich in 1309, when provision was also made for filling vacancies by co-option. Indirect elections, very likely with an element of co-option, probably occurred in many towns, as they did for instance at Exeter and Winchester. They are found in contemporary national politics and in towns abroad, and reflect the medieval desire to avoid domination either by cliques or by the mob, to procure representatives of weight and standing, and to achieve a harmonious consensus in conformity with custom and contemporary ideas of justice. In practice they could and sometimes did favour selfish oligarchies, but we should not assume that those who profited were always disingenuous in believing in these methods, or that the discontented were all frustrated democrats. Nor, given the failure of other systems to produce instant social justice, should we assume that believers in this one, more or less unsuccessful as it was, were unduly naïve. The apparently oligarchic nature of thirteenth-century town governments, where anything is discernible about them, and the long periods that councillors and some officers seem to have served, should not therefore be seen as a falling off from primitive or intended democracy.

Where councillors, like the aldermen of London, represented separate wards, leets, or quarters, elections need not have been either more or less popular. While a ward representative might be particularly aware of his constituents' interests, wardmotes could be advised whom to send and family influence could be so strong as to give an impression of inheritance. Inheritance has indeed been suggested for some twelfth-century London wards, but, except for Portsoken ward, of which the prior of Holy Trinity, Aldgate, was alderman, cannot be proved. As Urry remarks in connection with Canterbury: 'It is hardly a matter for surprise when the same office appears and reappears in a given medieval family'.[6]

In times of difficulty or stress the rulers of towns could also call on wider assemblies of their fellow burgesses to confer with them. In the larger towns completely open assemblies of all inhabitants were probably rare after municipal governments were set up, except in revolutionary times like the 1260s, when riotous mass meetings seized power in London. At other times in London the wards, and in Norwich the leets, regularly supplied panels of between two and twelve 'respectable men' (*probi homines*) or 'better and more discreet citizens' (*de melioribus et discretioribus civitatis*).[7] The members may have been nominated from above or have constituted permanent bodies within their wards or leets. In early fourteenth-century London representatives were sometimes summoned from crafts rather than wards. The political significance of this has been much debated and is discussed below: no contemporary examples from other towns have yet been noticed. Any consultation outside the regular twelves or twenty-fours seems to have been as yet largely *ad hoc*: the permanent 'common councils' of later centuries seem to be traceable only from the fourteenth century. Already, however, controversies about consultation were contributing to the need for a closer definition of who was a full citizen or burgess of his town and therefore eligible to be consulted.

The earliest view of burgesses (or citizens, as they were generally known in cathedral towns) was probably that they were occupiers of

[6] *Canterbury* [303], 102; cf. Williams, *Med. London* [373], 32–5; Rogers, *Making of Stamford* [419], 41. Cf. Wilkinson, *Med. Council of Exeter* [324], p. xxxii.

[7] Williams, 'London, 1216–1337' [372], 62–70; *Rec. of Norwich* [389], i. 191.

burgages, that is householders, and sometimes specifically resident householders, in towns. It seems to have been modified by 1086, as is shown by the bordars of Norwich, who were too poor to pay their dues and so did not rank as burgesses, but it did not disappear as a common assumption. The first attempts at exact definition appear in twelfth-century charters, apparently to ensure that as many people as possible contributed to royal dues, and that only those who did so would share in the privileges awarded. The restriction of full trading rights to resident townsmen paying 'scot and lot' evidently conformed to the wishes either of the whole community or of those who dominated it.[8] It was only in the thirteenth century, as commercial competition probably grew fiercer, immigrants multiplied, and townsmen began to gird against their own rulers, that burgess franchise seems to have become a matter of controversy within urban communities themselves.

How this happened has recently been described as 'one of the most mysterious problems of medieval urban history'.[9] In trying to solve it we should bear in mind two points. Firstly, the controversy did not affect all towns. At Wallingford, as in many other places, the merchant guild became integrated with the borough so that the freedom or full membership of the two became identical.[10] Such freedom was apparently secured by paying a lump sum down or granting an annual rent to the town, but many other people secured what seem to be the same trading rights by making annual subscriptions. In the earlier thirteenth century these *pactionarii* probably included a majority of the working inhabitants as well as a good many people from surrounding villages who came in to trade in the town. Although they did not count as 'free burgesses' and presumably did not share in the government of the town, there is no evidence of conflict between the two groups either in the thirteenth or fourteenth centuries. *Pactionarii* could apparently become 'free' as soon as they could make the appropriate down payment. Secondly, as the evidence from Wallingford suggests, medieval townsmen saw burgess-ship less in terms of political rights than of privileges in trade and law to be enjoyed by the members of the

---

[8] Above, p. 93–4; Liebermann, *Gesetze* [42], i. 523; *Liber de Ant. Leg.* [348], 238–9; *Brit. Bor. Ch. 1042–1216* [16], 101–11.

[9] Dobson, 'Admissions to Freedom of York' [438], 20; cf. Pollock and Maitland, *Hist. of Eng. Law* [221], i. 670–3.

[10] Herbert, 'Borough of Wallingford' [426], 98–107; cf. Platt, *Med. Southampton* [416], 18–19; Gross, *Gild Merchant* [136], i. 30–1, 123–6, 229.

privileged body in return for subscriptions, however those subscriptions might be paid. In London an official register of apprentices was started in 1274-5 (and there had been others earlier) because people who were not entitled to the freedom of the city were claiming it. It was stated then that there were three ways of becoming free: by patrimony, for those lawfully born in the city; by apprenticeship; and by redemption (i.e. paying a lump sum down). Since no record of citizens by patrimony was kept until well on in the fourteenth century the register still left room for dispute about that category, but, thanks to the scale of immigration, it was a relatively small one. Citizenship became therefore generally linked with a served-out apprenticeship and membership of a craft. Similar rules were being elaborated elsewhere. Complaints in Lincoln in 1267 that mayors had been making people who had been in scot and lot for a year and a day nevertheless pay for the liberties to which they were entitled suggest an unhappy halfway stage between old and new definitions.[11] The probability that definition was produced less by policy than by changing circumstances and the cases that happened to arise is illustrated by the mayor of London's surprise in 1244 when royal justices challenged the right of non-citizen owners of property in London to share the citizens' privilege of bequeathing city land by will. Though the problem of distinguishing real members of the town community from those who happened to have land there must have been particularly acute in London, and though some other towns had already specified that full rights belonged only to permanent residents, the Londoners had not yet thought to apply the rule consistently to all the liberties that had become encrusted in city tradition.[12] By 1300, however, it looks as if in all the larger towns such participation in government as the rulers allowed, together and more importantly with full trading and legal rights, were reserved to the sons—and, in trade, often the widows—of burgesses; to those who had served a full apprenticeship; and to those who paid a fee for it. In some cloth-making towns weavers and fullers were entirely excluded from burgess rights: this

[11] *Chron. Edward I and II* [346], i. 85–6; Williams, *Med. London* [373], 43–7; *Cal. London P. & M.R. 1364–81* [345], pp. xviii–xxx; Veale, 'Craftsmen and London Econ.' [367], 135–7; Martin, 'Borough of Ipswich' [327], 91–2; *Leet Jurisdiction in Norwich* [386], pp. lxxxv–lxxxviii; Hill, *Med. Lincoln* [333], 211–16, 302–3; *Brit. Bor. Ch. 1216–1307* [16], 132–44; Wilkinson, *Med. Council of Exeter* [324]; *V.C.H. Northants* [384], iii. 7; *Cal. Inq. Misc.* [19], i, no. 238 (12).

[12] *London Eyre of 1244* [356], no. 297.

looks like corruption of normal principles by the particular interest of cloth-merchants. Meanwhile, however, in the more homogeneous societies of some—perhaps most—of the smaller market towns the older qualification by residence and property still held good.[13]

THE SCOPE AND ACTIVITIES OF GOVERNMENT

The scope of municipal government was regulated by the liberties a town could acquire from the king. Even seigniorial boroughs were dependent on royal grant for the most important privileges. By the late twelfth century serious crimes, except when the criminal was caught in the act, were nearly always reserved to royal justices, though some towns were allowed to appoint their own coroners to keep records of crimes pending the arrival of the justices, and some to have accusations against burgesses tried within the town by all-burgess juries.[14] Many had extensive jurisdiction over their inhabitants in civil cases and followed customs which differed from the common law in various ways. Notable fields of activity in urban courts were the law merchant, including cases in what became known as 'piepowder courts' for quick actions concerning visiting merchants; the enrolment of deeds concerning town property; the enrolment or probate of wills, which was maintained more or less successfully against the ecclesiastical courts; wardship of orphans and some jurisdiction over the widows of burgesses and their rights; and nuisance cases, since gutters, party-walls, and so forth provided endless matter for dispute in urban conditions.[15] Altogether courts in the bigger and more privileged towns must have taken up a good deal of the time of the mayors and other officials who presided over them and of the councillors who, like the aldermen of London or the Twenty-four of Exeter, may have acted as jurors or assessors. The maintenance and recording of customs also involved them in correspondence. A charter of 1229 told the burgesses of Oxford to consult London about doubtful points and they did so on several occasions

---

[13] Lobel, *Bury St. Edmunds* [300], 80–1; Martin, *Early Court Rolls of Ipswich* [328], 35; Walsingham, *Gesta Abbatum* [405], ii. 166.

[14] *Brit. Bor. Ch. 1216–1307* [16], pp. lix–lx; *Borough Customs* [15], i. p. xx; *Cal. London E.M.C.R.* [343], pp. x–xiii; *Cal. London P. & M.R. 1323–64* [345], pp. xii–xxvi; *Rec. of Norwich* [389], i, p. cxxvi.

[15] Above, pp. 101–2; *Select Cases in Law Merchant* [53]; *Cal. London P. & M.R.* [345], *1323–64*, 7–8, 23–4, 169; *1381–1412*, pp. vii–xli; *London Assize of Nuisance* [355]; Pollock and Maitland, *Hist. of Eng. Law* [221], ii. 330–1; *Borough Customs* [15], ii, pp. cxxxviii–cxlv, 194–201. See Martin, 'Borough of Ipswich' [327] and Herbert, 'Borough of Wallingford' [426] for full discussions of court business.

later, with the honour and reverence 'which a daughter owes to her mother'.[16]

An important motive in the movement towards autonomy was to control trade and protect town traders and consumers against outside competition and extortionate tolls. Though records before 1300 are relatively scarce and some are unprinted, town authorities probably spent considerable time on trade regulations and disputes, and on the actual inspection of markets and merchandise. Weights and measures were inspected and some goods had to be weighed on the public scales or weigh-beam (*trona*, tron) and toll (tronage) paid to the king or the civic authorities. The defence of trading interests involved consultation between towns about customs, mutual recording of liberties, and sometimes fierce disputes about conflicting privileges. Exeter tried to extend its jurisdiction over the Exe to prevent its trade from being captured by downstream Topsham; the bailiffs of Reading sued the bailiffs of both Windsor and Newbury in defence of Reading men wanting to trade toll-free there; and London and Northampton indulged in periodic litigation, and their citizens in occasional violence, when the liberties of both prevented either from securing jurisdiction in suits between their respective citizens and burgesses.[17] At the same time as protecting their own traders towns needed in the conditions of the time to operate a continual siege-economy to ensure their food supplies. In what Pirenne called 'une sorte de socialisme municipale'[18] the control of prices, measures, and quality (especially freshness) of food was taken for granted in principle though often breached or disputed in particular.

Some regulation of town industries may also have been undertaken from the start, but it probably grew more strict as time went on. The thirteenth-century registration of apprentices, which may imply controls, has already been mentioned. The same principles and assumptions as prompted the protection of town traders, the control of food prices, and efforts to attract business from elsewhere, might also entail controls of manufacturing and other trades. In-

---

[16] *Cal. London P. & M.R.*, *1323–64* [345], 7–8, 23–24, 169.

[17] Jackson, 'Med. Exeter' [323]; *V.C.H. Berks.* [402], iii. 346; *Liber de Ant. Leg.* [348], 47–8; *Cal. London Letter Book C* [344], 40, 82, 85, 92–5, 100, 106, 133; *Cal. London P. & M.R. 1323–64* [345], 6–7.

[18] *Les Villes* [216], i. 197. See *Cam. Econ. Hist.* [79], iii. 157–206; and e.g. *Rec. of Norwich* [389], i. 174–5; *Leet Jurisdiction in Norwich* [386]; *Beverley Town Documents* [290], 8–9; *Rec. of Leicester* [331], i. 90.

cidentally, of course, it was extremely difficult to reconcile all four aims, legitimate as they all were, and the inevitable conflicts of interests between townspeople who were at once consumers, merchants, craftsmen, and even employees, contributed to many of the disputes mentioned below. The cloth industry is an example of early recorded regulation. Some towns are known to have fought hard to defeat the pretensions of weavers' guilds which had secured royal protection before the towns gained self-government.[19] Town authorities generally frowned on independent craft associations and preferred to authorize craft ordinances themselves. The mayor and aldermen of London approved ordinances about wages, materials and hours of work, apprenticeship, and so on, for various city crafts in the thirteenth century. Some other towns are known to have done likewise, while the prohibition of sectional guilds in others suggests that they too were watching over crafts and craftsmen in general.[20]

Public health and public works were also necessary parts of urban administration. Although medieval towns were dirty and unhealthy that was not because no attempt was made to improve conditions. Inadequate household sanitation, the practice of necessary but noxious trades, the keeping of essential draught animals, and the need to slaughter beasts near to where they would be eaten, all imposed intractable problems. Some of the earliest municipal records show efforts to control the waste from latrines and animal dung and from industries like butchery and tanning. In the late thirteenth century the authorities in London and Norwich were constantly worrying about hygiene. London had a conduit bringing fresh water from Tyburn by 1237, while Bristol had had its first piped water laid on about fifty years before. The folkmoot and wards in London were responsible for fire-watching by the twelfth century and the earliest set of building regulations for the city dates from the early thirteenth. Encroachments on roads were another concern, and so sometimes were road repairs in general. The duty to pave roads seems originally to have lain on the owners of adjoining property, but from the thirteenth century municipalities began to obtain powers of enforcement. They could also secure royal grants of pavage, or the right to take tolls in order to pave their streets. Public works were done on markets and market-places, bridges, and town walls. London Bridge was endowed with valuable city property to which a thirteenth-

---

[19] Carus-Wilson, *Med. Merchant Venturers* [81], 183–238.
[20] *Mun. Gild. Lond.* [357], ii. 78–9, 99–102; *V.C.H. Northants* [384], iii. 7; see p. 83.

century mayor added the revenues of the new Stocks Market, with its market hall, which he established. As with pavage, similar grants of tolls for the building or repair of bridges (pontage) and walls (murage) provide evidence of public works in other towns.[21]

In almost all its activities, judicial and administrative, a town was liable to interference from the central government. Town liberties were no defence against the king himself, and, moreover, entailed the execution of a mass of local duties on his behalf. As well as paying over the traditional dues of the 'borough farm' many of the bigger towns seem to have become involved, less formally though under only patchy supervision, in the assessment and collection of royal taxes. By 1300 they were also sending members to represent them in parliament. Since the purpose of this was that the local community as a whole, rather than the individuals comprising it, or even particular classes as such, should be represented, the method of election was left to the towns. It is reasonable to assume that the officers and assemblies which normally managed the more important municipal business were the effective electors. In London, assemblies comprising the mayor, aldermen, and representatives from the wards elected either the two members or a panel who selected two of themselves.[22]

Though burgesses did much judicial and administrative work without pay, and though some town officials might do well out of fees, towns needed revenues to carry out all their activities. Some came from tolls and local customs,[23] and from penalties imposed in the borough courts, and some towns owned property long before the later legal theories of incorporation would allow them to have done so. A symbiosis of borough and merchant guild could also provide useful funds from entry fees, penalties, and properties belonging to the guild. How many towns resorted to raising their own taxes or tallages is unknown, but the record of complaints against unfair assessment and collection shows that they were more numerous than those which formally secured royal permission to do so.

[21] *V.C.H. Northants* [384], iii. 26; *Mun. Gild. Lond.* [357], ii. 66; Lobel and Carus-Wilson, 'Bristol' [294], 9; *Leet Jurisdiction in Norwich* [386]; *Cal. London Letter Book A* [344], 183; *Cal. London E.M.C.R.* [343], 161–2; Sabine, 'Butchering in London' [360]; Platt, *Eng. Med. Town* [220], 48–51, 69–72; Liebermann, *Gesetze* [42], i. 657; *London Assize of Nuisance* [355], especially pp. xxvii–xxx; Salusbury-Jones, *Street Life* [239], 14–90; Williams, *Med. London* [373], 86–7; Turner, *Town Defences* [266].

[22] Young, *Eng. Borough and Royal Admin.* [285], 41–54; McKisack, *Parl. Repres. of Eng. Boroughs* [184], 11–16; above chapter 5 and (for tax records) pp. 50–1.

[23] e.g. Hill, *Med. Lincoln* [333], 214–16; *V.C.H. Northants* [384], iii. 25.

Here as elsewhere borough charters give a misleading impression of what really went on in the towns.

INTERNAL CONFLICTS AND DISORDERS

Evidence about the internal politics of English towns apart from London is scarce before the fourteenth century. Apart from Alderman Arnold fitz Thedmar's highly personal account of London affairs in the *Liber de antiquis legibus* (or *Chronicle of the mayors and sheriffs of London*), references to urban affairs in chronicles are rare and brief, while most surviving municipal records are too formal to record disputes or even discussions. Some conflicts can be deduced from the custumals or other documents which record attempts to resolve them, but most appear only when they became so bitter as to provoke royal intervention.

The interpretation of these often gnomic sources has varied, and often seems to have owed a good deal to the political preoccupations of the historian's own day. It may therefore be helpful to survey the evidence of some of the recorded episodes. More could be added, and some may well be found to invalidate the tentative conclusions drawn below, while the material for London is at once so abundant and so hard to interpret as to lay the sketch of it given here open to charges of over-selective distortion. Much more work on more towns is needed to allow any approach to certainty.

The first hints of internal dissensions have been found in the way in which weavers and fullers in several towns sought royal protection for their own separate guilds in the twelfth century, and in which town governments dominated by cloth-dealing entrepreneurs tried to keep the weavers and fullers in economic subservience later on. The London authorities tried, though in the end unsuccessfully, to get the local weavers' royal charter rescinded, while Winchester, Marlborough, Oxford, and Beverley all forbade working weavers to become burgesses and deprived them of commercial and legal privileges.[24]

The London campaign against the weavers came soon after the city secured its measure of independence in 1190–1.[25] There are

[24] Carus-Wilson, *Med. Merchant Venturers* [81], 222–38; Williams, *Med. London* [373], 173–4.

[25] For London: *Liber de Ant. Leg.* [348] and *Chron. de London* [347], both trans. by H. T. Riley as *Chronicles of Mayors and Sheriffs* (London, 1863); 'Annals of London' (possibly by Andrew Horn (d. 1328), city chamberlain) in *Chron. Edward I and II* [346]; *Rot. Hund.* [50], i. 403–33; Weinbaum, *London unter Eduard I und II* [370], ii. 164–96

known to have been disagreements in London in 1191, which are thought to be connected with some kind of internal revolution, but there is no evidence either of that or of any consistent 'parties' or political conflicts during or before 1191. In 1194, however, London suffered disorders provoked by unfair collection of taxes and in 1206 the king ordered an enquiry into abuses concerned with justice and taxation. Thanks to Alderman Arnold fitz Thedmar we know that London was beset by faction in Henry III's reign. The king's interventions to raise taxes and diminish the city's liberties complicated and exacerbated the quarrels, but it is difficult to detect anything but personal rivalries and maladministration behind them before 1258. In that year a royal enquiry was held into the mayor and aldermen's management of tallages. Panels of thirty-six men, elected in each ward in the absence, according to Arnold, of their aldermen, at first objected that the city's liberties would be infringed if they were to give information. The royal justices appealed to the mob, and in the end the juries produced several accusations, and the mayor, one sheriff, and several aldermen were deposed. Other miscellaneous grievances recorded in 1274 go back to about this time or earlier, notably some concerning encroachments on public roads by rich men's houses.

A few months after the tax enquiry London was caught up in the conflicts of king and barons which started with the parliament of Oxford and culminated in the battle of Evesham in 1265. The city authorities' lukewarm support for the barons was checked when they discovered that city liberties might suffer in the cause of reform. Humbler people in London, like people in the country at large, were, however, probably inspired to higher hopes than the baronial reformers intended by all the talk of justice and consultation, and by the serious efforts the barons made to redress grievances.[26] Successive appeals to open meetings of the folkmoot encouraged them further, and Thomas fitz Thomas (mayor 1261–5), according to Alderman Arnold,

so pampered the people of the city that, calling themselves the commune (*communa*) of the city, they had the first voice in its affairs. For the

(eyre of 1321); *Cal. London Letter book D* [344], 22, 24–6, 275–6, 283–4. For reference to other sources: Unwin, *Gilds* [366], especially pp. 61–81 (but see p. 166, n. 13; Williams, *Med. London* [373], fuller but often following Unwin; Reynolds, 'Rulers of London' [359].

[26] See, e.g., Jacob, *Studies in Baronial Reform* [157], especially pp. 281–9; Treharne and Sanders, *Documents* [24].

mayor decided and did all that he had to do through them, asking them: 'Do you want this to be done?', and if they said 'Ya, ya', so it was done. The aldermen and magnates of the city on the other hand were consulted little or not at all, but were as though they were not. Thus the people got so above themselves and inflated with pride that in the time of the troubles of the kingdom . . . they made themselves into gangs (*conventiculas*) and leagued themselves in hundreds and thousands by oath under pretence of keeping the peace which they so obviously disturbed.[27]

Arnold fitz Thedmar also accused the same mayor of authorizing new ordinances—'or rather abominations'—which were submitted for civic approval by some of the crafts and caused great loss to merchants visiting London and the English fairs and to the country at large. Just what was abominable about them is not clear. London mobs meanwhile attacked Jews, aliens, and royal supporters, and when Simon de Montfort made his headquarters in London in 1264 the city became committed to his cause. As a result it suffered severely after he was defeated and did not recover its liberties for some years. In 1272 trouble broke out again with the populace claiming 'We are the commune of the city and to us belongs the election of the mayor'. Arnold accused their successful candidate of judicial malpractices; of currying favour deceitfully over taxation; of allowing the bakers to sell too light loaves; and of granting charters to certain crafts without the assent of the aldermen and citizens, to the benefit of the rich members of the crafts concerned and to the injury of the poor.

During Edward I's reign discontents continued to be expressed, but frequent and heavy royal interventions, combined with the king's need for taxes and patronage of aliens, helped to unite the city as well as to allay disorders—though no doubt the disorders would look more serious to us if Alderman Arnold had survived longer to deplore them. When trouble broke out again in Edward II's reign, with popular irruptions into elections in 1313 and 1315, it was probably because conflicts in the country at large fomented old discontents. Perhaps too the apparent recrudescence of conflict owes something to the improved information provided by contemporary chroniclers at this stage, though, sadly, none is so detailed or opinionated as Arnold fitz Thedmar. Demands for popular participation were partially rewarded in 1319 by royal letters patent which confirmed various constitutional arrangements against the

[27] *Liber de Ant. Leg.* [348], 55.

wishes of the then mayor. These arrangements included the annual replacement of the mayor and aldermen, a prohibition against the holding of several offices together (a notable offence of that same mayor), restrictions on fees, and the supervision of key functions by non-aldermen (*communiarii*) elected by the community. It also restricted citizenship to those who were sponsored by a craft or were formally approved by the whole community. Alien candidates had to be approved in the husting. Assemblies representing crafts were at this time just beginning to be used occasionally to supplement those of ward representatives, but there does not seem to be much evidence to link the crafts as such with any particular grievances or with policies to remedy them. Most of the reforms of the period were indeed such as would have deserved conventional approval,[28] while most of the grievances, summed up in presentments to the last great visitation by royal justices in eyre in 1321, resemble those expressed for over a hundred years, except that they reflect the greater complexity of the city's government and the changed opportunities for corruption and oppression that it afforded.

Other towns meanwhile had been having their troubles too. The earliest example noted in a quite casual search, apart from what was implied in the weavers' laws mentioned above, comes from Oxford. In 1256–7, according to a later endorsement, the 'lesser burgesses' or 'burgesses of the lesser commune' (*de minori communia*) of Oxford submitted a petition to the king comprising twenty-nine accusations against the mayor, jurats, and 'greater or magnate burgesses'. Most concerned unfair assessment and collection of tallages and other imposts, but judicial grievances, the compelling of poor men to enter the merchant guild, the raising of tolls from fishmongers and other victuallers, unfair regulations on lesser burgesses' looms and weaving, and the holding of feasts at public expense, are all mentioned too. In 1258 and the following years complaints may have been encouraged by the barons' efforts to reform central and local government. In that year the baronial council issued trading regulations agreed by the common assent of the men of Grimsby after complaints by the poor there that a few rich men engrossed all the trade, especially in fish. Similar grievances were expressed at Scarborough a year later and provisions for fair and open trading for all burgesses were made by sworn middling people (*mediocres*) of the town. In

[28] See *Mun. Gild. Lond.* [357], ii. 16–25.

Canterbury there was a dispute in 1259 when all the citizens gathered as usual to elect the mayor but the choice of 'the greater and wiser part' was allegedly reversed. The revocation two years later of rates imposed on bakers' stalls and windows suggests continuing factions.[29] The popular disturbances of 1263-5, according to a royalist chronicler, spread from London through almost all the towns of England in a confederacy (*conjuratio*) of ribalds who called themselves bachelors and oppressed the mayors of cities and boroughs with violence.[30] Little is known of these revolutionary events outside the capital except that unrest seems to have been marked by attacks on Jews, as at Lincoln, Northampton, Winchester, and Worcester, and on ecclesiastical lords, as at Winchester, York, and Bury St. Edmunds, while the Cinque Ports, like London, lent vital support to Simon de Montfort in 1263-5.[31]

In Lincoln a royal enquiry of 1267, prompted by the city's failure to pay its fine for pardon after the civil wars, elicited grievances about irregularly held courts, misappropriated tolls and tallage, and about men in scot and lot being made to pay for the franchise. In the ragman or hundred enquiries of 1274-5 Lincoln was represented by three separate juries of great, middling, and lesser men (*magni, secundarii, minores*), but their respective presentments did not differ much: all alleged some maladministration by civic officials and some embezzlement of tallage and murage by a former mayor, and all were unanimous in their condemnation of any acts by outsiders that injured the trade and community of Lincoln. In 1290 some richer citizens of Lincoln were accused of selling the city's tronage without consent of the poor and of assessing tallages unfairly on them.[32] Municipal assessors of royal tallages were of such ill repute that a royal official was warned in 1268 that when any town agreed a lump sum with him he should stay to see it assessed in detail, so as to prevent the rich from being spared and the poor burdened as had often happened before. Allegations—not necessarily true—about unjust or misappropriated tallages, tolls, and murage

[29] *Cal. Inq. Misc.* [19], i, no. 238; *Cal. Charter R. 1257-1300* [17], 14-16; *Yorks. Assize Rolls* [410], 117-20; Urry, *Canterbury* [303], 90-1.

[30] *Ann. Mon.* [13], iv. 138; on 'bachelors', see Jacob, *Studies in Baronial Reform* [157], 134-7.

[31] e.g. *Ann. Mon.* [13], ii. 101, 363; iii. 226, 230; iv. 141-3, 170, 449; *Flores Hist.* [30], iv. 480, 482-3; Powicke, *Henry III* [227], 785-7; for conflicts with Church lords, see pp. 115-16.

[32] Hill, *Med. Lincoln* [333], 210-16; *Rot. Hund.* [50], i. 309-28; for these enquiries, see Cam, *Hundred and Hundred Rolls* [77].

have been noted in the later thirteenth century and the beginning of the fourteenth at Bristol, Gloucester, Leicester, Lynn, Northampton, Norwich, Oxford, Stamford, Winchester, and York. In most cases the accusations are made against the rich, great, or more powerful, and at Bristol, Lynn, and Norwich middling people (*mediocres, medius populus*) are mentioned as aggrieved. The Stamford complaint is unusual in alleging unfairness not as between rich and poor but as between tenants of two fees within the town. That from Northampton says that because burgesses with great rents would not contribute, fullers, weavers, dyers, drapers, glovers, skinners, and other craftsmen had left the town. At York in 1306 the oppressors had used the cover of a charitable guild to league together to maintain each others' interests in general as well as to impose taxes unjustly.[33] Other allegations of oppression of the poor, though not specifically by taxation, come from Carlisle and Scarborough (again), and of forestalling or engrossment of trade from Bristol, Grimsby (again), Ipswich, and Newcastle upon Tyne. Reforming ordinances passed at Ipswich in 1320 suggest some sort of malpractices by past bailiffs. At Bristol the internecine conflicts were complicated by a simultaneous dispute with the constable of the royal castle. This spurred the town to resist a royal tallage and led to full-scale sieges and counter-sieges of the castle and town in 1312–16. At Winchester the trespasses alleged against sixteen members of the Twenty-four in 1276 provoked a ruling from the king's court that in future the town's bailiffs should be chosen each year by two electors appointed respectively by the Twenty-four and the community. In 1312 certain citizens were said to have usurped the mayor's powers.[34]

The traditional interpretation of all these disputes used to be that English towns moved towards oligarchy from an archaic democracy. An alternative and more recent view, owing more to continental historians, is that oligarchical and mercantile 'patrician' governments were transformed by attacks from humbler or 'middle-class'

[33] Rymer, *Foedera* [52], 478; *Cal. Pat. R.* [20] *1281–92*, 23; *1301–7*, 325; Fuller, 'Tallage of Edward II' [292]; *Rot. Parl.* [51], i. 47; *Rec. of Leicester* [331], i. 165–6; *Rot. Hund.* [50], ii. 2–3; Madox, *Firma Burgi* [185], 94–5; *V.C.H. Hants* [431], v. 33–4, *V.C.H. Yorks: York* [444], 36.

[34] *Cal. Pat. R.* *1272–81*, [20], 476; Madox, *Firma Burgi* [185], 96; Fraser, 'Med. Trading Restrictions in N.E.' [381]; Martin, 'Borough of Ipswich' [327], 60–72; Mundy and Riesenberg, *Medieval Town* [43], 119–20; Fuller, 'Tallage of Edward II' [292], 181; *Rot. Hund.* [50], i. 263; *V.C.H. Hants.* [431], v. 33–4; see also Bond, 'Med. Const. of New Windsor' [432], 25.

craftsmen.[35] Whether the evidence will consistently support either interpretation is doubtful. As has already been suggested, twelfth- and thirteenth-century people are unlikely to have wanted either oligarchy or democracy for the reasons modern users of the words would expect. They believed that all government should preserve a harmonious consensus of interests and classes, that all rulers should consult with their subjects, and that all just interests should be justly reconcilable since the world was God's and he was just. There was plenty of room for argument about means but not yet much about ends. Moreover, because their society's traditions were more concerned with representing collectivities than individuals, most discontented subjects of town governments, like the discontented subjects of their kings, do not seem, despite their demands for more consultation, to have been particularly exercised about traditional methods of election or even about the exact composition of the consultative assemblies they demanded. The modern tendency to translate the neutral word *communitas* as 'commonalty' when it occurs in phrases like *maior ballivi et communitas* or *per communitatem eligantur* may imply too consistent and obvious an antithesis between rulers on the one hand and subjects—'commonalty' or 'commoners'—on the other.[36] A *communitas* included the mayor and bailiffs, who themselves represented as well as ruled it. When the London constitutions of 1319 distinguished aldermen from elected *communiarii* they showed that an acknowledged distinction was emerging, but even then the method of the commoners' election is left unspecified and in some clauses of the constitutions *communitas* is still used in its old and general sense. The conflict of interest between rulers and ruled was usually seen as the result of sinful misgovernment, not as something inherent in the relationship: with stricter rules and better rulers it might disappear, so there was no need to elaborate permanent methods of controlling future rulers. That is not to say that we know that there were no real ideological revolutionaries about in the thirteenth century, but we need to have hard evidence before we assume them.

The emphasis in more recent interpretations on the economic basis of urban conflicts can also look over-simplified. There was

[35] Tait, *Med. Eng. Bor.* [258], 302–38; Unwin, *Gilds* [366], 61–81; Hibbert, 'Origins of Med. Town Patriciate' [145] and in *Cam. Econ. Hist.* [79], iii. 198–206; Williams, *Med. London* [373].

[36] For other uses of the word, see pp. 103–4, 106–7, 108, 110, 114.

obvious scope for economic conflict in twelfth- and thirteenth-century towns, and it probably grew more intense as trade expanded and as townsmen themselves, with their own varying economic interests, gained control of town administration. Burgesses had common interests against non-burgesses, whether alien or 'foreign', visiting or resident; consumers against producers and sellers; employers against employees; and merchants against craftsmen. The last conflict has received particular emphasis and is certainly to be found in the cloth industry, where merchants were sometimes employers or virtual employers of weavers and fullers, but the categories of merchant and craftsman were by no means mutually exclusive in all industries and all towns. We do not know that the craft ordinances made by popular leaders in thirteenth-century London fulfilled any real class policy or even differed substantially from those made at other times, while the popular hostility to aliens may reflect an irrational and populist nationalism as much as any deliberate attack on the rich importers among the aldermen. Attacks on the aldermen seem to have been motivated by fiscal and political, not economic, grievances.

Doubts have already been cast in chapter four on how far a 'mercantile patriciate' existed in any real sense in London or elsewhere. If it did not exist then it cannot have been transformed by the rise of the crafts or by anything else. There is little evidence of any 'political drive of the crafts' as such or of any significant difference between new and old regimes. The 'craftsmen' who rose to power in late thirteenth-century London were the rich, often fishmongers and other victuallers, and once in power they behaved very like their predecessors. As G. A. Williams, whose interpretation of thirteenth-century London is in effect criticized here, admits: 'The one common feature [of the crafts] was an employers' front against employees; there were too many conflicts, too few points of contact'.[37] What his account graphically shows is the multifarious interests of the rich, their domination of the city in their own interests, and the jealous preoccupation of all citizens with the trading rights of citizenship, often attained through craft apprenticeship. When the crafts began to register batches of new freemen in the early fourteenth century, it was probably more because the protection of trade and trading privileges demanded better record-keeping than because the crafts undertook a 'drive for citizenship' so as to sway the city's

[37] *Med. London* [373], 275.

government by new voters. In all large towns, both in England and abroad, crafts were becoming more organized, partly as a means to control the economic privileges of burgess-ship, and partly in order to control trade and industry in other, equally conventional, ways. Though this could enable the crafts to provide a forum for popular discontent, and some were to do so later on, neither now nor later do they seem to have represented any coherent class interest.

What the evidence outlined here seems to suggest as the main cause of dissension was the political, judicial, and fiscal power of the richer citizens—the 'more powerful' or 'magnates' of the sources. It was not in economic interests that they were consistently opposed to their fellow burgesses, for most wage-earners were not burgesses, anyway, and only occasionally erupted into town politics. Given the assumptions of medieval society and politics, the richer burgesses— the more substantial citizens, the 'better and more discreet'—were bound to take the lead and hold municipal office. Where they comprised a distinct merchant class, whose interests might for instance be linked with those of outside producers or alien exporters or importers, then they might well try to see that the town pursued the sort of policies which could indeed injure local craftsmen and consumers.[38] But the conflict which was fundamentally inherent in the situation was that between taxers and taxed, rulers and ruled. Traditional methods of consultation and accounting could not withstand the temptations to corruption and a simple parish-pump love of power and prestige. Nor could town administrations, however improbably honourable, either control food supplies and prices or limit royal taxation, so as to satisfy consumers and tax-payers in bad times.

The discontents and disputes provoked by urban governments should not blind us to the cohesion within medieval urban society. All medieval governments were weak and lacking in means of repression by modern standards. They could not have survived or maintained order as well as they did without much willing submission, most of all by those who according to our standards were most unjustly treated. Town governments relied on affective bonds and voluntary obedience: the limited nature of popular demands and the rarity of real popular revolution show how far they got it. Much of the cohesiveness which sustained town government may look unattractive to modern eyes—the corollary of excluding non-burgesses, whether poor townsmen, country people, or aliens, from

[38] See below, pp. 182-5.

retail trade and so forth—but it had its virtues in contemporary eyes. The prohibition of sectional guilds and communes was not always or only designed to protect mercantile interests, but also to maintain the common unity, to bind the people of the town in 'one firm fellowship and one true friendship'.[39] Allowing, as we must, that servants, dependants, and most women were without question excluded, we should recognize that the community of a small town could be quite a real one, and should not react too far against the admittedly sentimentalized pictures that older historians used to draw of brotherly guildsmen and equal opportunities for all. Even in bigger places, where both politics and economics gave greater scope for conflict, many people probably did not feel all the class antagonisms that we may think their rational interests required. Their differences were not ideological. Their very faith in consensus and reconciliation may indeed have made it in some ways harder for them to resolve their conflicts, for it gave them no simple way to find and enforce just the right amount of consultation and control.

[39] Gross, *Gild Merchant* [136], i. 227.

7

The Later Middle Ages:
Demographic and Economic Change

THE PROBLEMS

With the fourteenth century both sources and secondary works on
English towns multiply, but so do problems of interpretation. Much
of what has been written about medieval towns is based on documents from the later Middle Ages and historians have sometimes
assumed, without much argument, either that earlier medieval
towns were rough drafts of later ones, or that they had changed in
some particular direction, but a direction which depends a good deal
on the preconceptions of the historian concerned. Earlier writers
tended to assume that the new records implied new growth, and
that, in M. M. Postan's words, 'things had to grow bigger and better
from generation to generation if they were to end as big and as good
as historians knew them to have been in Queen Elizabeth's time.[1]
More recently, led by Postan, many scholars have stressed the unhappy demographic, economic, and even climatic conditions against
which the better known political troubles of the fourteenth and
fifteenth centuries took place. Disagreements continue, and meanwhile a touch of gloom has spread over into the sixteenth century.
While it might be agreed that 'the economic function of almost all
English towns was transformed from 1500 to 1700',[2] recent work
stresses the troubles many underwent at the beginning of that period.
Unfortunately the tendency to study either the period before, or the
period after, some supposed moment of change, which hampers the
understanding of English urban history throughout the Middle Ages,
is even more pronounced at this stage. Few historians have considered the problems of the fifteenth and sixteenth centuries to-

[1] *Essays on Med. Agric.* [223], 196. For background e.g. *Cam. Econ. Hist.* [79], i–iii
(especially iii. 206–29); Bautier, *Econ. Dev. of Med. Europe* [64]; Heers, *L'Occident aux
xive et xve siècles* [141]; Reinhard, *Hist. de la pop.* [232]. Russell, *Brit. Med. Pop.* [238]
should be used with caution: see works in nn. 3–4.
[2] Clark and Slack, *Crisis and Order in Eng. Towns* [87], 10.

gether so as to explain the changes and continuities between them. The present work is not an exception. Though some material between 1500 and 1547 is included much of what is said here about the later Middle Ages may be vitiated by a failure to go much further than 1500. The ends of historical works, to adapt Maitland's phrase about their beginnings, have to tear the seamless web of history.

It seems likely that the Black Death, which hit England in 1348–9, and recurred with less ferocity thereafter, reduced the population by as much as a third. Whether numbers were still growing until 1348, were static, or had already declined from a high point at the end of the thirteenth century or even earlier, is not agreed. Postan sees the severe famine of 1315–17 as a symptom of Malthusian over-population and consequent depression, but the period between then and 1348 is too short, and the evidence is too patchy and uncertain, to suggest a general trend: there are local signs of both decline and prosperity. What seems clear is that in the long run the fourteenth-century reduction in population produced a shift in economic power from landlords and employers to tenants and workers, so that wages rose while prices and rents were low. The population nevertheless seems not to have risen for some time in the way that the better living standards suggest that it should have done. During the course of the sixteenth century it grew fast, but some historians would put the turning point in the fifteenth, others as late as the second decade of the sixteenth, while current work draws attention to the losses of the 1550s. Whatever date is correct the delay is hard to explain: plagues recurred in the fifteenth century but they seem to have been decreasingly virulent, increasingly local, and probably increasingly urban. The economic effects of the drop in population are also much debated, with some of the arguments about the interaction of demography and economy becoming confusingly circular. The general consensus among economic historians has been that the fourteenth and fifteenth centuries saw a general fall in economic activity, though A. R. Bridbury has argued that, in view of the reduced population, the level which was maintained constituted actual economic growth. Others have noticed the evidence of increased prosperity among the poorer classes, and most would agree that the changes in patterns of trade and industry included growth in some kinds and places as well as decay in others, even if agriculture—again with some exceptions—looks more generally depressed.[3]

[3] Bridbury, *Econ. Growth* [74]. Keen, *Eng. in Later Middle Ages* [164] surveys some

As all this suggests, evidence of late medieval population is very poor, though for towns, in contrast to parts of the countryside, it is a bit better than for the earlier period.[4] The most important new source in both town and country is provided by the poll taxes of 1377–81. The absence of comparative figures for towns at other dates before or after the Black Death makes the poll tax assessments, even where they are complete, a little difficult to use, but they are more helpful than anything else. After 1334 the normal parliamentary taxes (known as 'lay subsidies' or 'tenths and fifteenths'[5]) were not reassessed but levied as standard lump sums from each locality. From time to time places which established claims to have been particularly hard hit economically managed to get their quotas reduced. *Ex parte* evidence of reduced prosperity, which may imply reduced population, also comes sometimes from petitions for charters—illustrating once again the danger of using charters as evidence of urban growth. Petitions were also made for reductions in the traditional 'fee-farms'—the old 'borough farms'.[6] With the sixteenth century come the newly assessed Tudor subsidies and associated muster rolls in the 1520s and the chantry certificates and other records later on. Though individual towns may produce additional information of their own[7] it is largely these which enable historians to make some kind of comparison between fourteenth- and sixteenth-century figures. The numbers of people admitted to the freedom of towns have also been used as an index of population in the intervening period, but though they *may* reflect fluctuations in prosperity their relation to it and to total numbers is variable.[8] Much use has also been made of the relation between prices and wages to suggest changes in the total population, but this supposes a type of economy and a completeness of records which do not really exist. It

of the recent controversies but stops in 1485. On the early sixteenth century: Blanchard, 'Population Change' [71] and Cornwall, 'Eng. Population' [96]; Dyer, *Worcester* [434], 19–32; C. Phythian-Adams and E. A. Wrigley, speaking at the Past & Present Conference, 1975.

[4] Beresford, *Lay Subsidies and Poll Taxes* [2]. Varying interpretations: Hoskins, 'Eng. Provincial Towns' [150]; Cornwall, 'Eng. Country Towns' [95]; Darby, *New Hist. Geog.* [99], 178–84, 196, 241–7, and see Schofield, 'Geog. Distribution of Wealth, 1334–1649' [246], 500n, and 'Historical Demography' [247].

[5] See above, p. 51.

[6] e.g. *Cal. Chart. R. 1427–1516* [17], 5–6, 128–9; *Cal. Pat. R. 1436–41* [20], 266.

[7] e.g. Keene, 'Winchester: the Brooks Area' [430], 75–7; Heath, 'North Sea Fishing' [409], 65.

[8] Dobson, 'Admissions to Freedom of York' [438]; Veale, 'Craftsmen and London Econ.' [367]; D. J. Keene, review in *Archives*, xi (1974), 221–2.

Map 4
The larger towns of the later Middle Ages
(based on Darby, *New Hist. Geog.* [99], 243)

is moreover particularly difficult to use for individual places without interpolating material and assumptions from elsewhere which would invalidate any argument.

Towns moreover present problems, firstly, because changes in their populations were so liable to be affected by migration and, secondly, because it is so easy to confuse evidence of their population and prosperity. London seems to have grown in wealth during the fourteenth and fifteenth centuries and to have attracted migrants. Its population may therefore have increased intermittently but in 1501 was probably little if at all greater than it had been in 1377. No doubt this was largely because of plagues, which apparently struck the capital more fiercely and more often than any other place. If, as Sylvia Thrupp has suggested, successive generations of London merchant families barely replaced themselves, and if other classes were as unfortunate, then migration to London, combined with a relatively heavy death rate there, may have absorbed some of the natural increase of the immigrants' places of origin. Perhaps that, with proportional movement to other prosperous and intermittently growing towns like Norwich, Coventry, and Bristol, could help to explain the failure of national population to rise—particularly if immigrants to towns were young and unmarried. *A priori* arguments about both death rates and migration, however, like all other *a priori* arguments about such subjects, are dangerous, and need to be tested against the evidence, not merely from individual towns, but from towns and the regions which sustained them.[9]

The use of taxation records to illuminate population positively invites confusion between numbers and wealth. While Bristol and Norwich, for instance, grew in wealth, Norwich may have had no more inhabitants (about 10,000) in 1524 than it had had before the Black Death, and Bristol even fewer. Lavenham by the 1520s was the thirteenth richest place in the country but had fewer than a thousand inhabitants: though it was urban in its economy it was not a large town even by medieval standards. Prosperity and economic growth too, as Bridbury has shown, can be defined in varying ways, not all equally noticed by contemporaries or apparent in the sources. Southampton was a busy port but less of the wealth that passed through it stuck to local hands than did at Bristol. This has been

[9] Butcher, 'Origins of Romney Freemen' [403]; Thrupp, *Merchant Class* [364], 41–52, 191–210; 'Replacement Rates' [265]; cf. Wrigley, 'London's Importance, 1650–1750' [374]. On expectation of life, see Platt, *Med. Southampton* [416], 262–3.

established by the Southampton Brokage Books which record tolls on goods leaving the town by road; though the Southampton books seem to be exceptional in their detail, local customs and toll accounts elsewhere, where they exist, can help to establish levels of prosperity.[10] Sad tales of decay and of the inadequacy of municipal resources to pay the king's fee-farm, to which allusion has already been made, may deserve some scepticism: either over-traditional accounting or astute policy may on occasion have kept the funds which traditionally met a fee-farm lower than the wealth of the community, measured by other indices, suggests should have been necessary.[11] It is always worth noticing whether petitions for relief were granted: despite the pressures of corruption and influence contemporaries were in a better position to weigh claims than we are. Municipal or seigniorial accounts of urban property or dues may also give an exaggerated impression of decay because of the way they repeat items of traditional but uncollected income year after year without showing how other new items made up for them. A house described as ruinous may only have needed repair: such words in medieval accounts should evoke in modern terms the customary gloom of a surveyor's report rather than photographs of war-torn buildings. Evidence such as that of new bridges, parish churches, guildhalls, or even houses, where they or records of them survive; the paving of roads and construction of wharfs; and the conspicuous consumption of merchants and town corporations must be set against such evidence of decline. That is not, of course, to say that expenditure on buildings necessarily reflects prosperity: D. J. Keene sees the enlargement of Winchester's surviving churches as a sign of devotion, not of wealth.

The connection between the prosperity and population of a town and that of the surrounding country is also complex. Though plagues sometimes provoked flight to the country, famines or dangers outside could stimulate a move the other way. Market towns were naturally much affected by the fortunes of neighbouring agriculture while on the other hand a town of any size itself provided some stimulus to farming. A general shift in wealth from the midlands and east of the country to the south-west and south-east has been

[10] Campbell, 'Norwich' [385]; Coleman, 'Aspects of Southampton's Trade' [414]; Cobb, 'Local Customs Accounts' [3]; on ranking, see above n. 4, below n. 36.

[11] Dobson, 'Urban Decay' [108], doubts the evidence, but see *Southampton 3rd Remembrance Bk.* [418], i, pp. xxi–xxxi; Wilson, 'Port of Chester' [308]; *V.C.H. Warwicks.* [317], viii. 211 (payments by Trinity Guild).

noted, and while most towns grew proportionately richer than did the countryside, the shift must have affected towns in the different regions accordingly.[12]

All this makes it essential to study each town against a background of the general demographic and economic trends, even though the debates about the trends make it difficult to do so: circular arguments are as hard to avoid as wheels in a watch. Other external events affected many towns perhaps as much or more than plagues and their consequences. Firstly, as in earlier times, there were geographical changes like erosion and silting to bring decay to some ports and profits to their rivals. Ravenserodd, on the Humber, was destroyed by flood in the mid fourteenth century like Old Winchelsea three quarters of a century earlier; several of the Cinque Ports were decaying, and Chester was troubled by silting in the fifteenth century.[13] Secondly national politics—war and peace, taxation and so forth—affected towns in many ways, and more noticeably than in the earlier Middle Ages. Thirdly, the patterns of international trade were changing, and English towns were, as always, caught in a network of commercial relationships that were never static. The first of these subjects needs no further discussion here, but the second and third do.

WARS, TAXATION, AND THE WOOL AND CLOTH TRADES

War provides the most obvious way in which national and international politics affected towns. The Welsh wars, which had encouraged the fortification and modest growth of markets, first in the Marches and then—as the great castles were built—in Welsh Wales, were now more or less over. Scottish wars continued, bringing both profit and loss as well as fortification. The frequent presence of armies and court at York in the early fourteenth century may have stimulated the city's longer-term growth as well as benefiting local victuallers and armourers. The profit or loss sustained by the country as a whole from the Hundred Years War is disputed, and though there is no doubt about its impact on certain towns, here again the net balance is not always clear. The Channel ports enjoyed increased traffic at times but they also endured raids. Ports and ship-owners

[12] Schofield, 'Geog. Distribution of Wealth' [246]; Darby, *New Hist. Geog.* [99], 178–84, 196. For comparison e.g. Fourquin, *Les Campagnes de la région parisienne* [124]; Verhulst, 'L'Economie rurale' [270].

[13] *Melsa Chron.* [400], iii. 120–4. On the size of ships, see Scammell, 'Eng. Merchant Shipping' [242], 332–3; also Scammell, 'Shipowning, *c.* 1450–1550' [243].

lost money when ships were commandeered ('arrested') for carrying troops and provisions. Inland towns served as collection points for the heavy supplies shipped overseas, though again arrangements for payment could be damaging to suppliers. War added to the constant dangers—and possible profits—of piracy for ship-owners and merchants. More importantly it affected ports and producers by its interruptions of particular trades. The Gascon wine trade was especially vulnerable: when it revived in the later fifteenth century Boston never recovered its once large share, which passed to ports in the south and west.

The effects of the so-called Wars of the Roses on trade and urban life look fairly limited. Most of the periodic outbreaks of violence in towns were unconnected with national conflicts, and though some places, mostly in the midlands, were plundered and more took the precaution of improving their defences, many remained virtually unfortified. Cartloads of goods continued to trundle along the roads from Southampton as far as the midlands, and the links between discernible fluctuations in prosperity and the intermittent dynastic trouble are seldom easy to establish. International repercussions may have made more impact, through their effect on trade, as when Edward IV used Hanseatic ships in his invasion of 1471 and rewarded the German merchants with trading concessions in 1474: these included privileges at Hull, Boston, and Lynn, as well as in London, but the benefits were one-sided and did not include access to the Hanse ports for English ships.[14]

Closely linked to the effect of war itself was that of taxation and chiefly, since royal finance depended on them, of customs duties on wool. From 1336 Edward III increased the wool custom and otherwise manipulated the trade to such a degree that, despite the imposition of a relatively small cloth custom in 1347, the export of raw wool became less profitable, while the home manufacture and export of cloth were stimulated. One important aspect of royal policy was the establishment of a wool staple (or staples), that is, a place (or places) through which all wool must pass for taxation. After some experiments with staples in the Netherlands or at home—the lists of home staples providing some guide to the principal trading places

[14] Turner, *Town Defences* [266], 75–84; McFarlane, 'War, Economy and Social Change' [183]; Postan, *Essays on Med. Agric.* [223], 49–80; Hewitt, *Organization of War under Edward III* [144], 3–7, 15–21, 50–92; *Libelle of Eng. Polycye* [41] and extracts in *Eng. Hist. Docs.* [29], iv, pp. 1032–5; Power and Postan, *Studies in Eng. Trade* [226]; Carus-Wilson, *Med. Merchant Venturers* [81]; Lander, *Conflict and Stability* [168], 163.

—the wool staple was fixed at Calais in 1363. There the Merchants of the Staple established their long monopoly of the shrinking trade. Some exemptions from staple regulations were allowed, notably for wool going to the Mediterranean. Most of it was shipped by Italians who used first Sandwich and then Southampton as their chief ports of embarcation. Though Boston, Ipswich, and Hull retained significant shares of the trade for some time, the Italian trade and the location of the staple in Calais tended to concentrate the wool trade in London, while the Merchants of the Staple, buying directly from producers, largely bypassed other towns.[15]

The development of the late medieval cloth industry in England was therefore partly a consequence of the accidental protectionism of the wool custom. It not only benefited the English 'merchant adventurers' who, though their share of the market fell periodically, exported an increasing proportion of the English cloth, but also employed far more people than could live off the export of raw wool. They worked in many parts of the country, but most of all in the West Riding, York, Coventry, Norwich and nearby, Suffolk, Bristol and the Cotswolds, Wiltshire, Somerset, and Devon. The growth of the rural industry is sometimes connected directly with the decline of the old cloth towns of the twelfth century and the introduction of fulling mills, but these interpretations telescope events too much, just as that which attributes it solely to the protection of the wool custom oversimplifies them. Lincoln bewailed its shrunken industry from the thirteenth to the fifteenth century and beyond, while York's grew meanwhile. There had moreover always been some rural cloth-working, though it is poorly recorded before the fourteenth-century aulnage accounts. To see the late medieval industry as even largely rural is not only to ignore the contribution of York, Norwich, Salisbury, and other major towns, but to beg important questions of urban history. While places like Castle Combe or Lavenham may represent new trends in industrial development they were themselves surely towns in all but municipal constitution. It is only by determined anachronism that they can be denied a title that is customarily bestowed on some equally small places merely because they had been called 'boroughs' at a time when that word had little or no constitutional significance.[16]

---

[15] *Cam. Econ. Hist.* [79], iii. 316–40; Power, *Med. Eng. Wool Trade* [225]; Carus-Wilson and Coleman, *England's Export Trade* [22]; Gross, *Gild Merchant* [136], i. 141–2.
[16] Carus-Wilson, *Med. Merchant Venturers* [81], 143–82, 239–64, and 'Evidence of

Manipulation of the coinage and bullion regulations also affected the course of trade and notably, since wool most often attracted royal attention, hampered the wool trade from time to time. How far these and other signs of protectionism should be regarded as the product either of war or of the restricted conditions of trade, or even as essentially new at all, is doubtful. The alien subsidies of the mid fifteenth century and the 'hosting laws', which for a while required some resident aliens to lodge and register their transactions with Englishmen, produced records which survive as a useful guide to alien colonies and their trade in various towns, but individual towns had implemented similar regulations long before.[17] National enforcement, though new, was still sporadic, and the impact of official policies, as the customs duties illustrate, was often unintended. English merchants enlarged their share of the export trade in this period, though patchily and with setbacks, but it is not clear how much that was due to government encouragement. The impact of all these political circumstances needs to be weighed against other and perhaps less well-known factors.

CHANGING PATTERNS OF TRADE

It is extremely difficult to disentangle the various changes in directions, volumes, and methods of trade which took place in the later Middle Ages, and to assign a single cause, or any causes at all, to many of them. Contraction of economic activity in the wake of plagues surely accounted for some developments. The decay or disappearance of many markets, for instance,[18] and the concentration of maritime trade into fewer and larger ports might be partly explicable in this way. Other influences on urban life came from the development of mercantile techniques in, for example, credit transactions and communications. As early as the thirteenth century these were helping to make merchants increasingly sedentary and to undermine the great international fairs. Some foreign fairs continued to play an international role and some English ones were regionally important for centuries, but by the late fourteenth century royal purchases of cloth were made in London, Coventry, and other towns,

Industrial Growth' [80]; Darby, *New Hist. Geog.* [99], 222-8; compare Coornaert, 'Draperies rurales, draperies urbaines' [92]; Bautier, *Econ. Dev. of Med. Europe* [64], 209-16.

[17] *Cam. Econ. Hist.* [79], iii. 158-72, 206-29, 328-38; Giuseppi, 'Alien Merchants' [133]; Thrupp, 'Alien Population in 1440' [263].

[18] Compare later changes: Finberg, *Ag. Hist.* [122], iv. 466-77, 502-6.

not at the fairs. In 1416 the old rule that the London husting should close for Boston fair on St. Botolph's day was rescinded.[19]

Although aliens seem to have dominated England's foreign trade in the late thirteenth century, that may have been a recent phenomenon, and there is no great reason to talk in terms of either 'national advance' or 'national backwardness' in subsequent expansions or contractions of native participation. In addition to wars and fiscal policy and to fluctuations in local and individual enterprise, some particular influences derived from elsewhere, like the export of corn from the German east and the monopoly of Norwegian and Icelandic trade by the German Hanse. Both of these had started before 1300. English merchants were, however, active in the Baltic in the late fourteenth century. About a hundred of them claimed over £5,000 between them in compensation for goods seized during troubles in Prussia in 1385; York, Lynn, Norwich, Beverley, and London were strongly represented in the list, and men from Boston, Colchester, Coventry, Hadleigh, Nottingham, and Salisbury put in smaller claims.[20] A little later, ships from Lynn, Boston, Hull, and Bristol broke into the Icelandic and Norwegian trade, but both the northern seas and the Baltic were virtually closed again to English merchants from the mid fifteenth century. Other influences on the fortunes of English towns were the troubles of the Flemish cloth industry, intensified as they were by competition from Brabant, France, and Italy, as well as from England; the supplanting of English salt by that from the Bay of Bourgneuf and further south; the growing Italian use of direct sea transport; and other changes in the fortunes of towns and the methods of merchants both in Italy and all over Europe.[21]

THE PORTS

It is difficult to generalize about the east coast ports, for individual trades fluctuated variously in them all and it is easy to be misled by the patchiness of the information available. On the evidence of the records of trade and shipping, the international ports of Boston and

---

[19] *Cal. London Letter Book I* [344], 159; *V.C.H. Hunts.* [406], ii. 217; above, pp. 58–9.

[20] *Die Recesse der Hansetage, 1256–1430* [47], iii. 405–12.

[21] Above, pp. 47–8, 76–7, in addition to works in n. 1, see Holmes, 'Florentine Merchants' [148]; Mallett, 'Anglo-Florentine Commercial Relations' [188]; Heers, 'Les Genois en Angleterre' [142]; Fryde, 'Anglo-Italian commerce' [127]; Dollinger, *The German Hansa* [110]; for contemporary surveys see *Libelle of Eng. Polycye* [41] and Fortescue, 'Comodytes of Eng.' [31].

Lynn have been described as suffering severely from the decline of their wool and wine trades, the closing of the Baltic, and the growing dominance of London in overseas commerce. In Lynn, however, an extensive survey of the town's buildings and topography suggests doubts: though Lynn more or less stopped growing from the fourteenth century there is no evidence of depopulation except in one quarter. This lay inland and the decay there before 1557 was compensated by new streets along the water-front. The two most prominent guilds of merchants started to build halls in 1406 and 1424, churches were altered and enlarged, the walls and gates were repaired, and 'there was extensive rebuilding of houses in all sections of the community' until the sixteenth century, when a fairly short period of relative decay set in. The evidence for Hull does not seem to be very clear either. Though the volume of overseas trade there may have shrunk by three-quarters in the fifteenth century a good deal of it went in Hull ships, while the export of Yorkshire cloth, though fluctuating, seems to have supported some active local merchants. Moreover, though building apparently slackened in the fifteenth century and corporation rents 'decayed' after 1460, the Holy Trinity shipmen's guild put up a hall, almshouse, and chapel in the 1460s, and there was some building at both the town's churches during the century. Nearby, Grimsby, largely a coasting and fishing centre, has been described as 'a small town getting poorer' during the period, but the townspeople's complaints of poverty from depopulation look disingenuous. Newcastle relied on the coal trade and did much coastal shipping. It is said to have enlarged its trade in the fifteenth century. By the early sixteenth century, when there was a general though patchy revival, Newcastle, Hull, Ipswich, and Yarmouth were the most active ports.[22]

In the south-east Sandwich did well in the fourteenth century, especially from Italian ships, and Dover and nearby ports profited from the link with Calais and the frequent need to provision it from England. Here too, however, the fifteenth century may have seen some shrinkage.[23] Further down Channel, much of the trade through Southampton was handled by Italians, Londoners, and men from the midlands, Salisbury, and Winchester. All the same the port

[22] Parker, *Making of King's Lynn* [379], 4–5, 11–12, 30, but cf. ibid. 166 and Scammell, 'Eng. Merchant Shipping' [242], 329–30; Carus-Wilson, 'Ports of the Wash' [82]; *V.C.H. Yorks. E.R.* [329], i. 54–70, 72, 76, 398; Gillett, *Hist. of Grimsby* [326], 48–67; Carus-Wilson, *Expansion of Exeter* [320], 4–5 (on Newcastle).

[23] Ruddock, *Italian Merchants* [417], 20, 29, 47, 65–7; Butcher, 'Romney Freemen' [403].

presents a striking picture of activity. Both its documentary and its archaeological records are rich and have been well studied. They suggest that, despite a prolonged depression after the damaging French raid of 1338, the town retained some prosperous burgesses as well as entertaining many visiting traders from Italy and else-where. The late medieval townsmen did not build as much in stone as their twelfth- and thirteenth-century predecessors seem to have done, but that may have been more because building fashions changed than because they were poorer: they had some very fine and large houses. There was little industry but some local men had their own ships, many probably did well out of providing port services, and others engaged in the carting trade, particularly to other towns nearby. Just why and when prosperity ebbed and Southampton sank into a lethargy that lasted until the railway age is not clear: the gradual departure of the Italians in and after the late fifteenth century, and competition from London in the sixteenth, were both damaging, but in the meantime trade was intermittently buoyant and ships left for the Mediterranean and even for the New World.[24]

Exeter and Bristol, with some at least of the smaller south-western ports, also profited from the shift of wealth to the south-west and the growth of the cloth industry there. E. M. Carus-Wilson thinks that the fourteenth century, despite population losses, was a time of outstanding prosperity for Bristol, with cloth exports from the Cotswolds, the midlands, and its own industry all growing fast. During much of the fifteenth century the volume of trade through the port was lower but it rose to new heights at its end. E. M. Carus-Wilson judges that it was in this century that a 'distinctively mercantile class' emerged, with extensive overseas commerce and a big investment in shipping. Bristol ships, like some from the east coast, made successful forays to Iceland early in the century. There-after they made abortive ventures into the Mediterranean, enjoyed a growing traffic with Normandy, Brittany, Portugal, and above all Spain, and before 1500 had undertaken journeys across the Atlantic to the New World. Even so, only a small proportion of the town's inhabitants lived primarily off foreign trade, and many of those who did were in a very small way of business, like the sailors who took cargo space for their own wares instead of wages. Bristol also served

[24] Platt, *Med. Southampton* [416], 92–226; Ruddock, *Italian Merchants* [417]; Coleman, 'Aspects of Southampton's Trade' [414].

as a regional centre for much of the south-west, as its metal and leather trades, for instance, suggest. The rise of Exeter, therefore, may help to explain why Bristol had by 1524 ceded its place as the second town of the kingdom to Norwich.[25]

In the north-west Chester was still the chief port, though not a very large one. The town's own inhabitants do not seem to have been active in foreign trade, while urban industry was too slight, and the hinterland as yet too poor, to enrich them by other means. It has however been suggested that the port's chief trade, being coastal and Irish, was less vulnerable to the fifteenth-century depressions than was continental commerce, and that the townspeople's pleas of poverty were false in reasoning if not in substance.[26]

The history of London in this period is too well recorded but as yet too little analysed to be susceptible of a very useful summary here. Its population is thought to have been much the same size in 1501 as it had been in 1377, or, for that matter, before the Black Death, but intervening changes are largely a matter for guesswork. Recurrent plagues probably failed to diminish the numbers for long, and the growth which doubled total population during the first half of the sixteenth century may have gone on intermittently a good deal earlier. By the end of the period the city's tendency to absorb the overseas trade of the whole country was becoming pronounced, and London merchants were competing in several of the ports which remained active. Even before then the proximity of the government and frequent sessions of parliaments and councils gave the city a strong hold on luxury industries and victualling trades. The records of the crafts, now becoming organized under chartered livery companies, bear witness to this as well as to the troubles and rivalries of different groups within the city. The Great Fire destroyed much of the building of the period, but Kingsford estimated that over fifty parish churches were rebuilt or enlarged in the fifteenth century or very soon afterwards. The great Guildhall, built between 1411 and c. 1430, still stands, though shorn of the court-rooms, chapel, and so forth that were added to it as soon as it was up. The city and its companies afforded lavish displays and pageants to kings and their guests in the later Middle Ages, sometimes with wine flowing from the

[25] Carus-Wilson, *Expansion of Exeter* [320]; Finberg and Hoskins, *Devon Studies* [123], 231–7; Carus-Wilson, *Med. Merchant Venturers* [81], 1–98; Lobel and Carus-Wilson, 'Bristol' [294], 10–14; Sherborne, *Port of Bristol* [295].
[26] Wilson, 'Port of Chester' [308].

conduits. Both corporation and individual citizens repeatedly lent large sums of money to the Crown (as other towns and citizens did on a smaller scale), not always at interest, in evidence both of their wealth and of their loyalty.[27]

INLAND TOWNS

Just as overseas trade is better recorded than coastal or inland trade, so that of the inland towns—among which are included here Norwich and York, though both were still in some sense ports—is less well recorded than is that of the seaports. Here the customs accounts are less useful, while inland trade tended to produce fewer lawsuits of the kind that the dangers of the sea and of foreign wars provoked and that illuminate the history of maritime commerce. Compared with earlier centuries, however, the fourteenth and fifteenth provide much more information about crafts and marketing from guild and municipal records. Whether that is because there was more, or more specialized, industrial activity, because it was more regulated, or merely because there are more records, is a moot point.

Norwich moved from eighth to second place in wealth among English towns during this time. Though its population was much reduced by the Black Death and may have been slow to recover, it probably doubled between 1377 and 1524—though even that may not have brought it much above what it had been in the eleventh century. Even in the troubles of the fourteenth century the city remained an active centre of trade and industry. Its speciality was worsted, which was woven in and around the town and formed a high proportion of English cloth exports at this time: its importance, James Campbell suggests, has been underrated. The trade may have declined somewhat in the early fifteenth century, but revived later, when most exported worsteds were sent by road to London instead of by river to Yarmouth as before. Over a quarter of the citizens admitted to the freedom of Norwich in the early sixteenth century were connected with the industry. During the hundred years after the Black Death many parish churches were rebuilt and all four orders of friars put up extensive buildings. A fine new guildhall and other municipal buildings were erected in the early fifteenth century. More striking still is Campbell's suggestion that it was in the later

[27] Thrupp, *Merchant Class* [364]; Veale, 'Craftsmen and London Econ.' [367]; Barron, 'Gov. of London' [334] and *Med. Guildhall* [335]; Kingsford, *Prejudice and Promise* [165], 140–3.

Middle Ages that Norwich 'changed from being predominantly one storeyed to being predominantly two storeyed', and that in this town the 'great rebuilding' which transformed rural England in the sixteenth and seventeenth centuries was largely accomplished by 1558. At Colchester too there was extensive rebuilding of parish churches, and the cloth trade, well established there before 1300, seems not to have declined thereafter. There was new growth in Suffolk at the cloth-making centres such as Sudbury, Long Melford, Clare, and Lavenham, and in Essex at Thaxted, which during the fourteenth century grew from a village into a prosperous town on the basis of an apparently new cutlery industry. Burgess tenure had appeared by the mid fourteenth century but it was not until the sixteenth, when Thaxted had already passed its brief phase of wealth, that the town secured any self-government.[28]

Further north, York, as might be expected from the geographical shifts of prosperity and overseas trade, suffered fluctuating fortunes. Stimulated by the frequent presence of the court and armies in the early fourteenth century and then by the development of the cloth industry, the city may have reached a peak of prosperity about the end of the century, when it is thought to have been more populous than before the Black Death. Bows, bells, pewter ware, and glass were among the products sent from York over much of the north and beyond, while merchants from there seem to have become 'more ubiquitous and their activities more diverse', taking over much of the commerce transacted a hundred years before by aliens. With the fifteenth century the competition of West Riding cloth and the decline of the North Sea and Baltic trades combined against York: property values fell, there was much municipal anxiety about the state of trade, and by the sixteenth century the population may have dropped back to the pre-plague level, leaving the city no longer among the country's top ten. On the other hand York produces good examples of parish churches rebuilt or enlarged during the apparently depressed fifteenth century. The same kind of evidence, in the absence of much in the way of documents, has been adduced to show prosperity in late fourteenth–century and fifteenth–century Stamford after a relative decline in the earlier fourteenth century. Lincoln meanwhile produces signs of decay continuing from before 1300. Though there was some new building in the fifteenth century

---

[28] Campbell, 'Norwich' [385], 15–17; Martin, *Story of Colchester* [309], 28, 35–9; Newton, *Thaxted* [424].

the citizens had difficulty in maintaining the reduced number of parish churches, several areas of the city had become depopulated, and it seems that there were long delays in replacing the old guild-hall, which had been demolished in about 1390.[29]

In the midlands Coventry grew richer, moving from thirteenth to fourth richest town in the kingdom between 1334 and 1524. How far this was due to the attainment of municipal liberties or to the growth of either the cloth or metal industries is still debatable, though it now seems clear that the division between two lords, traditionally thought to have held back the town's development until 1345, was of fairly short duration and limited significance. Coventry had probably developed quite steadily during the twelfth and thirteenth centuries and by the early fourteenth century had a good number of prosperous wool merchants. By 1400 its growing cloth industry had produced drapers with far-ranging trade. An important proportion of the town's recorded craftsmen were cloth-workers, with metal, victualling, and leather trades also significant. Much building went on in both the fourteenth and fifteenth centuries and from 1340 the richer townspeople endowed and supported several guilds, which were soon amalgamated into two, the guilds of Holy Trinity and Corpus Christi. From the fifteenth century some of the crafts claimed to have difficulty in financing the Corpus Christi plays for which they were responsible, and by 1494 the complaints were general. By the sixteenth century the town as a whole was again declining in prosperity and population.[30] Competition from Coventry may have injured Warwick, where there were complaints of languishing trade in the mid fourteenth century, and some relief from taxes was granted in 1444–5. Northampton failed to get its fee-farm reduced in 1334, when it pleaded that the cloth trade was declining. Although the townspeople managed to get remissions in the later fifteenth century when half the town was said to be desolate and destroyed, it nevertheless seems to have maintained a varied trade, employing numerous tailors and other cloth-workers. Further references to ruin and decay in 1535 may be explained largely by a fire in 1516. Another in 1675 destroyed too

[29] V.C.H. Yorks: York [444], 84–113, 120–4; Bartlett, 'Expansion and Decline of York' [436]; Rogers, Making of Stamford [419], 51, and Buildings of Stamford [420]; Hill, Med. Lincoln [333], 250–87.
[30] Coss, 'Coventry before Incorporation' [312]; V.C.H. Warwicks. [317], viii. 151–6, 208–14; Crisis and Order [87], 58; Hilton, Eng. Peasantry in Later Middle Ages [146], 210–11.

much for us to be able to assess the evidence of buildings. At Oxford the Black Death and town-and-gown conflicts may have accelerated a decline of trade that had started well before 1300. Merton College and the founder of New College were able to buy once populated but now deserted sites cheaply in the later fourteenth century.[31]

In the south, Winchester, like Lincoln, provides a string of complaints from the thirteenth century, yet even here the cloth industry furnished employment and ephemeral signs of revival in the late fourteenth century, while at Salisbury 'apart from the years of plague there was no pause in development in the late Middle Ages'. The population apparently grew between 1377 and the 1520s and building continued on both new and old sites. It was financed by an extensive general trade and a large cloth industry in the city and round about. Only in the sixteenth century did the decay of Southampton begin to undermine the foreign trade of Salisbury's general merchants so that local clothiers began to replace them as civic leaders.[32]

CONCLUSION

Despite the brevity and gaps of the foregoing survey its implications preclude any simple conclusion. Neither the older view of late medieval towns burgeoning with life nor the new orthodoxy that 'in the fifteenth century Southampton, Bristol and London alone escaped the general blight on towns and trade' seems to make adequate sense.[33] The first, which still survives for example in suggestions that the appearance of 'craft guilds' reflects greater division of labour,[34] relies too much on the increase in municipal records and on the assumption that growth must have been inevitable and continuous. The second relies too much on the evidence of international trade in the customs accounts and on the assumption that the period was one of uniform economic decline. Slightly less sweeping generalizations—that, for instance, large ports did better than small, or that, whatever the fluctuating prosperity of existing centres, it was an age virtually without new beginnings—flounder respectively before the nuances of Southampton's and Lynn's histories on the one hand, and the rise of Thaxted and the cloth-working

[31] V.C.H. Warwicks. [317], viii. 481–2; V.C.H. Northants [384], iii. 19, 26–31; Pevsner, Northants [382], 314; Davis, 'The Ford, the River, and the City' [391].

[32] Keene, 'Winchester: the Brooks Area' [430], 168–87; Rogers, 'Salisbury' [407], 5–7.

[33] Coleman, 'Aspects of Southampton's Trade' [414], 9.

[34] Miller, 'Eng. Econ. in 13th Cent.' [195], 27–8: see pp. 62, 83, 165–6.

'villages' or 'manors' on the other. Some general points may however be made. New towns were far fewer than in previous centuries,
and few towns were indisputably larger in 1500 than they had been in
1300. At the same time it must be noted how the balance between
town and country shifted. Despite the undoubted troubles of many
towns more of the country's wealth—though possibly not of its
population—lay within them in 1524 than in 1334. It seems improbable
that the change occurred at the very end of the period and belonged,
as it were, to a post-medieval surge forward. While some places
were growing then, others were not. C. Phythian-Adams has drawn
attention to the troubles of many towns in the early and mid sixteenth
century, when a series of dearth years hit communities already in
trouble and the increasing expense of municipal office was driving
the rich away from them.[35] If we had more information for more
dates in the fourteenth and fifteenth centuries we should probably
be able to see more shifts in the prosperity and ranking of towns
between 1300 and 1500.[36] In any case such comparisons, suggestive
as they are, are vulnerable to many criticisms. Until more closely
analysed figures are published, the details of ranking, like the estimates of population, should not be pushed too far.

Clarification seems to depend as usual on more work on individual
towns which would set one type of evidence against another and
not take general trends for granted. At the same time the danger of
seeing towns in isolation is, as usual, as great as that of generalizing
about them. Hazardous though explanations may seem when one is
not sure what one is explaining, critical work might be more stimulated by trying to explain apparent trends, and the different ways that
towns joined or did not join in them, than by just describing the
trends. Everitt's suggestion that 'primary' towns survived better in
difficult circumstances than did those of later growth provokes
thought. Lincoln and Winchester, surviving all the troubles that they
bewailed, as well as market towns like Banbury which inspired the
suggestion, may be cases in point.[37] Perhaps we should not even take it
for granted that the 'late Middle Ages' constitute a definable and useful
period in the history of English towns. In other words we should not
assume that significant changes or halts in the nature and direction of

[35] At Past & Present Conference, 1975; see below, pp. 180–1.
[36] See, e.g., *Statutes of the Realm* [54], i. 165; *Gough Map* [36]; Hewitt, *Organization of War* [144], 48–9; *Rot. Parl.* [51], v. 231–3; Carus-Wilson and Coleman, *England's Export Trade* [22], 8.
[37] Everitt, 'Banburys of Eng.' [119], 35; above, p. 14.

their history came at any particular moment during the whole medi-eval period, and that this moment inaugurated the 'late Middle Ages' of English urban history in general. Important as the general demo-graphic and economic changes of the fourteenth century were, they do not seem to have been the only, or in some places even the chief, determinant. Perhaps the real break for the urban historian comes with the change not in the substance but in the materials of history, with the beginning of any considerable—and surviving—town archive. That beginning transforms the study of urban history by making it possible to ask and answer many more questions. Although it is certain that towns grew faster in the twelfth century than they did in the fifteenth, the biggest contrast for their historian is that he knows more, and knows different things, about them in the later century than in the earlier.

8

The Later Middle Ages:
Social and Political Change

THE PROBLEMS

It is tempting to discuss the social, political, and constitutional
changes and conflicts of late medieval urban life simply in terms of
the consequences of economic and demographic change. The previous chapter has argued, however, that a uniform contraction of all
urban economies cannot be assumed. Too often the growth of
oligarchy and protectionism which have been postulated, and might
be taken as natural consequences of it, cannot be proved either. Any
contraction of population and economy must surely have affected
social and political life in *some* way, but in just what way is not obvious. There is no reason to assume that this was the only source of
change. There is plenty of evidence, for instance, of a growing complexity, self-confidence, and ceremony in town life, which are far
from easy to correlate with either economic growth or decline.

THE CLASS STRUCTURE

Changes in the class structure are peculiarly subject to the usual
problems of interpretation: most of the information used to describe
it throughout the Middle Ages comes in fact from this later period,
so that suggestions of change are based on a combination of assumptions about the direction of change—in turn based on the assumed
causes—and of modern interpretations which may be quite in-
appropriate. Information about the occupations and wealth of
townsmen can be found in guild, municipal, and tax records, sometimes in deeds, and best of all in the wills which become less rare as
the period goes on.[1] Lists of those admitted to the freedom of craft

[1] The *Reports* of the Hist. MSS. Comm. 1870–1916 (see Martin and McIntyre,
Bibliog. of Brit. Munic. Hist. [9], i, p. 67; Gross, *Bibliog.* [4], 11–12) include abstracts of
town records (though see below, n. 23). *Eng. Hist. Docs.* [29], iv gives a few examples.
On guilds and freemen: Phythian-Adams, 'Records of Craft Guilds' [10] and D. M.
Woodward, 'Freemen's Rolls' [12], and above, p. 142, n. 8. For tax records see above,

or borough add to the valuable if shaky basis of statistics provided by the tax lists, and if one then adds the evidence of lawsuits and disputes about trade or local government, the shape and stresses of town society begin to appear, though so hazily that a good deal of them seems to lie in the eye of the historian. Not all differences of opinion result from prejudice or subjective judgement: the evidence is genuinely ambiguous.

On the one hand the evidence of apparently restrictive craft and municipal policies, and of conflicts between merchants and craftsmen, masters and journeymen, has often been taken to demonstrate a hardening of class divisions. On the other, A. R. Bridbury argues that a larger proportion of the reduced town populations was found among the masters now than during the overcrowded thirteenth century. Comparison of prices with the wages paid to building workers, moreover, strongly suggests that, after the troubles and disorders of the fourteenth century, the fifteenth was a good time for wage-earners. It is not clear, however, how closely most urban wages followed the trends of those in the building trades. In others, journeymen's and labourers' pay might be more effectively held down by municipal and craft restrictions in hard times.[2]

It is very difficult to be precise about class divisions. It has recently been estimated that forty per cent of those assessed in 1525 to the subsidy in Norwich were wage-earners, while sixty per cent of the town's wealth belonged to only six per cent of those assessed. The assessed were assumed, from arguments based on other towns, to represent two-thirds of the population, and on that basis it was estimated that about two-thirds of the whole population of Norwich 'lived below or near the poverty line'. Rather similar disparities between the few rich and the many poor have been postulated for other large towns at the same time, though in some cases the assumptions look stronger than the evidence. A. D. Dyer, in a detailed study of sixteenth-century Worcester, points out that the group he tentatively calls the 'middle/upper class' and estimates—again tentatively—at about twenty per cent of the total population, contained many gradations and few hard barriers to social contact and mobility. The real division came between the independent tradesmen

pp. 142–5. Of many useful classes of central government records the *Calendars* of Charter, Patent, and Close Rolls and of Chancery Inquisitions Miscellaneous are both printed and indispensable. The Chancery Miscellanea, unprinted, are often useful.

[2] Phelps-Brown and Hopkins, 'Seven Centuries of Prices' [215]; see above, p. 141, n. 3.

and the eighty per cent of the population which comprised employees and the poorest of the self-employed. How far the sixteenth-century pattern represents that of the fifteenth, or of more distant parts of the Middle Ages, is uncertain: while the general classification may well have been similar there was much scope for change in the relative size of the categories. The fact is that we lack earlier material closely comparable to the sixteenth-century subsidy assessments, and should suspect that demographic and economic conditions were changing fast when they were drawn up.[3] Whereas Bridbury sees fifteenth-century towns as full of opportunity and relatively free of class barriers, so that contrary social trends in the sixteenth century might plausibly be the product of contrary economic conditions, those who think that the fifteenth century was a time of conflict and repression must explain the apparent continuance of these tendencies in the sixteenth rather differently. Probably both general pictures try to take in too many towns in too many periods at once.

Hints of growing poverty around 1500 have been noted in the way some town governments were then worrying about unemployment and vagrancy.[4] It is difficult to distinguish a growing concern—or increasing records of concern—from a growing problem: some increase of toughness towards poor immigrants can be found a good deal earlier, in the restriction of the traditional right of villeins to enfranchisement in towns.[5] This was probably not very damaging in practice, however, and in 1391 the knights of the shires in parliament failed in an attempt to abrogate the right entirely. That was in the aftermath of the Peasants' Revolt. What had happened then reminds us not to discount all possibility of class conflict, and perhaps growing class conflict, during the fourteenth century. Nevertheless, though the panicky rumours that the rising evoked emphasize the gulf between chroniclers and the poor, nothing that happened in the towns suggests very radical discontents or objectives.[6] Some kind of class conflict was in the air but it was outweighed by the traditional bonds of lordship, deference, and—perhaps even more important in towns—by craft and household loyalties.

[3] Pound, 'Soc. Structure of Norwich' [388], 49–50; Dyer, *Worcester* [434], 174–6. For subsidies, see above, p. 142, n. 4.

[4] Below, pp. 178–9; cf. Jordan, *Philanthropy in Eng.* [163], 56–7, 66–72.

[5] *Rot. Parl.* [51], iii. 296; see below, pp. 171–2.

[6] See below, p. 183.

Political and economic conflicts are discussed later in the chapter, but it should be noted here that the fifteenth-century journeymen's guilds, with their attempts at collective bargaining, and the conflicts between crafts, suggest some solidarity and discontent, if again very limited aims and rather blurred class divisions. Sylvia Thrupp describes the 'drawing apart of merchants as a superior social class'[7] in London and her argument that the merchants increased their political hold on the city in the fifteenth century may imply a widening of the division between them and the lesser citizens. The same social exclusiveness of the richest burgesses, among whom merchants were usually prominent, has been noted elsewhere, though differences in wealth and presumably in style of life were much less in smaller towns. It should also be remembered that the representation of separate classes in urban government was much rarer in England than, for instance, in Italy, which suggests that divisions were less deep.

Now that surnames had become for the most part hereditary, geographical mobility can no longer be deduced from simple lists of names. Other sources, and particularly wills, help to make up for this. The apparently short survival of urban families, where they can be traced, gave scope to rising newcomers, while the tradition of leaving sometimes as much as a third of movable property (which included money, merchandise, and debts) to religious and charitable purposes discouraged the maintenance of capital. Apprenticeship probably provided a road to advancement only for a few: Sir Richard Whittington (d. 1423), who incidentally did not acquire his cat until a hundred and fifty years after his death, came, like many other successful immigrants, from respectable landowning stock. Sylvia Thrupp points out that a significant number of immigrant apprentices in 'the greater London companies came from families already engaged in industry and trade, mostly in the smaller towns and villages'. There was also movement between provincial towns. It is sometimes said that social mobility between the upper classes of the towns and the landed gentry was increasing. It may well be so, though there is little hard evidence except in a few, perhaps unrepresentative, cases. The growing self-confidence and display in urban life may have facilitated mutual acceptance, while Miller suggests that in York declining opportunities in trade could also, by

---

[7] Thrupp, *Merchant Class* [364], 29.

encouraging investment in land, have speeded movement into the gentry.[8]

RELIGION, GUILDS, AND EDUCATION

Until monasteries and chantries were dissolved in the sixteenth century, parish churches, religious houses, and guilds continued to provide much of the framework of local activity which was sketched in chapter four. Though some urban parishes disappeared, many of the churches which survived were enlarged and their aisles, altars, and services were enriched by the multiplication of chantries for intercession on behalf of the living and the dead. Though the endowment of chantries did not enrich the beneficed clergy directly, Londoners at least are known to have made bequests to their parish churches and clergy too, so that many London livings seem to have become richer in the later Middle Ages. Some of the multiplying chantries had permanent endowments and' specially constructed chapels, and many were more or less closely connected with guilds and fraternities of multifarious kinds.[9]

Merchant guilds are still mentioned in some towns, where they seem to have embodied the whole community of enfranchised burgesses under another name. More often they seem to have atrophied, while a newer association, generally an ordinary social and religious guild or fraternity by origin, came to gain a dominant position as the top people's club. Some boasted eminent and even royal members from outside. In Ludlow the dominant guild was called the Palmers' Guild and included in its confraternity merchants and gentry from the midlands, the west country, and Wales. In a number of places the guild of Corpus Christi took the lead, though at Coventry prosperous burgesses transferred from Corpus Christi to the Holy Trinity guild as they moved up the municipal ladder. Where a town was still under seigniorial control a guild of this sort could provide the same sort of forum as merchant guilds had done before: indeed the differences between the two sorts of guild may be more obvious to historians than they were to contemporaries.[10] In larger towns a

[8] Ibid. 191–222, 223n, 312; Barron, 'Sir Richard Whittington' [338], 198–9; Imray, 'Membership of the Mercers' Co.' [353], 167–8; Butcher, 'Origins of Romney Freemen' [403]; *V.C.H. Yorks: York* [444], 109–13; Dyer, *Worcester* [434], 178–9.

[9] *V.C.H. London* [368], i. 208, 224, 226–31, 238; and see e.g. Hamilton Thompson, *Eng. Clergy in Later Middle Ages* [261] and Heath, *Eng. Clergy on the Eve of the Reformation* [140].

[10] *V.C.H. Salop.* [377], ii. 134–40; Phythian-Adams, in *Crisis and Order* [87]; *V.C.H. Leics.* [332], iv. 50–1, 366–7.

whole network of other guilds and fraternities, some connected more or less closely with particular parish churches, catered for other groups. Some admitted women to more or less full membership and some accumulated a good deal of property.

By this time many trades and crafts were coming to be regulated and controlled by organizations of their practitioners, whose powers were, in effect if not explicitly, delegated from the town authorities. These bodies are usually now described as craft guilds though oddly enough the word guild is used less often of them in the sources than in modern literature. The more usual words were the obvious ones—craft or trade (*officium*) or mistery (*mestera, misteria* etc.: from *ministerium*). The word mistery denoted not an association of masters as such (though it was certainly the masters who ran the organizations) nor a mystery in the religious sense (despite the modern talk of 'mystery plays'), but a calling or *métier*.[11]

Most of the guilds of craftsmen, notably weavers and bakers, that are referred to in twelfth-century and early thirteenth-century sources seem to have become submerged when autonomous town governments established their authority. Some guilds and fraternities particularly connected with individual trades no doubt survived, or came and went, but most of the trade organizations of the later Middle Ages seem to have developed anew, as municipal authorities delegated authority to 'searchers' or inspectors in the various trades and industries, and as these powers fell into the hands of leading practitioners of each trade. Since such men might often have a guild or fraternity of their own, with the usual social and religious functions, it might then become the effective governing body of the trade. The balance of power between the town and any particular trade organization varied, and rubs were not infrequent, though friction could be lessened by the way in which members of the more influential merchant crafts tended to dominate town governments too. In 1389 suspicion of secret societies seems to have combined with hope of fiscal profit to prompt a government enquiry into guilds. Its immediate results—apart from returns which are very interesting to historians—are unclear, but in 1437 an act of parliament required guilds and fraternities to register with their local authorities. This probably helped to fortify the dominant guilds while assuring municipal control over them. Subordinate groups within crafts had their own separate fraternities too, which

[11] *Oxford Eng. Dict.* vi (2), 537, 815–16.

were tolerated provided that they were not subversive. Guilds or fraternities of journeymen, of course, easily fell under suspicion, and were banned at moments of conflict when their members might use them for more than the conventional purposes.

To the confusion of historians the sources seem sometimes to use the words guild, company, society, mistery, and craft almost interchangeably for all these bodies.[12] But just because words like guild, fraternity, and society were used so widely, the associations they describe could be very various. Historians have themselves deepened their own confusion by their odd convention of using the word guild in preference to all the others, and then assuming that all guilds were basically trade associations. An elementary barrier to the understanding of late medieval urban associations and their purposes would be removed if those who discuss them would use the key words as they are used in the sources and not beg the question of their meaning.

The most famous trade or craft associations are the London livery companies, as they came to be known.[13] Some London crafts had begun making and registering ordinances by the 1260s, and conflicts both between crafts and between the crafts and the city's rulers are recorded from then on. During the fourteenth century they become better recorded: trouble then revolved around rival claims to trade monopolies, rights of search, and so forth, with some crafts outflanking their opponents by getting royal charters to support their claims. After the disorders of the 1380s all guilds and fraternities fell under suspicion of fostering subversion, which prompted more London crafts to get royal recognition of their ruling guilds—though not always yet explicit recognition of the guild's control over its craft. The possibilities of playing off king and mayor became remote after the statute of 1437 and gradually most of the lines of demarcation became agreed. The internal organization of the crafts was meanwhile becoming more fixed and hierarchical, formally integrating the ruling guilds. Some greater companies were absorbing lesser ones, and the survivors became formally entrenched in the government of the city. Though these processes are sometimes equated with the change from old 'guild'

---

[12] *Eng. Hist. Docs.* [29], iv, pp. 1068, 1088, 1094–5; works cited above, p. 81, n. 23, and Coornaert, ' "L'Origine" des communautés de métiers' [92].

[13] Veale, *Eng. Fur Trade* [268], 101–32 and 'Craftsmen in London Econ.' [367] supersede the old standard interpretation of Unwin, *Gilds* [366], which is very tenuously related to the sources.

to new 'livery company' contemporaries might not have recognized that the concepts differed. The London companies were exceptionally rich and influential but their distinctiveness really came later. There was as yet no clear legal distinction between companies and other craft organizations. In other towns too, though the elaboration and independence of craft organizations varied, some crafts—whether 'incorporated' or not by royal charter—held property, sponsored candidates for burgess freedom, and issued a special dress or 'livery' for their full members to wear on ceremonial occasions.

Some guilds can thus be seen in this period to have served more distinctly sectional interests within towns than are generally discernible in the meagre records of the earlier Middle Ages. In particular the regulation of industry seems to have become more rigid and protectionist in about the same centuries as town governments began to delegate it to the trades or crafts, sometimes though not always organized by guilds. This explains the common belief that 'craft guilds' caused the economic decline of medieval towns through their restrictive practices—or, in some versions, vice versa. Craft associations had a natural tendency to protectionism which they indulged the more readily either when town governments gave them supervisory duties or when economic problems multiplied. Both happened now, though not everywhere and not always at the same time. The formal recognition of trade associations might be a sign of growth, showing that there were enough craftsmen to band together, and perhaps too many and too various for the town to supervise them all directly and together. Or it might be a sign of increasingly fierce competition induced by conditions of saturation or economic decline. No simple or general explanation is likely to fit all cases, but the records would probably respond to more imaginative questions about the causes, purposes, and results of the formation and recognition of trade associations than seem as yet to have been asked in most cases.

All guilds and fraternities continued to serve much more than economic purposes. Burials, masses for the dead, and conviviality for the living were all primary functions. Charity to decayed members or their dependants and public works for the community were secondary but still important. From the mid fifteenth century the Ludlow Palmers' Guild supported a school, contributed to the building and decorating of the parish church as well as paying its choir, and looked after almshouses which had been founded by a member for the brethren. Elsewhere bridges, causeways, and roads were objects of solicitude, while Bristol even had a guild to look after the town records. Guilds frequently held processions on the feast days of their patron saints and, as is well known, crafts in some towns were responsible for shares in regular plays and pageants. Some of the most famous of these were performed at Corpus Christi, a feast first proclaimed in the mid thirteenth century. As it fell in midsummer, a relatively safe time for out-of-door events in England, plays and pageants, some of older origin, tended to accumulate around the Corpus Christi processions enjoined by the papacy. The splendour and expense the festival demanded may well account for the high status of Corpus Christi guilds in many places. In London the procession was provided by the skinners, whose leading fraternity was dedicated to Corpus Christi. In York Corpus Christi plays were organized by the city and performed by the crafts, while the Corpus Christi guild was in charge of the Creed play, which was performed every ten years in the later fifteenth century. There was also a periodical Pater Noster play under the care of its own Pater Noster guild. All this could be very expensive, so that complaints about the burden provide a guide to the relative prosperity of the various guilds or craft organizations and indirectly to that of the trades they more or less accurately represented. In Coventry some of the crafts were from time to time allowed to join together to reduce their expenses.[14] These amalgamations did not affect the work of the actual trades the members practised, which incidentally illustrates the dangers of using craft or guild records to illuminate economic history.

Earlier in the Middle Ages one may guess but cannot prove that literacy in towns was relatively high. Now it increased and so does the evidence for it, not least in the widespread clerical competence displayed in proliferating borough records. A few fifteenth-century towns even had lending libraries. Many towns had elementary or grammar schools by the fourteenth century, and permanent endowments were appearing, so that some of the schools we hear of are more likely to have lasted longer. Foundations multiplied during the fifteenth century, reaching about twelve in each decade by the early sixteenth. Many children must in any case have learnt to read

[14] Stow, *Survey of London* [362], i. 15–16, 91–103; Craig, *Eng. Relig. Drama* [97], 138–44; Johnston, 'Plays of Relig. Guilds of York' [440]; *Crisis and Order* [87], 57–85; *Eng. Hist. Docs.* [29], iv, pp. 1062–7, 1095–6.

and cast accounts in the home or workshop. In 1422 the brewers of London decided to keep their records in English because many of them could read English but not Latin or French. Later in the century some city companies required apprentices to be literate, and Sylvia Thrupp estimates that half the laymen (but not women) of London could probably read. In 1503 a York glazier left to his apprentice 'all my books that is fit for one prentice of his craft to learn by'. Meanwhile the records of commercial lawsuits show English merchants mastering the sophisticated techniques of international credit and exchange which the Italians developed and which the English learned from them both at home and abroad.[15]

Expanding literacy helps to explain the spread of heresy in late medieval England, though both urban and ecclesiastical historians still confront the problems why England—and even its towns—had so little heresy before the late fourteenth century, and how far Lollardy, when it began, took deeper root in towns than in the country. There is no doubt that from the late fourteenth century Bristol, Coventry, Leicester, and of course London—but oddly enough not Norwich—provided reservoirs of dissent and trouble for the hierarchy. In London the parish clergy exacerbated their problems by attempts to increase the amount of offerings made by the citizens under a thirteenth-century commutation of their tithes. In 1514 a London man named Richard Hunne, who was in trouble with the church authorities, was found hanged in his cell in the bishop's prison. The resulting furore revealed widespread anticlericalism in the city, if not, as the bishop alleged, rampant heresy. Much of what is labelled heresy in ecclesiastical sources may have been little more than scepticism and anticlericalism, fanned in London and some other towns by friars who preached against the vices and wealth of the secular clergy. Though more could probably be discovered about individual urban heretics, the evidence of heresy and early protestantism, such as it is, has been relatively well explored, and little more can probably be discovered about its extent.[16]

[15] Orme, *Eng. Schools* [206], 190–217, 272–90, and list of schools pp. 293–322; *Eng. Hist. Docs.* [29], iv, pp. 833, 835–6, 907–22, 1084; *V.C.H. Yorks.: York* [444], 94; *Cal. London P. & M.R. 1381–1412* [345], pp. xxx–xli.

[16] See McFarlane, *John Wycliffe* [182]; Thompson, *Later Lollards* [262] and 'Tithe Disputes in London' [363]; Platt, *Eng. Med. Town* [220], 170–4; Dickens, *Eng. Reformation* [104], 13, 27–33.

Most townsmen, at least among the property-owners, remained within the framework of conventional religion well into the sixteenth century. Borough, guild, and parish records, together with surviving wills, show the traditional ceremonies being held and even elaborated, and the traditional bequests for chantries and other pious purposes being made. In Norwich, despite the poverty of the city's livings, citizens' sons continued to take them up, there was little pluralism, and the number of graduate clergy increased, helped by charitable bequests for their education. The fifteenth century also saw a number of anchorites and anchoresses in Norwich, and for a while two groups of women lived a semi-communal life like the continental béguines without coming under official disapproval or suspicion of heresy.[17] Because of the widespread continuance of conventional piety, and because of the way in which religious practices pervaded urban institutions, the dissolution of the chantries in 1547 and the subsequent attacks on traditional religious ceremonies dislocated the pattern of urban life as much, perhaps, as any event since the Black Death. The statute dissolving chantries condemned the celebration of masses and the maintenance of lights on behalf of the dead, and went on to confiscate such property of all chantries, hospitals, guilds, and fraternities as was devoted to 'the continuance of the said blindness and ignorance'. Guilds and companies for trade were excepted but had to redeem the property that they had hitherto used for 'superstitious' purposes. Most schools and almshouses seem to have been saved or recovered in the end.[18] Whether or not most townspeople now believed wholeheartedly in the doctrines condemned now and in the following decades, their corporate life was surely affected by the amputation of many of the ceremonies that formed the outward and visible sign of a town's inward and social community. The dissolution of the monasteries in the 1530s left physical voids in the centre of many towns. The dissolution of the chantries, followed as it was by the gradual repression of most of the traditional plays and processions, left social voids. Much conviviality and some ceremonies, shorn of their religious content, of course survived, but the religious changes begun and symbolized by the Chantries Act marked as clear a break as any between medieval and later town life.

[17] Tanner, 'Popular Religion in Norwich' [259], 116–29.
[18] 1 Edward VI, c. 14; Dickens, *Eng. Reformation* [104], 205–17 (ref. to printed chantry certificates, ibid. n. 11).

THE STRUCTURE OF GOVERNMENT

Town governments, like other governments, became more complex in the later Middle Ages, officials multiplied, and systems of control were elaborated. Most discussion of the subject has revolved around the question whether they also became more oligarchical or more democratic. Each side has based its contention on assumptions about the character and purpose of earlier arrangements which, as was argued in chapter six, lack much basis in the sources.[19] Although ideological differences may now have been becoming more real, that is not very easy to prove. Some of those who promoted the 'close corporations' of the late fifteenth century and the sixteenth may have been deliberately trying to exclude and muzzle their critics, but many of the constitutional changes which were made during the period seem to have been designed simply to formulate old rules more precisely. They were perfectly compatible with the old, and not quite threadbare, ideals of harmonious hierarchy and consensus.

The trouble about talking in terms of oligarchy and democracy is that oligarchy is a pejorative word: it traditionally implies not merely government by the few, but selfish government by the few. Modern writers tend to assume that all governments of the few must be selfish. Medieval townsmen, however, like Aristotle, thought that government by the few best men—that is, the more prosperous and able as well as the more virtuous—would be good and benevolent: it would be aristocracy and not oligarchy. Fortified by their Christianity, they were also more optimistic than Aristotle in hoping that proper rules for consultation would make it practicable. The conflicts to be discussed in the last part of this chapter did not unambiguously prove them wrong.

Full citizenship—the burgess franchise—was by now generally restricted in larger towns to those who had earned it by apprenticeship, patrimony, or redemption. The new explicitness of this gives an appearance of greater exclusiveness to borough government. That may be only an appearance, though it is given some substance

<hr />

[19] Tait, *Med. Eng. Bor.* [258], 302–38; Bridbury, *Economic Growth* [74], 52–79. Most sources used hereafter for London, Lynn, Norwich, Shrewsbury, and Worcester are cited by Tait. For London, also Thrupp, *Merchant Class* [364]; Bird, *Turbulent London of Richard II* [341]; Barron, 'Gov. of London' [334] and 'Ralph Holland' [336]; for Lynn: *Cal. Inq. Misc. 1399–1422* [19], no. 517; for Worcester: Dyer, *Worcester* [434]. Other works not separately cited below include *V.C.H. Warwicks.* [317], viii and *Coventry Leet Book* [313]; *V.C.H. Yorks. E.R.* i [329]; Hill, *Med. Lincoln* [333]; Platt, *Med. Southampton* [416]; *V.C.H. Yorks.: York* [444].

by a weakening of the old rule that a year and a day's residence in a town enfranchised a villein. The rule was under attack in the early fourteenth century and was abrogated, at least in London and Bristol, in the fifteenth.[20] Changing conditions and concepts made this less damaging to immigrants than it looks. The rule had always been intended to apply only to those in 'scot and lot' in a town. Relatively few unfree immigrants may ever have reached that position, though lords had cared less about recovering fugitive villeins in the old days of plentiful labour. In the meantime many villeins probably still achieved effective freedom at common law by living in towns, though most, as before, did not achieve the status now more clearly defined as the freedom of the borough. Moreover some towns resisted seigniorial suits against villeins in the late fourteenth century and the attempt made in parliament to forbid them to do so was not successful. A hundred years later villeinage had practically disappeared.

In practice towns varied in their policy of enfranchisement. Fourteenth-century weavers and fullers were admitted as burgesses in some towns which had excluded their predecessors. Both London and Oxford objected to enforcing a statute of 1406 requiring apprentices to come from families with at least 20s. annual income, and London got exemption for all persons of free condition, so that poor children, if not villeins, could at least start on the road to citizenship.[21] When York, for instance, raised the fees for citizenship in the late fifteenth century it was probably because trade was bad; the city may have been attracting fewer immigrants anyway. Other variations in policy may have sprung from less obvious motives, and of course some inhabitants of towns preferred not to enjoy a privilege to which onerous duties were attached. The borough franchise might incidentally also be given to influential outsiders, though probably less often than was membership of a guild. A full freemen's list, where it exists, can tell something about the political and economic conditions within which the borough community lived, but it speaks in a very different language from that of a modern electoral register.[22]

There was some trend towards uniformity in the structure of

---

[20] Thrupp, *Merchant Class* [364], 215–17; *Little Red Book of Bristol* [293], i. 37–8; above pp. 100, 123–5.

[21] Thrupp, *Merchant Class* [364], 215–17.

[22] See above, p. 142, n. 8.

urban offices and councils, but it must not be exaggerated. Norwich acquired a mayor in the course of remodelling its constitution on that of London, but Colchester and Worcester, for instance, continued to be ruled by pairs of bailiffs. Other towns showed the early influence of a guild merchant in the survival of one or two aldermen either as substitutes for mayors or in some slightly lower but still senior position. Since guilds were useful sources and custodians of funds the alderman of the guild merchant might, for instance, act as borough treasurer. Systems of consultation also show local variations, partly through the ancient framework of courts within which most councils grew up. In Coventry, for example, government was conducted through the court leet, and in Hereford three 'inquests' represented the townsmen. Some towns, like Worcester, Shrewsbury, and no doubt many smaller places, still seem to have had no permanent council interposed between the community and its officers. Others, like Wilton and, for most of the period, Exeter, had a single council and summoned open assemblies of all the burgesses when fuller consultation was needed. A good many towns, however, were by now ordering their affairs through two concentric rings of counsel; York even had three.

The inner councils, successors of those formally called portmen or jurats, generally numbered twelve or twenty-four members who served for life and were often former mayors or other officers. They were sometimes called the mayor's brethren and tended to be renamed aldermen in later charters of incorporation, occasionally being allocated to separate wards at the same time. Examples of outer councils, which came to be called common councils, can be found from the fourteenth century. They were designed to answer the need for wider consultation that large towns with single councils had already felt in the thirteenth century but had then met by *ad hoc* assemblies. At first they did not necessarily supersede occasional open meetings of burgesses, but might be intended to ensure a minimum, sober, and representative attendance at them. Common councils usually had to be summoned for important elections, the disposal of borough property, and the presentation of annual accounts. Since they generally seem to have deliberated jointly with inner councils it was strictly the joint body, not the outer one alone, that formed the 'common council' of the borough.

It might seem natural to expect that common councils, if not all councils, would be directly elected by the burgesses. This was not always so, but not because of deliberate plots to emasculate them. In London both councils were always elected, though the methods varied. The members of the upper council, that is the aldermen, were elected by wards, generally for life. A requirement of annual elections in 1319 seems to have remained a dead letter until 1376, when it was buttressed by a prohibition against immediate re-election. Though this came at a time of political conflict in the city it did not have very significant results: there was no noticeable widening of the field of aldermen and by 1394 the old system was back. In the fifteenth century vacancies were filled by wards sending in a panel of four names from which the remaining aldermen chose one. The common council was meanwhile becoming fixed as a regular part of the city's constitution. In 1322 a decision was remitted to a meeting of ward representatives from a 'very great commonalty' so as to save the commonalty trouble. In 1376 election by misteries replaced the usual election by wards. That had happened before and it is easy to see how misteries may have been the most cohesive units of civic life as well as the most relevant to current conflicts. Unfortunately the change probably exacerbated the conflicts and, after some discussion of the rival merits of the two systems, ward elections were resumed for good in 1384.

Elsewhere councillors might be chosen by open meetings of burgesses, by an electoral committee, or by the aldermen or borough officers themselves. Borough records nevertheless stress their representative character and it seems unlikely that this emphasis was entirely disingenuous. The very documents that lay down apparently oligarchical systems of co-optative and indirect election result from conflicts about past malpractices. They usually specify elaborate financial checks on the officers, sometimes provide for secret ballots, and often exclude present or recent office-holders from the council. The same mixture of election and co-option appears in the elections of members of single councils. Hull for instance seems to have had a permanent council only from 1440; its members served for life and vacancies were filled by the whole community choosing from two names submitted by the surviving aldermen. Elections of officers were made in the same way and all these meetings, like those to elect members of parliament or transact other important affairs, were summoned by the town bell. Secret ballots were used on occasion. Altogether it seems misleading to draw too hard a line between the 'popularly elected common councils' of London and

Norwich (which copied the forms of London) and the 'not elected' councils of other towns.

The election of councillors needs to be seen alongside the systems of electing and controlling borough officers. In London the election of the mayor was commonly made in an especially large assembly or congregation which was obviously intended to represent the whole community. It comprised mayor, aldermen, common councillors, and additional representatives of the commonalty, though those not summoned were from time to time forbidden to attend. By 1467 most, if not all, of the extra commoners summoned were sent by misteries rather than by wards. From 1475 only the mistery representatives attended, wearing their liveries. How far the requirement of livery was deliberately designed to restrict attendance to an élite is uncertain: companies would prefer to send their more substantial members anyway.[23] That the purpose of controlling attendance was rather to avoid disorder than deliberately to muzzle public opinion is suggested by the elaborate arrangements for voting. By the fifteenth century, and probably earlier, the commoners—both common councillors and others—were to assemble apart from the aldermen and submit the names of two aldermen who had served as sheriffs through the common serjeant as their spokesman. He conveyed their choice to the mayor and aldermen, who withdrew and selected one of the two by secret ballot under the supervision of the common clerk and recorder. To judge from the procedure at Norwich, which was copied from London, the commoners' election was by majority of voices and thus more open to pressures than was the second stage. It is, however, clear that the separation of the stages was designed as much to prevent the influential few from intimidating the humble as to stop the unruly masses from intimidating the aldermen.

In the early fifteenth century the system was copied by Norwich and Lynn with local variations including the free participation of all burgesses at the first stage. Lynn, however, very soon reverted to its older method whereby the alderman of the guild merchant nominated four burgesses who co-opted eight others. This electoral committee, who were not to include members of the council of twenty-four (at that time the only council), then chose the mayor, councillors, and other officers. Like the election of members of

[23] *Cal. London Letter Book L* [344], 132; Thrupp, *Merchant Class* [364], 12–13, 29; Imray, 'Membership of Mercers' Co.' [353], 173–6.

parliament, which was made in rather the same way, this might take place in a large assembly and does not seem designed to avoid all popular participation whatsoever.[24] Norwich too, after forfeiting its liberties because of a riot in 1443, amended the system so that nominations for mayor and sheriff were made by the common councillors and ward constables, not by an open meeting. Elsewhere similar restrictions of participation begin to accumulate, but one may notice that successive ordinances at Shrewsbury, while finally leaving the town council closed and co-optative, at the same time devoted much attention to the regulation of fees and administration in general and to the elaboration of financial checks on the officers. The Worcester ordinances of 1466 are more precise about the avoidance of peculation and undue influence than about methods of election.

This sketchy and inevitably subjective survey suggests that most of the consultative and electoral arrangements of the later Middle Ages still reflected the preoccupations noted in chapter six: to allow such participation by the body of respectable and solid citizens as would equally avoid corruption, domination by cliques, and the disorders of mob rule. Towards the end of the period, however, as constitutional arrangements begin to be precisely set out in new charters of incorporation, more councils became co-optative, more chief officers were to be chosen by councillors.[25] The characteristic 'close corporations' which were to be abolished by the Municipal Corporations Act in 1835 were coming into existence. The acts of parliament which excluded the public from borough elections at Leicester and Northampton blamed divisions and discords there and in other boroughs on the way in which 'such multitude of the said inhabitants, being of little substance and havour [i.e. possessions] and of no sadness [i.e. soberness], discretion, wisdom, nor reason . . . often exceed in their assemblies others that be approved, discreet, sad, and well disposed persons'.[26] Evidently official fear of dissension, disorder, and the lesser burgesses as a whole, outweighed other considerations. Perhaps a deliberate policy of oligarchy was beginning to develop, but the exclusion of office-holders from councils, continued demands for full accounting, and the fact that open meetings

---

[24] For a typically censorious interpretation: Hist. MSS. Comm. *11th Rep.* [378], app. 3, pp. 146–51, 169–70.
[25] *Brit. Bor. Ch. 1307–1660* [16].
[26] *Rot. Parl.* [51], vi. 431–2.

were not always abolished, all suggest that motives at first were far from clear cut.[27] We should not assume that all the irresponsibility and corruption that came to be associated with close corporations were intended or achieved when the constitutional arrangements that introduced them were first set out.

THE ACTIVITIES OF GOVERNMENT

The increasing evidence of municipal activity seems to embody rather a difference of degree than a difference of kind from earlier times. There are few, if any, subjects of concern which are not foreshadowed in the sparser records of the thirteenth century. Many more boroughs can now be seen worrying over public health and public works, and trying to regulate trade and industry. Towns were acquiring much more property and had to spend more time in managing it and more care in accounting for the profits. In some cases property belonged to an élite guild rather than to the town itself, in which case the duties of accounting might be easier but very much the same people would be responsible. Time may have been saved on the day to day supervision of trade and industry when town authorities left it largely to craft and trade associations, but mayor and councillors were still periodically embroiled when inter-craft disputes or trade recessions made the regulations both more controversial and more necessary.

It is sometimes said that towns were becoming more protectionist. Many of their economic controls were, however, imposed for traditional purposes which were individually uncontroversial in principle, though mutually incompatible and likely to injure particular interests in practice. The protection of burgesses' trade was always as much a duty of the community as was the securing of cheap supplies. Which took precedence in individual towns depended on the balance of influence in the town council and on circumstances which varied from place to place and from time to time. Economic policies were in any case liable to be both inconsistent and ineffective, partly because of the difficulties of the economic problems, partly because of the need to balance interests, and partly because towns could not always enforce what they decided. Suburbs and enclaves of ecclesiastical jurisdiction, for instance, housed traders who were exempt from craft controls, though this was a

---

[27] Below, pp. 185–7; on later developments, Thomas, *Town Gov. in 16th Cent.* [260]; Clark and Slack, *Crisis and Order* [87], 20–5 *et passim*.

smaller problem than it became after the Dissolution when the sites of religious houses were built over.

In 1353 staple courts, which dealt mainly with merchants and their debts, were set up in a number of important trading places. The list varied slightly from time to time, and so did the relationship between staple and borough courts, but they seem to have become gradually integrated into local merchant life. The mayors of the Westminster and Bristol staples at least were often mayors or ex-mayors of London and Bristol respectively, so that staple courts seem to have given leading townsmen further scope for work and influence.[28] Many borough courts meanwhile gained in jurisdiction and became more uniform as they acquired their own sessions of the peace, in which typically the mayor, the recorder, and perhaps some of the aldermen became justices. Some of the more archaic customs like compurgation were beginning to go, and intermittent distinctions were beginning to be made between the legal and administrative business of town assemblies.

One apparently new subject of concern was common rights in the land around the town, which might become controversial when landowners sought to enclose their holdings and extinguish common rights over them. In Coventry for instance the extensive Lammas and Michaelmas lands (respectively open to grazing at these dates each year) were incompatibly valuable both to graziers producing wool for the cloth industry, and to the numerous burgesses who counted on their common rights to feed the odd horse or cow and to give themselves fresh air and exercise. Not surprisingly the attitude of the leet is described as 'persistently ambivalent', for it winked at riots against outside enclosers, but was severe to those which protested against enclosures made by a prominent guild or townsman. At York the poor mayor, caught between landowners and commonalty, was carpeted by the king in 1494 and told that if he did not control his townsmen, 'I must and will put in other rulers that will rule and govern the city according to my laws'.

Another apparently new or enlarged threat to public order came from beggars and vagabonds. In August 1418 the civic authorities in London ordered vagrant beggars to go away and help with the harvest. In November 1475 another order to expel them was presumably more directed at the maintenance of local order than at the shortage of agricultural labour. Romney from 1484, Coventry

[28] Rich, 'Mayors of Staples' [235]; *Staple Court Books of Bristol* [296], 50–63.

from the 1490s and repeatedly from 1517, and York from 1501 were trying to get rid of vagabonds. The problem of beggars and poor relief was to absorb an increasing amount of urban and indeed national attention in the sixteenth century.[29]

There are far fewer references in borough records to national politics than the beginner in urban history tends to expect. Men and money had of course to be found in wartime and the larger towns in particular lent the government large sums. All this furnished subject for discussion and occasional acrimony, while the supposed or real needs of defence in troubled times produced miles of new or repaired walls. The impulse to improve defences came quite often from royal command rather than from burgess timidity, and some towns tried to economize on their walls or to secure state aid towards them. Coventry spread the construction of its large circuit over more than a century. In the event few towns suffered much from either French raids or civil wars. There is little evidence that their rulers took much interest in national conflicts except so far as local interests might be affected. Parliamentary elections were probably rarely contested and some boroughs accepted representation by the growing number of outsiders who offered to pay their own expenses.[30]

Where the activities of town governments seem to change most is in their development of dignity and ceremony. This is unlikely to be just an illusion of better records. Civic pride and patriotism, at once the cause and effect of local autonomy, naturally grew as urban institutions, both political and social, became more established. The records of Colchester burst into sudden panegyric over the achievements of a bailiff of 1373–4: his beautification of the guildhall, his provision of a new market and revival of an old fair, his skill at securing good terms in town leases and at getting outsiders to contribute to town taxes, and even his benevolence to prisoners in the town gaol. The record looks as if it was inspired or even composed by the bailiff himself. Its combination of civic patriotism with personal enjoyment of success and influence conveys the essence of established and secure town life.[31] With self-confidence came

[29] Cal. London Letter Book I [344], 196; ibid. L, 136; Butcher, 'Origins of Romney Freemen' [403]; and see above, p. 171, n. 19.
[30] Eng. Hist. Docs. [29], iv, pp. 562–3, 580–5, 1104–6; Turner, Town Defences [266], 80–4; Keen, Eng. in Later Middle Ages [164], 341; Barron, 'Gov. of London' [334], 324–35.
[31] Red Paper Book of Colchester [310], 5–11.

ceremony, stimulated by a growth of conspicuous consumption and display which went all through late medieval life. It was in the fifteenth century that the mayor of London began to be called lord mayor and gained precedence, while in the city, even over the archbishops and the king's brothers. Insults to mayor and aldermen in London and in lesser towns were often treated with a solemnity which to us verges on the ridiculous. Pomposity may have seemed the more necessary because powers of enforcement were weak and because burgesses, being so much of a rank, could rely relatively little on the habitual deference of a stratified society to protect the dignity of their officers.

Town councils spent a good deal of time therefore in organizing processions and pageantry as well as in feasting and liveries. The Corpus Christi and other plays at Chester, Coventry, York, and elsewhere, of which records and texts survive, bear witness to the rich ceremonial life which developed in medieval towns and of which the modern lord mayor's show is a fossilized relic. Fifteenth-century references to the mayor of London's annual swearing-in at Westminster suggest that it was then becoming an occasion for an important civic procession. As yet it was fairly formal, however, and the more exciting displays were reserved to the midsummer watch, royal visits, and so forth. Feasting too served as what the sociologically inclined call 'structurally integrative commensality', promoting unity and good fellowship among townsmen. Participation in ceremonies was thus a duty as well as a privilege and both individuals and crafts sometimes felt aggrieved by the costs imposed upon them. Economic benefits might of course follow: ideally pageants and plays, like modern 'festivals', not only proclaimed but promoted prosperity by attracting business to the town. Even kings and queens attended the Coventry plays sometimes in the fifteenth century.[32]

It has been suggested that by the early sixteenth century the burden of time and money which the multifarious activities and ceremonies of municipal government imposed was driving prosperous citizens out of the towns, and that this, rather than the restrictions of councils and guilds, was what created a crisis in many sixteenth-century towns.[33] Lincoln and York were certainly worried by refusals to hold office in the mid fifteenth century, Worcester

[32] See above, p. 168, n. 14.
[33] See above, p. 158; cf. Dobson, 'Urban Decay' [108].

doubled the fine for refusal between 1466 and 1496, and other examples could be cited. Reluctance to serve might be explained by economic difficulties: the fewer the prosperous burgesses the greater the burden they had to share. The uncertainties of the economic trends, however, turn this into a circular argument. It is important to notice chronology and to distinguish the fixing of penalties from evidence of actual evasion of office—and the reason for it. Refusal to serve was almost unknown in Worcester by the mid sixteenth century, and in contemporary Oxford a burgess who refused office was nevertheless allowed—and apparently willing—to take the appropriate part in processions. Evidently it was not always ceremony that repelled.[34] If the phenomenon really increased it may have reflected as much a change in attitudes as in the wealth and numbers of the burgesses. In 1383 and 1414 two burgesses of Southampton had secured royal grants of exemption from local service. One, who served as mayor nine times, does not appear to have used it, and the other did so only after being bailiff as often. Public spirit may have been wilting by the sixteenth century. The evidence deserves further investigation.

ECONOMIC AND POLITICAL CONFLICT

Conflict, both political and economic, is sometimes said to have become more intense in urban society during the later Middle Ages. It certainly becomes more visible in the sources and that may well reflect a more conscious acceptance of its existence by contemporaries, if not an intensification of the phenomenon and its causes. To some extent, however, historians may simply have found what they were looking for: whereas English towns of the earlier Middle Ages have been studied too much in isolation from each other and from towns overseas, some of the textbook versions of their later history suggest too ready an acceptance of analogies drawn from elsewhere.[35] The theory that a revolution of 'the crafts' against 'the patricians' left most towns both more democratic and more protectionist is taken from older accounts of great cities in the Netherlands, Germany, and Italy. Since few English towns had either industries of comparable size and organization or merchant capitalists on the same scale there are plenty of reasons why the model

---

[34] Thomas, *Town Gov. in 16th Cent.* [260], 35–6.
[35] As Gross pointed out: *Gild Merchant* [136], ii. 109.

should not fit them. In fact it has meanwhile been modified by some
of those who have more recently studied some of the original
exemplars.[36] Chapter four has already argued that it is unhelpful to
call dominant townsmen patricians, chapter six that the evidence of
economic or class conflict between governors and governed in
thirteenth-century towns is slight. Many of the cautions expressed
there apply to the later period too. Uncertainty about the whole
theory is enhanced by the way it seems to be applied with equal
facility to both thirteenth-century and fourteenth-century towns in
very varying economic conditions. Nevertheless the growing
evidence of apparently economic conflicts, both within and between
crafts, needs some further examination.

It is reasonable to suppose that in those towns where trade
contracted in the later Middle Ages economic jealousies may have
become more acute, for instance between competing masters in the
same craft, between crafts with overlapping interests, between
merchant-importers and local craftsmen, and between masters and
servants. The delegation of municipal controls over trade and industry to craft organizations, together with the proliferation of
separate societies and fraternities for separate groups within the
crafts, enabled all these organizations to express their discontents
more coherently and to get them recorded. Perhaps they therefore
came to formulate and develop them more radically. One class can,
however, be disposed of quite easily: the journeymen, apprentices,
and other wage-earners, most of whom were not burgesses and thus
remained outside the town community. One would imagine that
they had most reason of all for discontent, but the evidence about
them seems to be scarce. That may partly be because, unlike the
evidence concerning the peasants, it has not been very much
searched for and studied. On present knowledge one can only conclude tentatively that so far as there was an English urban pro-
letariat, it was less revolutionary than were the peasants.

The first recorded conspiracy to put up wages seems to be one by
carpenters in London in 1299, but they were probably master
craftsmen rather than servants of the usual wage-earning sort. There
was a flurry of prosecutions of London masters and servants under
the labour legislation after the Black Death and a trickle of similar

---

[36] For foreign towns see above, pp. 119, n. 3, and 140, n. 1; Lane, *Venice* [169];
Mollat and Wolff, *Ongles bleus, Jacques et Ciompi* [198]: Eng. trans. (1973) not recom-
mended; Reimann, *Unruhe und Aufruhr in Braunschweig* [231].

cases can be found in various towns thereafter.[37] Nevertheless there seems to be remarkably little evidence of widespread response to the Peasants' Revolt from the urban poor. Canterbury, Rochester, and Norwich were all invaded by rebels and some townspeople joined in the rioting. At Yarmouth the destruction of a town charter implies jealousies from outside, and at Bridgewater, Bury, Cambridge, St. Albans, and Winchester hostility was directed against ecclesiastical lords or liberties, not against a ruling group within the urban community. The exceptions were York, Beverley, Scarborough, and of course London. In the first three the rising seems to have given opportunities to those already embroiled in disputes; where a class element appears it was the lesser burgesses, not the actually unenfranchised, who played the revolutionary part. If, as R. B. Dobson suggests, the attacks on the walls and gates of ecclesiastical liberties at York reflect resentment at the liberties' exemption from economic regulations, then they are all the more likely to have been mounted by freemen of the city. In London both chronicles and records suggest that a small number of prosperous dissidents combined with many poorer men. Disorder of the kind the capital suffered would naturally be most beguiling to the poorest, but even so the evidence is really too slight to support suggestions that the rebels in general or most of them came 'from the lowest classes' or the non-citizens.[38]

During the fifteenth century masters are recorded on occasion as trying to keep wages down and journeymen as trying to raise them, but conflicts seem less open. At Coventry journeymen were allowed to form associations provided that they registered them with the mayor. Beyond that we may guess that apprentices, journeymen, and other 'foreigns' joined in such riots and protests as the century afforded, but we have no reason to suppose that they contributed more, or as much, to them as did their employers, the burgesses, themselves. Whether or not any 'craft revolution' brought greater democracy, pressure from the unenfranchised poor was not very significant.

At first sight London seems to fit the model of a craft revolution against the old oligarchy quite well. Throughout the fourteenth

[37] *Cal. London E.M.C.R.* [343], 25; *Mun. Gild. Lond.* [357], i. 33–4, 52, 99; *Cal. London P. & M.R. 1323–64* [345], 108, 225–35; *1364–81*, 291–4.

[38] Dobson, *Peasants' Revolt* [107], 13–14, 32, 127–8, 139–41, 145–7, 239–42, 256, 269–96, and 'Admissions to Freedom of York' [438], 12–13; Bird, *Turbulent London* [341], 52–6, 132–3.

century the crafts were often the vehicle of grievances against the
city's rulers and they ended with formal representation in its
constitution. On closer inspection, however, the troubles of the
fourteenth century seem to have sprung from a tangle of different
conflicts which had no ideological or even political motivation
except to assuage particular grievances. Various groups, particularly
those selling provisions, tried to establish trade monopolies and were
resisted by consumers; merchants dependant on overseas trade were
caught between aliens and home producers, and tended to side with
the former; crafts like the saddlers and saddle-tree-makers or the
skinners and tawyers skirmished between themselves; and the mass
of relatively poor citizens—mostly craftsmen—girded intermittently, as they had done for well over a hundred years, at the corruptions
and oppressions of the rich. Ruth Bird, studying the city in Richard
II's reign, showed that the apparent triumph of the crafts or 'non-
victualling party' in 1376 reflected many of these cross-currents.
Like Thomas fitz Thomas, a rather similar popular reformer of the
thirteenth century,[39] the leader, John of Northampton, was soon
ousted and his constitutional measures were largely reversed, so that
power and influence returned to the city's traditional rulers. As they
were mostly merchants one might say it was a victory of the mercantile interests but that would be over-simple and unfair. The city
government did not thereafter crush the non-mercantile craftsmen
in any crude way. In the 1440s, for instance, it handled a dispute
between the influential and merchant drapers and the less influential
and mainly artisan tailors with fair restraint, considering the dangerous way the tailors' leader attacked its authority. The crafts meanwhile continued to operate under civic control and though the
freedom of the city was attained through membership of a company,
freedom to trade in any commodity was not restricted to members of
the appropriate company. The pressures of influence and corruption
seem to have been more complex and latterly more restrained at a
corporate level than the model of a craft revolution implies.

Elsewhere the model fits even less well, which is not surprising
considering how few in most towns were really rich men with
distinctively mercantile interests: the majority of burgesses everywhere depended on relatively small-scale industries and local trade.
Economic policies varied from time to time and sometimes aroused
bitterness, but they were seldom supported by consistent parties or

[39] See pp. 131-2.

groups. Part of the attraction of the 'craft revolution' for historians may have been that it imposes meaning on disparate scraps of information which are otherwise difficult to evaluate. In 1430 Winchester allowed anyone except butchers and fishmongers to trade freely, even retail, but the measure was reversed at an unknown date probably soon after.[40] It looks simply like a desperate and unsuccessful attempt to overcome the prolonged depression from which the town suffered. Coventry applied demarcation between crafts and trades more strictly than London did, but it is no easier here than in London to determine how far that reflects the particular interests of particular classes, or even any consistent and deliberate economic policy at all. The structure of medieval industry did not favour the development and expression of economic class interests any more than did the values of medieval government. Urban society, while undoubtedly stratified, resembled a trifle rather than a cake: its layers were blurred, and the sherry of accepted values soaked through them. People seem to have resented not inequality but the misuse of authority by *potentes* over *inferiores*.

As in the preceding period, therefore, it was the control of power that was the basic issue in most recorded conflicts, and misgovernment rather than discontent with the political system as such that provoked them. There are hints that the repetition of grievances was beginning to provoke firmer statements on both sides, but these hover on the verge of radicalism rather than plunging into it. It is easier to find evidence of deliberate attempts to exclude the mass of burgesses from sharing power than of the burgesses' desire to assume regular responsibility. In Norwich persistent complaints, characteristically of rigged elections, unfair trading, and fiscal malversation by the rich and powerful, provoked the response that the complainants alleged 'that every person of the least reputation... should have as much authority and power in all the elections and other affairs . . . as the most sufficient persons'.[41] If they really made such a claim they were undoubted revolutionaries, but we may doubt whether most, if any, of them seriously believed in political equality. At York the commonalty claimed in 1475 that 'forasmuch as we be all one body incorporate, we think that we be all alike privileged [including any] of the commonalty which has borne none office in the city', but this was the preamble to a demand that chamberlains should be appointed only from former bridgemasters, and bridge-

[40] Gross, *Gild Merchant* [136], ii. 261–2.   [41] *Rec. of Norwich* [389], i. 81.

masters from 'the most able men in goods and discretion'. Riots and disorders when they occurred nearly all happened at mayoral elections—the one time when all burgesses normally had a right and duty to turn out and protest against wrongs—provided that they *were* burgesses and did not riot. The royal government, noble and ecclesiastical arbitrators, and many townsmen alike recognized the force behind many of these protests: wrongs were committed which they thought could best be righted by requiring strict accountability to as full and representative a body of burgesses as could be trusted not to cause disorder.

When conflicts became bitter, as at Norwich and Lynn in the early fifteenth century, then attitudes hardened. At Lynn one mayor recognized the political possibilities of the franchise and gave it to persons of small worth and reputation in return for support. A Chancery decree during his mayoralty acknowledged the irreconcilability of groups within the town when it gave separate representation on a council to the more powerful, the middling, and a category called '*inferiores* not burgesses', who seem to have lived outside the borough proper under the bishop's jurisdiction. The system evolved for mayoral elections in London recognized the permanence of potential conflict between rulers and commonalty by the two separate stages of voting and the two separate spokesmen. During the 1440s London elections were in fact repeatedly disturbed by disputes between the aldermen and a rebellious section of the commonalty representing the artisan misteries. At one stage a leading malcontent was alleged to have said that the mayor was not mayor of those who had not elected him, so that those excluded from the election could withdraw their obedience. He denied it, however, and the revolt petered out.

The general impression left by the records which have been consulted is that most subjects demanded only the traditional and accepted right of consultation and objected only to the traditional evils of peculation and misgovernment. A wider and deeper search through the records might well produce a different conclusion. If, however, it is true that radicalism did not develop far, then the reason may be that, whether because of stricter controls or for economic and social reasons, and despite the increased opportunities of corruption afforded by enlarged borough property, town government in the fifteenth century looks rather less corrupt than it had been earlier—or than it was to be later, when councils had got used to being 'closed'. The corporate solidarity of rulers which was beginning to produce closed corporations, in so far as it was corrupt, shows as yet the simple corruption of individuals by power and fear of trouble rather than a deliberate desire to keep the fruits of office for a ruling class against the common interest. The old political values may have been wearing out but they had not yet been replaced by anything else.

CONCLUSION

Writers about late medieval society have sometimes been tempted to award marks to it, or withhold them, for being better or worse than the twelfth and thirteenth centuries. The result is subjective. Even if we could agree on a measurement of welfare or happiness we know far too little about the towns of late medieval England to be able to apply it. Much more could be learnt from the surviving records, but even when they have been fully explored, so that the questions posed here—and many others—can be better answered, it would probably be wiser to think in terms of change than of improvement or degeneration. In the meantime it may not involve falling into the same trap to suggest that, despite reductions in population and economic vicissitudes, the corporate life of English towns became more complex and richer, perhaps thereby giving a new confidence to their prominent citizens. Sir William de la Pole (d. 1366), first mayor of Hull, was 'the first merchant promoted to the high military rank of banneret for mainly *financial* services to the crown, while his son Michael provided the earliest recorded example of a merchant's son raised to the peerage'.[42] Sir Richard Whittington (d. 1423) seems to be the first townsman to become a national folk-hero. Whether or not ceremony weighed too heavily on urban society and economy by 1500, there is no doubt that it meanwhile helped townspeople to sustain their dignity against the outside world in a way that was important to them at the time. When the lord treasurer of the kingdom was given precedence over the mayor of London at a city dinner in 1464 the mayor withdrew quietly with most of the aldermen and laid on an equally splendid feast 'both of cygnet and other delicacies enough' in his own house at a moment's notice. 'And so the worship of the city was kept and not lost.'[43]

---

[42] Fryde, *Wool Accounts of William de la Pole* [128], 4.
[43] *Eng. Hist. Docs.* [29], pp. 1103–4.

9

A Postscript on Topography

So far this book has only touched in passing on the physical appearance and layout of towns. To many people that must seem extraordinary and wrong, for much of the most interesting work published recently on English medieval towns has dealt with archaeology, town plans, and other aspects of urban topography. Even a book like this, which concentrates on towns as societies, and on their political and economic institutions, must use topographical evidence to give form to disembodied statements, just as the urban archaeologist, for instance, relies on written sources to recreate the society and thoughts of those who lived in the structures he excavates. One can no more separate the topographical history of a town, its streets and buildings, from the history of urban society than one can separate the physical appearance of a human being from his personality. Both aspects are essential and interdependent. Unfortunately it is not very practical to try to be equally well-informed—let alone expert—on all the disciplines that the ideal urban historian needs. This chapter, therefore, sketches some of the most obvious subjects for urban topographical study from the point of view of those who, like myself, start from documentary evidence, are primarily concerned with urban society, and have no archaeological or architectural expertise. Even from this starting point there is a good deal that we can learn—and that we cannot afford to do without—if we use maps, eyes, and feet.[1]

The information about a town's medieval past that can be derived from looking at it today is at once greater and more difficult to interpret than is always realized. It must of course be supplemented by maps, views, and straight documentary sources. The very few maps and views from before 1500 are too formalized to be much use, but later ones can tell a lot about the medieval state of a town pro-

---

[1] See e.g. Hoskins, *Making of Eng. Landscape* [152] and *Local Hist. in Eng.* [151]; Beresford, *Hist. on the Ground* [66] and *New Towns* [67]; Dymond, *Archaeology for the Historian* [116] and *Archaeology and History* [115].

vided they are combined with as much information as possible about the intervening changes. The outward appearance of most towns changed much more in the past than popular belief allows. The nostalgic image of 'Old London', 'Old Barchester', or 'Old Anywhere' is unreal. Buildings were always being put up, taken down, and altered, and many which are locally reputed to be medieval or Tudor are not. Nevertheless property units, street plans, and the backs and insides of houses change more slowly than street fronts; when they do change they often leave traces which may appear in later maps or in air photographs. For this reason a basic tool for the topographer is a large-scale Ordnance Survey map—and, unlike earlier maps, the Ordnance Survey covers every town in the country. The first edition of the 25-inch and 6-inch maps was produced between 1840 and 1893 and some towns were surveyed on a still larger scale. Even in places which had been outwardly transformed since 1500 these maps or plans form an indispensable companion to topographical field-work concerned with the Middle Ages.[2]

Traditionally historians have not used either maps or feet enough. In trying to remedy this, and to learn as much as possible from the geographer, archaeologist, and architectural historian, the local historian must remember not to be so blinded by the dazzle of other disciplines that he forgets his own. If he does he is useless to his colleagues, who need his critical study of written sources. Co-operation is essential. The archaeological information about early Anglo-Saxon towns would be much less revealing and much harder to date precisely without Bede's account of seventh-century bishops and kings. We could deduce a good deal from the map about how St. Albans grew, but the abbey chronicle tells us when it happened and how the abbot encouraged it. The excavations of Winchester set a new standard at least partly because of the equally skilled and critical study of documentary evidence with which they are combined.[3] It is often difficult to weigh one sort of evidence against another and particular care must be taken with what is sometimes called 'topographical evidence'. Topography can much more often show what was likely than prove what actually happened. The geographer can deduce from analysing a large-scale plan how a town may have developed, and the historian can learn much from a skilled

[2] Barley, *Guide to Brit. Topog. Colls.* [1]; Lobel, 'Early Maps' [7]; Harley, *Maps for the Local Historian* [5]; Harley and Phillips, *Historian's Guide to O.S. Maps* [6].

[3] e.g. Keene, 'Winchester: the Brooks Area' [430]; and see above, pp. 11, 23, 33-4.

geographer's observations. But he must not take on trust that that
is what did happen. Geographers occasionally base their deductions
on what to the historian may seem inadequate evidence and super-
ficial knowledge of medieval conditions. It is up to the historian to
say so, and to provide the geographer with better information and
constructive criticism.[4]

The first and most obvious question to ask of a town's topography
is how, when, where, and why the town started, and the next is how
it grew and changed. It is of course essential to look outside the
town as well as inside for the answers, and to consider its situation
against the background of its immediate neighbourhood and region.
Roads, rivers, and county and parish boundaries, all of which may
have changed course and cannot be taken on trust in their modern
form, are often suggestive. The importance to Salisbury of Harnham
Bridge can be appreciated only if successive changes in the roads out
of the town to the south and west are understood,[5] just as the origin
of Salisbury itself can be understood only in relation to Wilton and
Old Sarum. The relation between external roads and rivers and the
plan of streets inside can suggest the relative importance of through
traffic, though here too successive changes can make connections
obscure. Roman Colchester was built, like other Roman towns,
around a cross-roads, but G. H. Martin points out how the block-
ing of the west gate in the fourth or fifth century has determined
the town's rather curious plan ever since.[6]

Within a town, maps and documents can often between them be
interpreted to reveal an original focal point or points. Bridges,
market-places, and churches are obvious examples, though all
present problems. A bridge may have been moved or may replace an
earlier ford on a different site. While topography can suggest the
best early fording or bridging point, only excavation or documents
can prove which was actually used. Central market-places may have
shrunk or disappeared through progressive encroachments, but their

---

[4] For a good example of the geographer's approach, see Conzen, *Alnwick* [288], and of
confirmation of deductions from topography by archaeology and documents, see Ramm,
'Twelfth-century Town Planning in York' [442]; R. Com. Hist. Mon. *York* [443], iii.
125; Addyman, 'Excavations in York' [435], 227. *The Atlas of Historic Towns* [60] com-
bines maps and commentaries with varying degrees of synthesis between topographical
and documentary evidence.

[5] Clearly described in Rogers, 'Salisbury' [407], 3 (cf. *V.C.H. Wilts.* [408], iv. 255,
257), though not shown on accompanying map.

[6] Dickinson, 'Town Plans of E. Anglia' [106]; Martin, 'The Town as Palimpsest'
[191], 160.

old extent may still be discernible on a map. Islands of buildings inside former market-places often started as market stalls which then gradually became more substantial; their origin may be betrayed by their lack of yards or gardens.[7] As for churches, many towns had several by the twelfth century or so, and successive rebuildings and the scarcity of documentary evidence before 1086 (or even later) may make the earliest hard to identify. The proximity of an early market-place is one possible clue, while the shape of parishes sometimes suggests how one has been cut out of another. Given the pressures against alterations, many of the parish boundaries marked on the first large-scale Ordnance Survey maps may have been unchanged, or changed only in detail, since the parishes were formed. It is, however, important to use maps surveyed before the nineteenth-century rationalizations begun by the Divided Parishes Act, 1876; to combine them with earlier evidence like medieval deeds which mention the parishes in which identifiable properties lay; and to remember that the presumption of stability is only a presumption. Alan Rogers has used topography, documents, and parish boundaries inside and around the two towns to postulate the sites of the original Danish boroughs of Nottingham and Stamford, and of the Norman castles, boroughs, and markets alongside. He suggests that parishes including large areas of the town's lands outside are likely to be early, and that purely urban parishes, particularly where they look like enclaves cut from others, are likely to be later. Early boundaries are more likely to follow 'natural features or roads, later ones the backs of tenements.[8]

Few towns have grown steadily from a single focal point. An earlier generation of continental historians talked of the 'topographical duality' of north European towns, which they thought derived from the combination of an old 'pre-urban nucleus' with a mercantile suburb. Now their successors find evidence that many towns developed around several simultaneous or successive nuclei. English towns may have been less complex at first than the towns of Gaul, for instance: here the earliest churches could often be put right inside Roman walls, whereas there they had first been established outside. Churches also multiplied sooner in Gaul than

[7] Martin and McIntyre, *Bibliog. of Munic. Hist.* [9], i, pp. 393–5; Martin, 'The Town as Palimpsest' [191], 163.

[8] Rogers, 'Parish Boundaries and Urban Hist.' [237]; Campbell, 'Norwich' [385], 4–5, 9, 23 (a warning on unrecorded boundary changes); Tanner, 'Popular Religion in Norwich' [259], 11–30.

they did in England, so that some towns in Merovingian Gaul were
surrounded by a network of focal points for future urban growth.
Other post-Roman developments, however, affected England too,
like the shift from road to river transport, which added riverside
suburbs to York and Lincoln just as it did to Lyons. The whole
relationship between Roman and medieval topography, in fact, sets
a series of problems to which archaeology is beginning to provide
some rather surprising answers.

Although English towns started on sites which were relatively
uncomplicated by 'pre-urban nuclei', there is no doubt that they
developed their own complications later. Norman castles and separate
Norman boroughs are obvious examples, while new bridges, new
markets, and new or enlarged churches came to distort old plans
and stimulate new growth. From about 1100 the bishop and the
cathedral priory of Norwich each owned part of Lynn (now King's
Lynn), and the two halves, separated by a water-course, developed
around their respective churches and market-places. A third unit,
South Lynn, with yet another church just beyond another water-
course, remained a largely agricultural suburb.[9]

Some of the new growth of the twelfth century and later, both in
old towns and new, is often talked of as 'planned'. That is because
many new towns are known to have been fostered or 'planted' by
kings and other landowners, and a 'planted' town is sometimes
assumed to be the same as a 'planned' town—that is a town with a
completely planned layout. Presumably some degree of planning on
the ground always accompanied a foundation on a virgin site, but
most often it amounted to no more than the laying out of a market-
place bordered by a row of burgage tenements, possibly of uniform
dimensions. If the town flourished, more streets would be added,
but generally without any further planning or co-ordination. The
original 'plan' might still be detectable in the layout of the town
centre, though proof of deliberate planning would probably demand
documentary confirmation.

Some plans were more extensive, taking the form of a rectilinear
grid or chequer-board of streets, generally centred on a market-
place and sometimes leaving a whole chequer or 'island' for a church.
Salisbury and New Winchelsea spring to mind from the thirteenth

---

[9] See above, pp. 9–10, 14, 20, 26; Colvin, 'Domestic Architecture and Town-
Planning' [90], i. 52–3; Parker, *Making of King's Lynn* [379], 19–24. Detection of an
early church and its influence on topography: Lambrick, 'Abingdon' [286], 26–34.

century, though as M. W. Beresford points out they are very un-
typical: most foundations of the period were much less ambitious.
It has been suggested that as early as the tenth century some at least
of the boroughs fortified by the West Saxon kings were also given
grid plans.[10] That is quite likely, for it accords well with the impression of royal authority conveyed by the planning and execution
of the fortifications, but we should note that the topographical
evidence of a grid plan, whether in the tenth century or later, is not
always unambiguous. Approximate grids can, for instance, develop
gradually around a cross-roads, particularly if it is surrounded by a
rectangle of walls.

We should not be made anxious to find grid plans everywhere by
thinking of them as a particular achievement or mark of aesthetic or
technical advancement, and by contrasting the classical, planned grid
with the quaint medieval simplicity of an unplanned town like
Lavenham, where 'simple carving of the trusty oak was a pleasant
frill . . . but there is no urban style . . . [and] building materials and
methods were poorly adapted to making sophisticated experiments'.[11] Though surveying techniques were as yet primitive, a
society which produced parish churches like Lavenham's—let alone
the cathedrals—or even one which constructed the tenth-century
boroughs, could certainly lay out a simple grid plan. A town plan is
as much the product of undivided authority, exercised on a site attracting enough tenants to justify it, as of either a particular tech-
nique or a particular aesthetic. That a town looks to us tidily or
untidily laid out is not sufficient evidence that its ground plan was or
was not determined at a single moment.

The difficulty of analysing and dating medieval town plans is not
merely one of finding documentary evidence of purpose to corrobor-
ate topographical evidence of results, but of assessing the topographical evidence itself. W. H. St. J. Hope, writing in 1909, suggested that
Ludlow had been laid out after the Conquest on a grid plan which
had then become distorted by the enlargement of the castle in the
west and the disappearance of two streets to the south. M. R. G.
Conzen, in a preliminary study based on scrutiny of the modern Ordnance Survey plans, was able to detect five 'plan units', which he

[10] See above, pp. 30–1; Beresford, *New Towns* [67], 150 *et passim*; Biddle and Hill,
'Late Saxon Planned Towns' [69]; Biddle, 'Winchester: Development of Early Capital'
[429], 248–54.
[11] Johns, *British Townscapes* [159], 54. For a rare example of a street planned in
elevation: Martin, *The Town* [190], pl. 6.

suggested might represent different stages of development. His analysis is far more subtle than Hope's and is informed by increased knowledge and experience of similar studies elsewhere. Even so it is fair to note that his thirteenth-century 'planned southward extension', like Hope's single twelfth-century plan and lost southward roads, depends entirely on judgement of topographical probabilities. Neither study is—or claims to be—based on evidence of what in fact happened: whether such evidence exists is another matter.[12]

There are many possible pointers to the stages of a town's growth, though most may be maddeningly absent in any given case. Deeds and other documents may mention street names, which are helpful even if the first occurrence of a name comes, as it well may, many years after the street itself was there. Both names and courses of streets may, however, have changed more readily in the Middle Ages than they do now, so that it can be very misleading to talk of 'the medieval name' of a street and to base topographical deductions on its distinct and permanent identity.[13] The foundation of churches and the division of parishes are suggestive of growth despite the loose correlation between population and parishes. The boundaries of urban jurisdiction—often farther out than the walls or ditches though with enclaves within—are also significant, though they are often hard to establish, and their appreciation demands knowledge of changing legal, constitutional, and probably ecclesiastical conditions.[14] The walls themselves may or may not indicate the limit of the built-up area at any one time: that depends whether they were inherited from the Romans or laid out thereafter; whether this was before or after the town started to grow; whether it then grew as expected; and whether if it did they were then enlarged or not. Vanished walls and gates have often left traces, most obviously in a wide wedge-shaped street leading out from a gate, often with a suburban church and early ribbon development beside it.[15]

The existence of suburbs does not, of course, imply that the space inside a town was full. Relative costs, the needs of shipping, and jurisdictional boundaries alike encouraged suburban growth. London still had many open spaces long after it was ringed with housing

---

[12] 'Ancient Topography of Ludlow' [376]; 'Use of Town Plans' [91].

[13] Ramm, 'Town Planning in York' [442], especially on Monkgate; Campbell, 'Norwich' [385], 24–5.

[14] See above, p. 84; Webb, *Eng. Local Gov.* [276], ii. 279, 288–90; *V.C.H. Yorks.: York* [444], 311–20; Campbell, 'Norwich' [385], 23.

[15] Martin, 'The Town as Palimpsest' [191], 159–63; Turner, *Town Defences* [266].

outside the walls. Canterbury, Lincoln, Norwich, and York, for instance, all had suburbs by the eleventh century. Some intramural
open spaces were essential to a town's main functions, like market-
places, some of which had to accommodate large numbers of cattle,
or tenter grounds where cloth was hung to dry after fulling. Other
spaces were used as gardens, orchards, arable, and pasture, or
formed enclosures attached to religious houses. All these uses help to
account for the large spaces at Norwich: Campbell points out that
the medieval walls there enclosed an area as big as London's but
probably not a quarter of the population. It is in fact impossible to
generalize about the density of building or population in medieval
towns: excavation in Winchester has shown one street frontage completely built up by c. 1150 and the site behind it covered a hundred
years later, while elsewhere this sort of infilling only took place centuries afterwards. One pointer to past bounds of built-up areas is the
siting of leper hospitals, which were usually intended to be isolated.
Another, though less reliable, is that of friaries. Many towns were at
their largest in the later thirteenth century and the early fourteenth,
when most of the friaries were founded, and quite often—though not
always—the friars settled on cheap unoccupied land on the edge of
the town. In some cases, however, they bought up and cleared
surrounding properties as they grew richer: first impressions conveyed by their sites can be misleading.[16]

It is reasonable to look for topographical evidence of shrunken
populations in a good many late medieval towns. When documents
speak of uninhabited streets, vanished parish churches may help to
suggest where they lay. Nevertheless it would be as mistaken to look
only for decay in the later period as to look only for growth earlier
on. Town governments were now spending more on public works—
guildhalls, bridges, wharfs, conduits, and street-paving—which all
have to be studied in their physical setting and related to it even
where they have themselves disappeared. The relationship between
a town's prosperity and the size and distribution of its population
could moreover be complex. Norman castles and cathedrals cut
swathes through houses during one age of urban expansion and the
Norwich friaries did the same while the city was flourishing two
centuries later. Changing religious fashions could help to close
churches, and the most vulnerable would not always be those in the

---

[16] See above, pp. 48–50, 51; Campbell, 'Norwich' [385], 11; Martin, *The Town* [190],
15; Platt, *Eng. Med. Town* [220], 37–51.

least populous neighbourhoods. In Southampton the prosperous burgesses favoured different parishes at different times. While some of their reasons are likely to remain mysterious, others may be guessed from the history of the quays and fortifications.[17]

Topographical evidence thus has much to contribute to the social and economic history of a town, as well as to that of its individual trades and industries; where it is backed by detailed work on individual buildings the physical setting of urban life begins to come alive for us. From the twelfth century, deeds sometimes refer to stone houses in towns. A few even survive from this date, and more, whether stone or timber-framed, from later on, while others have left foundations for excavation. The combination of architectural, archaeological, and documentary study is now beginning to produce a body of knowledge about medieval town houses which seems much greater than its formerly separate parts.[18] It seems that individual buildings were altered and replaced quite frequently; at Winchester property boundaries between them changed too—a warning against assuming automatically that modern boundaries are the same as medieval ones and can be taken as evidence of them. Among several thought-provoking discoveries are the reversion from stone to timber in the richer houses of both Winchester and Southampton, and the suggestion that Norwich had become a city of substantial two-storey buildings by 1558. Even historians who are not qualified to carry out excavations or architectural surveys themselves must be stimulated by this new work to try to contribute to it from their own knowledge and critical skills. We may not be able to discover and contribute as much as we should like, but we are at least made aware how much we do not know.

[17] Chapters 7, 8, *passim*; Platt, *Med. Southampton* [416], 165–6.
[18] Colvin, 'Domestic Architecture' [90], i. 67–77; Pantin, 'Med. Eng. House Plans' [209] and 'Some Med. Eng. Town Houses [210]; Keene, 'Winchester: the Brooks Area' 430]; Wood, *Eng. Med. House* [282], 14–15; above, pp. 152, 154–5.

Glossary

alderman: derived from O.E. *ealdorman* and surviving in urban usage to describe the holder of a senior civic office. Two main usages are (1) the chief officer of a guild: occurs in the earlier Middle Ages and later in surviving merchant guilds; (2) the member of a town council, particularly an upper council: increasingly common in the later Middle Ages, probably under London influence. For London aldermen, see pp. 94, 119.

bordar: usually, in rural contexts, a relatively humble peasant occupying a cottage with little or no arable attached. For bordars in Norwich, 1086, see p. 43.

borough: as *burh* (O.E.) or *burgus* (Lat.) at first used of any fortified place, not necessarily a town (pp. 24, 31); by the eleventh century the word had strong urban connotations (see p. 34–6). For later usages, see pp. 99–100, 112, 114.

burgage: a unit of property in a borough, generally comprising a house but not much appurtenant land, held for a money-rent and according to the more or less standard rules of burgage tenure. See pp. 93, 98–100.

burgess (Lat. *burgensis*): the member of a town (borough) community, generally a householder paying his share of any communal dues and thus participating in communal privileges and possessing the 'freedom of the borough', 'burgess franchise', or 'borough franchise' (see pp. 123–126).

burgus (Lat.): see borough.

burgware (O.E.): the inhabitants of a *burh*.

burh (O.E.): see borough.

burhgemot (O.E.): a court held in a *burh* (see p. 92).

chantry: an institution, often endowed by will or supported by subscriptions through a guild, to pay for the regular saying of masses for the souls of the founder(s) and of friends and relations.

citizen (Lat. *civis*): used in a sense corresponding to burgess (q.v.) for the inhabitants of towns known as cities (*civitates*).

city: see *civitas*.

civitas (Lat., pl. *civitates*): a unit of government in the Roman empire, comprising not only the central settlement, probably more or less urban, but the surrounding territory, with its other settlements: e.g. *civitas* of the Cantiaci (roughly the later Kent). In the Middle Ages, a town of high status, usually fortified, and often of Roman origin or possessing a cathedral.

cnihta (O.E., pl. *cnihtan*): the word from which the later 'knight' is derived, but with humbler and less military connotations than it had later in the Middle Ages. See pp. 28, 82.

common council: a lower, or outer, town council in the later Middle Ages, or the inner and outer councils meeting together (see p. 173).

commune (Lat. *communio, communia, communa*): a derivative of *communitas* used particularly in the twelfth century for a sworn association of townspeople, often led by a mayor, which campaigned for corporate liberties (see p. 103-4). Not thereafter much used in England, though cf. *communitas*.

communiarii (Lat.): commoners. See p. 133.

communitas (Lat., pl. *communitates*): used to describe many affective associations including towns in their corporate characters, though not with any very exact meaning before the late Middle Ages when charters, later described as charters of incorporation, used the word *communitas* (later translated corporation). See pp. 113-14, 116.

craft or mistery (Lat. *misteria, mestera, officium*): an industry or trade, generally involving particular skills transmitted through apprenticeship under a master of the craft. By the later Middle Ages crafts were normally regulated, under municipal supervision, by their leading practitioners, who might be united in a guild, q.v.: hence the modern usage, 'craft guild': see pp. 165-6.

customs: used in three senses: (1) the customary rules and procedures of a town, especially in legal matters; (2) 'the king's customs', i.e. the early medieval customary dues, like landgable and tolls, owed to the king; (3) customs duties on the import or export of merchandise, including both local customs imposed in a particular port for its own profit and the national customs imposed 1203-6 and from 1275.

eyre or general eyre: a travelling court of royal justices, periodically sent round the country in circuits to enquire into royal administration and to hear both civil and criminal cases.

farm (Lat. *firma*): a fixed annual payment. The 'borough farm' or 'fee-farm' (*firma burgi*) was the basic lump sum from a town which had to be paid into the Exchequer each year either by the sheriff of the county or by the town's own officials.

fee-farm: see farm

franchise: see burgess.

frankpledge, view of: courts held, generally twice a year, either by the sheriff in each hundred or by lords with frankpledge jurisdiction in their manors, which dealt with minor criminal matters, e.g. breaches of the assizes of bread and ale, minor assaults etc.

gavel (Lat. *gablum*; O.E. *gafol*): see landgable.

geld or **danegeld**: a tax paid in the eleventh and twelfth centuries to the king.

guild (gild): a word used in the Middle Ages for associations of many purposes, but nearly always including mutual charity, general sociability (including drinking), and religious celebrations: see pp. 80–4, 164–8. For the 'guild merchant', or guild of traders, see pp. 82, 164; for 'craft guilds', see pp. 165–6.

hanse: an association of merchants who have secured corporate exemption from tolls and other dues; in twelfth-century England sometimes used interchangeably with 'merchant guild'. By the later Middle Ages the German Hanse was a formal association of towns, as well as of merchants.

hundred: an area of local government intermediate between the county and the village.

husting: the chief court of London.

journeyman: a wage-worker, generally assumed to be one who has served out an apprenticeship.

jurats (Lat. *jurati*): in a town, the sworn councillors.

landgable (derived from O.E. *gafol*): a payment, normally made to the king or other lord at a standard figure, from each house in a town in the earlier Middle Ages.

leet: in some towns, a ward or division of the town; also used in the later Middle Ages for courts with similar jurisdiction to frankpledge courts, q.v.

mistery: see craft.

moot (O.E. *gemot*): a court or meeting, as in *burhgemot*, q.v., portmoot or portmanmoot—common names for town courts (see port), or the London folkmoot and wardmotes.

murage: a toll charged to pay for the building or repair of town walls.

oppidum (Lat.): used by Roman writers to describe fortified non-Roman settlements which to them seemed to lack the attributes of a civilized town (*urbs*).

patrician, patriciate: used by modern historians to describe the governing classes of medieval towns, especially during the twelfth and thirteenth centuries: see pp. 67–8, 181.

pavage: a toll charged to pay for the paving of a town's streets, or some of them.

Pipe Rolls: annual rolls of the accounts presented at the Exchequer by the sheriffs, and including the farms of shires and boroughs.

pontage: a toll charged to pay for the building or repair of a bridge.

port (Lat. *portus*): a trading-place, not necessarily for water-borne trade, whose inhabitants were in O.E. *portware* or *portmenn*. Thus sometimes used as a synonym of 'borough' or 'town'. Portmoot or portmanmoot remained a common name for a town court. By the thirteenth century the town councillors were sometimes called portmen (or chief portmen).

reeve (O.E. *gerefa*; Lat. *praepositus, prepositus*): the usual word for an O.E. official, including the *scirgerefa* (sheriff) and *portgerefa* (port reeve, town reeve); continued to be used in towns after the Norman Conquest (later sometimes interchangeably with 'bailiff'), generally for the officials responsible for paying the king's or lord's dues.

scot and lot: a traditional expression for borough dues; those paying scot and lot were normally householders paying their full dues and thus ranking as members of the town community: see pp. 124, 134.

soke (from O.E. *soc*: jurisdiction): in London, the estate within the city of a lord who retained some jurisdiction over his tenants.

staple: a place with a monopoly of a particular trade, which must all pass through it. The Merchants of the Staple were the wool merchants trading through the wool staple (at Calais from 1363). Staple courts were established in 1353 with jurisdiction in mercantile cases in towns then designated as wool staples, and continued (generally in the same places) after the wool staple was moved to Calais.

tallage: an occasional direct tax of a relatively arbitrary kind, taken from those who (like villeins) were personally unfree or (like towns) had a customary obligation to pay; thus distinguished from aids, which were regarded as more freely granted. In towns, used in two main senses: (1) royal tallages, i.e. lump sums levied by the king before they were superseded by parliamentary taxes; (2) town or borough tallages levied by town authorities for their own use.

thegn (thane): a member of the late O.E. noble or upper class.

toll: a payment either on goods, vehicles, or persons passing a particular point, e.g. a bridge, ford, gate, or quay, or on the buying and selling of goods at a market or fair.

tron: a public weigh-beam or scales which had to be used for some goods and for which tronage was charged.

urbs: see *oppidum*.

vicus (Lat.): a settlement; often an unfortified and rural settlement (village or hamlet); sometimes a street or quarter of a town; also apparently used around the North Sea and Channel in the early Middle Ages for a merchant settlement or trading place: see *wik* and pp. 14, 19.

villein: a peasant who, by definitions established *c.* 1200, was unfree to the extent that, although not a chattel of his lord, he could not leave his holding and owed services for it which were limited only by custom and his lord's court, not by the royal courts.

wergeld: a monetary value, scaled according to rank, which was put on a person's life in the early Middle Ages.

wik (O.E. *wíc*, *wih*): a merchant settlement or town, probably originally unfortified and thus different from a *burgus* or *civitas*; apparently used in this sense (though also in others) in the North Sea trading area in the Dark Ages; see *vicus* and pp. 19, 24–7.

List of Works Cited

The following list contains only the works cited in the footnotes; it is not intended to be a full bibliography. In many cases the work chosen for citation is the most recent, or the most readily available, in which can be found references to earlier works and to original sources. The list is arranged as follows: I. General works (including works both on more than one English town and on individual towns abroad): (a) Bibliographies and guides to sources, (b) Printed primary sources, (c) Secondary works. II. Works on individual towns, with both primary and secondary sources arranged alphabetically under each town.

The following abbreviations are used:

Am. H.R.	*American Historical Review*
Annales E.S.C.	*Annales: Économies, Sociétés, Civilisations*
Ant. Jnl.	*Antiquaries' Journal*
Arch. Jnl.	*Archaeological Journal*
Ec. H. R.	*Economic History Review*
E.H.R.	*English Historical Review*
Jnl. Ec. H.	*Journal of Economic History*
Med. Arch.	*Medieval Archaeology*
P. & P.	*Past and Present*
Revue belge	*La Revue belge d'histoire et de philologie*
Rev. hist.	*La Revue historique*
T.R.H.S.	*Transactions of the Royal Historical Society*
V.C.H.	*The Victoria History of the Counties of England*

I. GENERAL WORKS

(a) *Bibliographies and guides to sources*

[1] BARLEY, M. W., *A Guide to British Topographical Collections* (London, 1974).

[2] BERESFORD, M. W., *Lay Subsidies and Poll Taxes* (Bridge Place, Kent, 1963: reprinted from *The Amateur Historian*, iii–iv, 1958–9).

[3] COBB, H. S., 'Local Port Customs Accounts to 1550', *Jnl. Soc. of Archivists*, i (1958).

[4] GROSS, C., *A Bibliography of British Municipal History* (New York, 1897).

[5] HARLEY, J. B., *Maps for the Local Historian* (London, 1972: reprinted from *The Amateur Historian*, vii, 1966–7).

[6] HARLEY, J. B. and PHILLIPS, C. W., *The Historian's Guide to Ord-nance Survey Maps* (London, 1964: reprinted from *The Amateur Historian*, v, 1961–3).

[7] LOBEL, M. D., 'The Value of Early Maps as Evidence for the Top-ography of English Towns', *Imago Mundi*, xxii (1968).

[8] MARTIN, G. H., 'The Origins of Borough Records', *Jnl. Soc. of Archivists*, ii (1961).

[9] MARTIN, G. H. and McINTYRE, S., *A Bibliography of British and Irish Municipal History*, i: *General Works* (Leicester, 1972).

[10] PHYTHIAN-ADAMS, C., 'Sources for Urban History: Records of Craft Guilds', *The Local Historian*, ix (1971).

[11] SAWYER, P. H., *Anglo-Saxon Charters: an Annotated List and Biblio-graphy* (London, 1968).

[12] WOODWARD, D. M., 'Sources for Urban History: Freemen's Rolls', *The Local Historian*, ix (1970).

(b) *Printed Primary Sources*

[13] *Annales Monastici*, ed. H. R. Luard (5 vols. Rolls Series, 1864–9).

[14] BEDE, *Historia Ecclesiastica*, ed. and trans. B. Colgrave and R. Mynors (Oxford, 1969).

[15] *Borough Customs*, ed. M. Bateson (Selden Soc. xviii (1904); xxi (1906)).

[16] *British Borough Charters, 1042–1216*, ed. A. Ballard; *1216–1307*, ed. A. Ballard and J. Tait; *1307–1660*, ed. M. Weinbaum (Cambridge, 1913–43).

[17] *Calendars of Charter Rolls, 1226–1516*.

[18] *Calendars of Close Rolls, 1227–1485*.

[19] *Calendars of Inquisitions Miscellaneous, 1219–1422*.

[20] *Calendars of Patent Rolls, 1226–1509*.

[21] *Cartae Antiquae: Rolls 11–20* (Pipe Roll Soc. xxxiii (1960)).

[22] CARUS-WILSON, E. M. and COLEMAN, O., *England's Export Trade, 1275–1547* (Oxford, 1963).

[23] *Councils and Synods: The English Church*, ii. *1205–1313*, ed. F. M. Powicke and C. R. Cheney (Oxford, 1964).

[24] *Documents of the Baronial Movement of Reform and Rebellion*, ed. R. F. Treharne and I. J. Sanders (Oxford, 1973).

[25] *Domesday Book* (3 vols., London, 1783–1816).

[26] EDDIUS STEPHANUS, *Life of Bishop Wilfrid*, ed. and trans. B. Colgrave (Cambridge, 1927).

[27] *Elenchus Fontium Historiae Urbanae*, i, ed. C. van de Kieft and J. F. Niermeijer (Leiden, 1967).

[28] *English Gilds: Original Ordinances of the Fourteenth and Fifteenth Centuries*, ed. Toulmin Smith (Early Eng. Text Soc. xl (1870)).

[29] *English Historical Documents*, ed. D. C. Douglas: i: *c. 500–1042* (London, 1955); ii: *1042–1189* (1953); iii: *1089–1327* (1975); iv: *1327–1485* (1967).

[30] *Flores Historiarum*, ed. H. R. Luard (3 vols., Rolls Series, 1890).

[31] FORTESCUE, J., 'The Comodytes of Englond' in *Works of Sir John Fortescue*, ed. Clermont (London, 1869), pp. 549–54.

[32] *Gesta Stephani*, ed. and trans. K. R. Potter (London, 1955).

[33] GILDAS, *De Excidio Britanniae*, ed. H. Williams (Cymmrodorion Record Series, iii, 1899–1901).

[34] *Glanvill*, ed. and trans. G. D. G. Hall (London, 1965).

[35] GLASSCOCK, R. E., *The Lay Subsidy of 1334* (London, 1975).

[36] *The Gough Map:* Facsimile, with Introd. by E. J. S. Parsons and F. M. Stenton (Oxford, 1958).

[37] *Hansisches Urkundenbuch*, i, ed. K. Höhlbaum (Halle, 1876).

[38] HILL, D., 'The Burghal Hidage: the Establishment of a Text', *Med. Arch.* xiii (1969).

[39] *The Laws of the Earliest English Kings*, ed. and trans. F. L. Attenborough (Cambridge, 1922).

[40] *The Laws of the Kings of England from Edmund to Henry I*, ed. and trans. A. J. Robertson (Cambridge, 1925).

[41] *The Libelle of Englyshe Polycye*, ed. G. Warner (Oxford, 1926).

[42] LIEBERMANN, F. ed., *Die Gesetze der Angelsachsen* (3 vols., Halle, 1916).

[43] MUNDY, J. H. and RIESENBERG, P., *The Medieval Town* (Princeton, 1958).

[44] PARIS, MATTHEW, *Four Maps of Great Britain, designed c. 1250* (British Museum, London, 1928).

[45] PEGOLOTTI, F. B., *La Pratica della Mercatura*, ed. A. Evans (Cambridge, Mass., 1936).

[46] *Pipe Rolls: 31 Henry I* and *2–4 Henry II* ed. J. Hunter (London, 1833, 1844); other rolls of *Henry II*, and of *Richard I, John*, and *2 and 14 Henry III* (Pipe Roll Soc., 1884–1964).

[47] *Die Recesse der Hansetage, 1256–1430*, iii (Leipzig, 1875).

[48] *Regesta Regum Anglo-Normannorum*, ed. H. W. C. Davis and others (4 vols., Oxford, 1913–69).

[49] RICHARD of Devizes, *Chronicle*, ed. and trans. J. T. Appleby (London, 1963).

[50] *Rotuli Hundredorum* (3 vols., Record Commission, 1812–18).

[51] *Rotuli Parliamentorum* (6 vols., Record Commission, 1783).

[52] RYMER, T., *Foedera* (2nd edn. Record Commission, 1816–30).

[53] *Select Cases in the Law Merchant* (Selden Soc. xxiii, xlvi, xlix, 1908–32).

[54] *Statutes of the Realm*, i: *1235–1377*, ii: *1377–1509*, iii: *1509–47* (Record Commission, 1810–17).

[55] *Three Old English Elegies*, ed. R. F. Leslie (Manchester, 1961).

[56] *Two Lives of St. Cuthbert*, ed. B. Colgrave (Cambridge, 1940).

[57] WILLIAM of Malmesbury, *Gesta Pontificum*, ed. N.E.S.A. Hamilton (Rolls Series, 1870).

[58] WILLIAM of Malmesbury, *Gesta Regum Anglorum*, ed. W. Stubbs (2 vols., Rolls Series, 1887–9).

(c) *Secondary Works*

[59] ADDLESHAW, G. W. O., *The Development of the Parochial System from Charlemagne to Urban II* (York: St. Anthony's Hall, pub. no. 6, 2nd edn. (1970)).

[60] *The Atlas of Historic Towns*: vol. i (as *Historic Towns*), ed. M. D. Lobel (London, 1969); vol. ii, ed. M. D. Lobel and W. H. Johns (London, 1975).

[61] BALLARD, A., 'The Laws of Breteuil', *E.H.R.* xxx (1915).

[62] BASS, G. F. ed., *A History of Seafaring, Based on Underwater Archaeology* (London, 1972).

[63] BATESON, M., 'The Laws of Breteuil', *E.H.R.* xv (1900).

[64] BAUTIER, R. H., *The Economic Development of Medieval Europe* (London, 1971).

[65] BENTON, J. F., *Town Origins; the Evidence from England* (Problems in European Civilization: Boston, 1968).

[66] BERESFORD, M. W., *History on the Ground* (London, 1957).

[67] BERESFORD, M. W., *New Towns of the Middle Ages* (London, 1967).

[68] BIDDLE, M., 'Archaeology and the History of British Towns', *Antiquity*, xlii (1968).

[69] BIDDLE, M. and HILL, D., 'Late Saxon Planned Towns', *Ant. Jnl.* li (1971).

[70] BLAIR, P. H., *An Introduction to Anglo-Saxon England* (Cambridge, 1962).

[71] BLANCHARD, I., 'Population Change, Enclosure, and the Early Tudor Economy', *Ec.H.R.* 2nd ser. xxiii (1970).

[72] BLOCH, M., *Feudal Society* (London, 1961; pub. in Fr. 1939–40).

[73] BOSWORTH, J. and TOLLER, T. N., *An Anglo-Saxon Dictionary* (Oxford, 1898).

[74] BRIDBURY, A. R., *Economic Growth: England in the Later Middle Ages* (London, 1962).

[75] BRIDBURY, A. R., *England and the Salt Trade* (Oxford, 1955).

[76] BROOKS, N., 'The Unidentified Forts of the Burghal Hidage', *Med. Arch.* viii (1964).

[77] CAM, H. M., *The Hundred and the Hundred Rolls* (London, 1930).

[78] CAM, H. M., *Liberties and Communities in Medieval England* (Cambridge, 1944).

[79] *The Cambridge Economic History of Europe*, ed. M. M. Postan and others, vols. i (2nd. edn. 1966), ii (1952), iii (1963).

[80] CARUS-WILSON, E. M., 'Evidence of Industrial Growth on some Fifteenth Century Manors', *Ec.H.R.* 2nd ser. xii (1959-60).

[81] CARUS-WILSON, E. M., *Medieval Merchant Venturers* (London, 1954).

[82] CARUS-WILSON, E. M., 'The Medieval Trade of the Ports of the Wash', *Med. Arch.* vi-vii (1962-3).

[83] CARUS-WILSON, E. M., 'Towns and Trade', in *Medieval England*, ed. A. L. Poole, i (Oxford, 1958).

[84] CENTRE pro CIVITATE, *Libertés urbaines et rurales du xie au xive siècle: Colloque internationale, Spa, 1966* (Spa, 1968).

[85] CLANCHY, M. T., 'The Franchise of Return of Writs', *T.R.H.S.* 5th ser. xvii (1967).

[86] CLANCHY, M. T., 'Had Henry III a Policy?', *History*, liii (1968).

[87] CLARK, P. L. and SLACK, P. ed., *Crisis and Order in English Towns, 1500-1700* (London, 1972).

[88] CLARKE, R. R., *East Anglia* (London, 1960).

[89] COLLINGWOOD, R. G. and MYRES, J. N. L., *Roman Britain and the English Settlements* (Oxford, 1936).

[90] COLVIN, H. M., 'Domestic Architecture and Town-Planning', in *Medieval England*, ed. A. L. Poole, i (Oxford, 1958).

[91] CONZEN, M. G., 'The Use of Town Plans in the Study of Urban History', in *The Study of Urban History*, ed. H. J. Dyos (London, 1968).

[92] COORNAERT, E., 'Draperies rurales, draperies urbaines', *Revue belge*, xxviii (1950).

[93] COORNAERT, E., 'Les Ghildes médiévales', *Rev. hist.* cxcix (1948).

[94] COORNAERT, E. ,'Une question dépassée: "l'origine" des communautés de métiers', *Tijdscrift vor Geschiedenis*, lxv (1952).

[95] CORNWALL, J., 'English Country Towns in the 1520s', *Ec.H.R.* 2nd ser. xv (1962-3).

[96] CORNWALL, J., 'English Population in the Early Sixteenth Century', *Ec.H.R.* 2nd ser. xxiii (1970).

[97] CRAIG, H., *English Religious Drama of the Middle Ages* (Oxford, 1955).

[98] CUNNINGHAM, W., *The Growth of English Industry and Commerce during the Early and Middle Ages* (Cambridge, 5th edn. 1910).

[99] DARBY, H. C. ed., *A New Historical Geography of England* (Cambridge, 1973).

[100] DARBY, H. C. and others ed., *The Domesday Geographies of Eastern, Midland, Northern, South-east, and South-west England* (as 5 separate works: Cambridge, 1954-67).

[101] DAVISON, B. K., 'The Burghal Hidage Fort of Eorpeburnan', *Med. Arch.* xvi (1972).

[102] DHONDT, J., 'Les problèmes de Quentovic' in *Studi in onore di A. Fanfani*, i (Milan, 1966).

[103] DHONDT, J., 'Les Solidarités médiévales', *Annales E.S.C.* xii (1957).

[104] DICKENS, A. G., *The English Reformation* (London, 1964).

[105] DICKENS, B., 'The Cult of St. Olave', *Saga Book of the Viking Soc.* xii (1937–45).

[106] DICKINSON, R. B., 'Town Plans of East Anglia', *Geography*, xix (1934).

[107] DOBSON, R. B. ed., *The Peasants' Revolt of 1381* (London, 1970).

[108] DOBSON, R. B., 'Urban Decline in Late Medieval England': paper read to R. Hist. Soc., 6 Feb. 1976.

[109] DOLLEY, R. H. M. ed., *Anglo-Saxon Coins: Studies Presented to F. M. Stenton* (London, 1961).

[110] DOLLINGER, P., *The German Hansa* (London, 1970: pub. in Fr. 1964).

[111] DONKIN, R. A., 'The Disposal of Cistercian Wool', *Citeaux in de Nederlanden*, viii (1957).

[112] DOPSCH, A., *Economic and Social Foundations of European Civilization* (London, 1937: pub. in German, 1923–4).

[113] DUBY, G., *The Early Growth of the European Economy: Warriors and Peasants* (London, 1974; pub. in Fr. 1973).

[114] DUBY, G., *Rural Economy and Country Life in the Medieval West* (London, 1968; pub. in Fr. 1962).

[115] DYMOND, D. P., *Archaeology and History: a Plea for Reconciliation* (London, 1974).

[116] DYMOND, D. P., *Archaeology for the Historian* (Helps for Students of History, London, 1967).

[117] EKWALL, E., *Old English wīc in Place-Names* (Lund, 1964).

[118] ENNEN, E., *Die europäische Stadt des Mittelalters* (Göttingen, revised edn. 1975).

[119] EVERITT, A., 'The Banburys of England', *Urban History Yearbook* (1974).

[120] FINBERG, H. P. R., gen. ed., *The Agrarian History of England and Wales:* vol. iv, ed. J. Thirsk (Cambridge, 1967).

[121] FINBERG, H. P. R., *Gloucestershire Studies* (Leicester, 1957).

[122] FINBERG, H. P. R., *Lucerna: Studies of Some Problems in the Early History of England* (London, 1964).

[123] FINBERG, H. P. R. and HOSKINS, W. H., *Devonshire Studies* (London, 1952).

[124] FOURQUIN, G., *Les Campagnes de la région parisienne à la fin du moyen âge* (Paris, 1964).

[125] FRERE, S., *Britannia* (London, 1969).

[126] FRERE, S., 'The End of the Towns in Roman Britain', in *Civitas Capitals of Roman Britain*, ed. J. S. Wacher (Leicester, 1966).

[127] FRYDE, E. B., 'Anglo-Italian Commerce in the Fifteenth Century', *Revue belge*, i (1972).

[128] FRYDE, E. B., *The Wool Accounts of Sir William de la Pole* (York: St. Anthony's Hall, pub. no. 25 (1964)).

[129] GANSHOF, F. L., 'A propos du tonlieu à l'époque carolingienne', in *La Citta nell' alto Medioevo* (Settimane del Centro di Studi sull' Alto Medioevo vi (1959)).

[130] GANSHOF, F. L., 'A propos du tonlieu sous les Merovingiens', in *Studi in onore di A. Fanfani*, i (Milan, 1966).

[131] GANSHOF, F. L., *Étude sur le développement des villes entre Loire et Rhin* (Paris, 1943).

[132] GELLING, M., 'Place-Names derived from wīchām', *Med. Arch.* xi (1967).

[133] GIUSEPPI, M. S., 'Alien Merchants in the Fifteenth Century', *T.R.H.S.* 2nd ser. ix (1895).

[134] GRAS, N. S. B., *The Early English Customs System* (Cambridge, Mass. 1918).

[135] GRIERSON, P., 'Commerce in the Dark Ages: a Critique of the Evidence', *T.R.H.S.* 5th ser. ix (1959).

[136] GROSS, C., *The Gild Merchant* (Oxford, 1890).

[137] HARMER, F., 'Chipping and Market: a Lexicographical Investigation', in *The Early Cultures of North-West Europe*, ed. C. F. Fox and B. Dickins (Cambridge, 1950).

[138] HARVEY, P. D. A., 'The English Inflation of 1180–1208', *P & P.* 61 (1973).

[139] HAVIGHURST, A. F. ed., *The Pirenne Thesis* (Problems in European Civilization: Boston, 1958).

[140] HEATH, P., *The English Parish Clergy on the Eve of the Reformation* (London, 1969).

[141] HEERS, J., *L'Occident aux xive et xve siècles* (Paris, 2nd edn. 1966).

[142] HEERS, J. 'Les Genois en Angleterre', in *Studi in onore di A. Sapori* (Milan, 1957).

[143] HEMMEON, M. de W., *Burgage Tenure in Medieval England* (Cambridge, Mass., 1914).

[144] HEWITT, H. J., *The Organization of War under Edward III* (Manchester, 1966).

[145] HIBBERT, A. B., 'The Origins of the Medieval Town Patriciate' *P. & P.* 3 (1953).

[146] HILTON, R. H., *The English Peasantry in the Later Middle Ages* (Oxford, 1975).

[147] HILTON, R. H., *A Medieval Society: the West Midlands at the End of the Thirteenth Century* (London, 1966).

[148] HOLMES, G. A., 'Florentine Merchants in England, 1346–1436', *Ec.H.R.* 2nd ser. xiii (1960).

[149] HOSKINS, W. G., *Devon* (London, 1954).

[150] HOSKINS, W. G., 'English Provincial Towns in the Early Sixteenth Century', *T.R.H.S.* 5th ser. x (1956).

[151] HOSKINS, W. G., *Local History in England* (London, 2nd edn. 1972).

[152] HOSKINS, W. G., *The Making of the English Landscape* (London, 1955).

[153] HUGHES, D. O., 'Urban Growth and Family Structure in Medieval Genoa', *P. & P.* 66 (1975).

[154] HYDE, J. K., *Society and Politics in Medieval Italy, 1000–1350* (London, 1973).

[155] JACKSON, K., *Language and History in Early Britain* (Edinburgh, 1953).

[156] JACOB, E. F., *The Fifteenth Century* (Oxford, 1961).

[157] JACOB, E. F., *Studies in the Period of Baronial Reform and Rebellion* (Oxford Studies in Soc. and Legal Hist. viii, 1925).

[158] JAMES, M. K., *Studies in the Medieval Wine Trade* (Oxford, 1971).

[159] JOHNS, E., *British Townscapes* (London, 1965).

[160] JONES, A. H. M., 'Cities of the Roman Empire', *Recueils de la société Jean Bodin*, vi (1954).

[161] JONES, A. H. M., *The Later Roman Empire* (3 vols. Oxford, 1964).

[162] JONES, G., *A History of the Vikings* (London, 1968).

[163] JORDAN, W. K., *Philanthropy in England, 1480–1660* (London, 1959).

[164] KEEN, M. H., *England in the Later Middle Ages* (London, 1973).

[165] KINGSFORD, C. L., *Prejudice and Promise in Fifteenth-Century England* (Oxford, 1925).

[166] KNOWLES, D., *The Religious Orders in England* (3 vols., Cambridge, 1948–59).

[167] KNOWLES, D. and HADCOCK, R. N., *Medieval Religious Houses: England and Wales* (London, 2nd edn. 1971).

[168] LANDER, J. R., *Conflict and stability in Fifteenth-Century England* (London, 1969).

[169] LANE, F. C., *Venice: A Maritime Republic* (Baltimore, 1973).

[170] LATOUCHE, R., *The Birth of the Western Economy: Economic Aspects of the Dark Ages* (London, 1961; pub. in French, 1956).

[171] LE GOFF, J., 'Ordres mendiants et urbanisation dans la France médiévale', *Annales E.S.C.* xxv (1970).

[172] LE GOFF, J., 'The Town as an Agent of Civilisation', in *The Fontana Economic History of Europe: The Middle Ages*, ed. C. M. Cipolla (London, 1972).

[173] Lestocquoy, J., *Aux origines de la bourgeoisie : les villes de Flandre et d'Italie sous le gouvernement des patriciens : xie–xve siècles* (Paris, 1952).

[174] Lestocquoy, J., 'De l'unité à la pluralité', *Annales E.S.C.* viii (1953).

[175] Lestocquoy, J., *Études d'histoire urbaine* (Arras, 1966).

[176] Levison, W., *England and the Continent in the Eighth Century* (Oxford, 1946).

[177] Little, A. G., 'Personal Tithes', *E.H.R.* lx (1945).

[178] Lopez, R. S., 'An Aristocracy of Money in the Early Middle Ages', *Speculum*, xxxviii (1953).

[179] Lopez, R. S., *The Commercial Revolution of the Middle Ages, 950–1350* (Englewood Cliffs, N. J., 1971).

[180] Loyn, H. R., *Anglo-Saxon England and the Norman Conquest* (London, 1962).

[181] Loyn, H. R., 'Towns in late Anglo-Saxon England', in *England Before the Conquest*, ed. P. Clemoes and K. Hughes (Cambridge, 1971).

[182] McFarlane, K. B., *John Wycliffe and the Beginnings of English Nonconformity* (London, 1952).

[183] McFarlane, K. B., 'War, Economy, and Social Change', *P. & P.* 22 (1962).

[184] McKisack, M., *The Parliamentary Representation of the English Boroughs during the Middle Ages* (Oxford, 1932).

[185] Madox, T., *Firma Burgi* (London, 1726).

[186] Maitland, F. W., *Domesday Book and Beyond* (Cambridge, 1897).

[187] Maitland, F. W., *Township and Borough* (Cambridge, 1898).

[188] Mallett, M. E., 'Anglo-Florentine Commercial Relations, 1465–91', *Ec.H.R.* 2nd ser. xv (1962).

[189] Martin, G. H., 'The English Borough in the Thirteenth Century', *T.R.H.S.* 5th ser. xiii (1963).

[190] Martin, G. H., *The Town* (London, 1961).

[191] Martin, G. H., 'The Town as Palimpsest', in *The Study of Urban History*, ed. H. J. Dyos (London, 1968).

[192] Mayer, T. ed., *Studien zu den Anfängen des europäischen Städtewesens* (Vorträge und Forschungen, iv, 1958).

[193] Mellinkoff, R., 'The Round Cup-shaped Hats on Jews in B.M. Cotton Claudius B. iv', *Anglo-Saxon England*, ii (1973).

[194] Michaud-Quantin, P., *Universitas : expressions du mouvement communautaire dans le moyen âge latin* (Paris, 1970).

[195] Miller, E., 'The English Economy in the Thirteenth Century', *P. & P.* 28 (1964).

[196] Miller, E., 'The Fortunes of the English Textile Industry in the Thirteenth Century', *Ec.H.R.* 2nd ser. xviii (1965).

[197] MITCHELL, S. K., *Taxation in Medieval England* (New Haven, 1951).

[198] MOLLAT, M. and WOLFF, P., *Ongles bleus, Jacques et Ciompi* (Paris, 1970).

[199] MORRIS, J., 'Dark Age Dates', in *Britain and Rome*, ed. M. G. Jarrett and B. Dobson (Kendal, 1965).

[200] MURRAY, K. M. E., *The Constitutional History of the Cinque Ports* (Manchester, 1935).

[201] MUSSET, L., *The Germanic Invasions* (London, 1975; pub. in French, 1965).

[202] MUSSET, L., 'Peuplement en bourgages et bourgs ruraux en Normandie', *Cahiers de civilisation médiévale*, ix (1966).

[203] MYRES, J. N. L., *Anglo-Saxon Pottery and the Settlement of England* (Oxford, 1969).

[204] NIELSON, N., *Customary Rents* (Oxford Studies in Soc. and Legal Hist. ii, 1910).

[205] OMAN, C., *The Coinage of England* (Oxford, 1931).

[206] ORME, N., *English Schools in the Middle Ages* (London, 1973).

[207] PACKARD, S. R., 'The Norman Communes', *Am.H.R.* xlvi (1941).

[208] PACKARD, S. R., review of Petit-Dutaillis, *Les Communes*, in *Speculum*, xxiv (1949), pp. 609–14.

[209] PANTIN, W. A., 'Medieval English House Plans', *Med. Arch.* vi–vii (1962–3).

[210] PANTIN, W. A., 'Some Medieval English Town Houses', in *Culture and Environment: Essays in Honour of Sir C. Fox*, ed. I.Ll. Foster and L. Alcock (London, 1963).

[211] PELHAM, R. A., 'Timber Exports from the Weald during the 14th cent.', 'The Foreign Trade of Sussex, 1300–50', 'Some Further Aspects of Sussex Trade', 'The Exportation of Wool from Sussex in the late 13th cent.', *Suss. Arch. Coll.* lxix, lxx, lxxi, lxxiv (1928–33).

[212] PERROY, E., 'Le Commerce anglo-flamand au xiiie siècle: la Hanse flamande de Londres', *Rev. hist.* cclii (1974).

[213] PERROY, E., 'Les origines urbaines en Flandre', *Revue du Nord*, xxix (1947).

[214] PETIT-DUTAILLIS, C., *Les Communes françaises* (Paris, 1947).

[215] PHELPS-BROWN, E. H. and HOPKINS, S. V., 'Seven Centuries of the Prices of Consumables, Compared with Builders' Wage Rates', *Economica*, 2nd ser. xxiii (1956): reprinted in *Essays in Econ. Hist.* ed. E. M. Carus-Wilson, ii (London, 1962).

[216] PIRENNE, H., *Les Villes et les institutions urbaines* (2 vols., Paris and Brussels, 1939).

[217] PIRENNE, H., *Mohammed and Charlemagne* (London, 1940; pub. in Fr. 1937).

[218] PIRENNE, H., *Medieval Cities : their Origins and the Revival of Trade* (Princeton, 1925).

[219] PLANITZ, H., *Die deutsche Stadt im Mittelalter* (Graz, 1954).

[220] PLATT, C., *The English Medieval Town* (London, 1976).

[221] POLLOCK, F. and MAITLAND, F. W., *The History of English Law before the Time of Edward I* (Cambridge, 2nd edn. 1911).

[222] POOLE, A. L., *From Domesday Book to Magna Carta* (Oxford, 1951).

[223] POSTAN, M. M., *Essays on Medieval Agriculture and General Problems of the Medieval Economy* (Cambridge, 1973).

[224] POSTAN, M. M., *The Medieval Economy and Society* (London, 1972).

[225] POWER, E., *The Medieval English Wool Trade* (Oxford, 1941).

[226] POWER, E. and POSTAN, M. M. ed., *Studies in English Trade in the Fifteenth Century* (London, 1933).

[227] POWICKE, F. M., *King Henry III and the Lord Edward* (2 vols. Oxford, 1947).

[228] PROU, M., 'Une ville-marché au xiie siècle', in *Mélanges d'histoire offerts à H. Pirenne*, ii (Brussels, 1926).

[229] RASHDALL, H., *The Universities of Europe in the Middle Ages*, ed. F. M. Powicke and A. B. Emden (Oxford, 1936).

[230] REANEY, P. H., *The Origin of English Surnames* (London, 1967).

[231] REIMANN, H., *Unruhe und Aufruhr im mittelalterlichen Braunschweig* (Brunswick, 1962).

[232] REINHARD, M. R., ARMENGAUD, A., and DUPAQUIER, J., *Histoire générale de la population mondiale* (Paris, 3rd edn. 1968).

[233] REYNOLDS, R. L., 'In Search of a Business Class in Thirteenth-century Genoa', *Jnl. Ec. Hist.* suppl. 5 (1945).

[234] REYNOLDS, R. L., 'Some English Settlers in Genoa', *Ec.H.R.* iv (1933).

[235] RICH, E. E., 'The Mayors of the Staples', *Cambridge Hist. Jnl.* iv (1933).

[236] RICHARDSON, H. G., *The English Jewry under the Angevin Kings* (London, 1960).

[237] ROGERS, 'Parish Boundaries and Urban History', *Jnl. of Brit. Archaeol. Assoc.* 3rd ser. xxxv (1972).

[238] RUSSELL, J. C., *British Medieval Population* (Albuquerque, 1948).

[239] SALUSBURY-JONES, G. T., *Street Life in Medieval England* (Oxford, 1938).

[240] SAWYER, P. H., *The Age of the Vikings* (London, 2nd edn. 1971).

[241] SAWYER, P. H., 'The Wealth of England in the Eleventh Century', *T.R.H.S.* 5th ser. xx (1965).

[242] SCAMMELL, G. V., 'English Merchant Shipping at the End of the Middle Ages: Some East Coast Evidence', *Ec.H.R.* 2nd ser. xiii (1960–1).

[243] SCAMMELL, G. V., 'Shipowning in England, *c.* 1450–1550', *T.R.H.S.* 5th ser. xii (1962).

[244] SCHLESINGER, W., *Beiträge zur deutschen Verfassungsgeschichte des Mittelalters* (2 vols., Göttingen, 1963).

[245] SCHLESINGER, W., 'Stadt und Burg im Lichte der Wortgeschichte', *Studium Generale*, xvi (1963).

[246] SCHOFIELD, R. S., 'The Geographical Distribution of Wealth in England, 1334–1649', *Ec.H.R.* 2nd ser. xviii (1965).

[247] SCHOFIELD, R. S., 'Historical Demography: Possibilities and Limitations', *T.R.H.S.* 5th ser. xxi (1971).

[248] SMITH, A. H., *English Place-Name Elements* (Eng. Place-Name Soc. xxv, xxvi, 1956).

[249] SOUTHERN, R. W., *The Making of the Middle Ages* (London, 1953).

[250] SOUTHERN, R. W., *Western Society and the Church in the Middle Ages* (Harmondsworth, 1970).

[251] STEERS, J. A., *The Coastline of England and Wales* (Cambridge, 2nd edn. 1964).

[252] STENTON, D. M., *English Society in the Early Middle Ages* (London, 1951).

[253] STENTON, F. M., *Anglo-Saxon England* (Oxford, 3rd edn. 1971).

[254] STENTON, F. M., *The First Century of English Feudalism, 1066–1166* (Oxford, 3rd edn. 1971).

[255] STEPHENSON, C., *Borough and Town* (Cambridge, Mass., 1933).

[256] STRAHM, H., 'Stadluft macht frei', in *Das Problem der Freiheit*, ed. T. Mayer (Vorträge und Forschungen, ii, 1953).

[257] SUMPTION, J., *Pilgrimage: an Image of Mediaeval Religion* (London, 1975).

[258] TAIT, J., *The Medieval English Borough* (Manchester, 1936).

[259] TANNER, N. P., 'Popular Religion in Norwich with Special Reference to the Evidence of Wills, 1370–1532' (unpublished D. Phil. thesis, Oxford, 1973).

[260] THOMAS, J. H., *Town Government in the Sixteenth Century* (London, 1933).

[261] THOMPSON, A. H., *The English Clergy and their Organization in the Later Middle Ages* (Oxford, 1947).

[262] THOMPSON, J. A. F., *The Later Lollards* (Oxford, 1965).

[263] THRUPP, S. L., 'The Alien Population in England in 1440', *Speculum*, xxxii (1957).

[264] THRUPP, S. L., 'Medieval Gilds Reconsidered', *Jnl.Ec.H.* ii (1942).

[265] THRUPP, S. L., 'The Problem of Replacement Rates in Late Medieval English Population', *Ec. H. R.* 2nd ser. xviii (1965).

[266] TURNER, H. L., *Town Defences in England and Wales, 900–1500* (London, 1971).

[267] UNGUREANU, M., *La Bourgeoisie Naissante* (Arras, 1955).

[268] VEALE, E. M., *The English Fur Trade in the Later Middle Ages* (Oxford, 1966).

[269] VERHULST, A., 'La Laine indigène dans les anciens Pays Bas', *Rev. hist.* ccxlviii (1972).

[270] VERHULST, A., 'L'Économie rurale et la depression du bas moyen âge', *Études Rurales*, x (1963).

[271] VERMEESCH, A., *Essai sur les origines et la signification de la commune dans le nord de la France* (Heule, 1966).

[272] *V. C. H. of Essex*, i (1903), ed. H. A. Doubleday and W. Page. Introduction to Domesday by J. H. Round.

[273] *V. C. H. of Wiltshire*, ed. R. B. Pugh and E. Crittall, ii (1955): Anglo-Saxon Wiltshire, by R. R. Darlington.

[274] WACHER, J. S., *The Towns of Roman Britain* (London, 1975).

[275] WALEY, D., *The Italian City Republics* (London, 1969).

[276] WEBB, S. and B., *English Local Government*, ii (London, 1908).

[277] WEINBAUM, M., *The Incorporation of Boroughs* (Manchester, 1936).

[278] WESTLAKE, H. F., *The Parish Gilds of Mediaeval England* (London, 1919).

[279] WILLARD, J. F., 'Taxation Boroughs and Parliamentary Boroughs' in *Historical Essays in Honour of James Tait* (Manchester, 1933).

[280] WITT, R. G., 'The Landlord and the Economic Revival of the Middle Ages in Northern Europe, 1000–1250', *Am. H. R.* lxxvi (1971).

[281] WOLFF, P., 'Les Luttes sociales dans les villes du midi français', *Annales E. S. C.* ii (1947).

[282] WOOD, M., *The English Medieval House* (London, 1965).

[283] WOOD-LEGH, K., *Perpetual Chantries in Britain* (Cambridge, 1965).

[284] WRIGLEY, E. A., *Population and History* (London, 1969).

[285] YOUNG, C. R., *The English Borough and Royal Administration, 1130–1307* (Durham, N. Carol., 1961).

II. INDIVIDUAL TOWNS

Abingdon

[286] BIDDLE, M., LAMBRICK, G., and MYRES, J. N. L., 'The Early History of Abingdon and its Abbey', *Med. Arch.* xii (1968).

[287] LAMBRICK, G., 'The Impeachment of the Abbot of Abingdon', *E. H. R.* lxxxii (1967).

Alnwick

[288] CONZEN, M. R. G., *Alnwick, Northumberland: A Study in Town-Plan Analysis* (Inst. of Brit. Geographers, xxvii, 1960).

Barnstaple

[289] REYNOLDS, S., 'The Forged Charters of Barnstaple', *E. H. R.* lxxxiv (1969).

Beverley

[290] *Beverley Town Documents*, ed. A. F. Leach (Selden Soc. xiv, 1900).

Bristol

[291] *Bristol Charters, 1378–1499*, ed. H. A. Cronne (Bristol Rec. Soc. xi, 1946).

[292] FULLER, E. A., 'The Tallage of 6 Edward II and the Bristol Rebellion', *Trans. Bristol and Glos. Arch. Soc.* xiv (1894–5).

[293] *The Little Red Book of Bristol*, ed. F. Bickley (2 vols., Bristol, 1900).

[294] LOBEL, M. D. and CARUS-WILSON, E. M., 'Bristol', in *The Atlas of Historic Towns*, ii, ed. M. D. Lobel and W. H. Johns (London, 1975).

[295] SHERBORNE, J. W., *The Port of Bristol in the Middle Ages* (Bristol, 1965).

[296] *The Staple Court Books of Bristol*, ed. E. E. Rich (Bristol Rec. Soc. v, 1934).

[297] WILLIAM of Malmesbury, *Vita Wulfstani*, ed. R. R. Darlington (Camden Soc. 3rd ser. xl, 1928).

Bury St. Edmunds

[298] DAVIS, H. W. C., 'The Commune of Bury St. Edmunds', *E. H. R.* xxiv (1909).

[299] JOCELIN of Brakelond, *Chronicle*, ed. and trans. H. E. Butler (London, 1949).

[300] LOBEL, M. D., *The Commune of Bury St. Edmunds* (Oxford, 1935).

Cambridge

[301] *V. C. H. of Cambridgeshire*, iii, ed. J. P. C. Roach (1959).

Canterbury

[302] JENKINS, F., 'St. Martin's Church at Canterbury', *Med. Arch.* ix (1965).

[303] URRY, W., *Canterbury under the Angevin Kings* (London, 1967).

Chester

[304] *Cheshire in the Pipe Rolls* (Lancs. and Ches. Rec. Soc. xcii (1938)).

[305] *Chester County Court Rolls* (Chetham Soc. lxxxiv (1925)).

[306] DOLLEY, R. H. M., 'The Mint of Chester', *Jnl. Chester Arch. and Hist. Soc.* xlii (1955).

[307] WEBSTER, G., 'Chester in the Dark Ages', *Jnl. Chester Arch. and Hist. Soc.* xxxviii (1951).

[308] WILSON, K. P., 'The Port of Chester in the Fifteenth Century', *Trans. Hist. Soc. of Lancs. and Ches.* xvii (1965).

Colchester

[309] MARTIN, G. H., *The Story of Colchester* (Colchester, 1959)

[310] *The Red Paper Book of Colchester*, ed. W. G. Benham (Colchester, 1902)

Coventry

[311] CAZEL, F. A., review of J. C. Lancaster, *Godiva of Coventry* in *Am. H. R.* lxxiv (1968), pp. 135–6.

[312] COSS, P. R., 'Coventry before Incorporation: a Reinterpretation', *Midland History*, ii (1974).

[313] *The Coventry Leet Book*, ed. M. D. Harris (Early Eng. Text Soc. cxxxiv–cxxxvi, cxlvi, 1907–13)

[314] DAVIS, R. H. C., 'An Unknown Coventry Charter', *E. H. R.* lxxxvi (1971).

[315] LANCASTER, J. C., 'Coventry', in *The Atlas of Historic Towns*, ii, ed. M. D. Lobel and W. H. Johns (London, 1975).

[316] ROBERT of Gloucester, *Metrical Chronicle*, ed. W. A. Wright (Rolls Series, 1887).

[317] *V. C. H. of Warwickshire*, viii, ed. W. B. Stephens (1969).

Dunstable

[318] *The Taxation of 1297*, ed. A. T. Gaydon (Beds. Hist. Rec. Soc. xxxix (1958)).

[319] *V. C. H. of Bedfordshire*, iii, ed. W. Page (1912).

Exeter

[320] CARUS-WILSON, E. M., *The Expansion of Exeter at the Close of the Middle Ages* (Exeter, 1963).

[321] FOX, A., *Roman Exeter* (Manchester, 1952).

[322] GRIFFITHS, M. and BIDWELL, P., *Cathedral Close Excavations* (Exeter City Archaeological Field Unit Report, 1973).

[323] JACKSON, A. M., 'Medieval Exeter', *Trans. Devon Assoc.* civ (1972).

[324] WILKINSON, B. and EASTERLING, R. C., *The Mediaeval Council of Exeter* (Manchester, 1931).

Gloucester

[325] HURST, H., 'Excavations at Gloucester, 1968–71: First Interim Report', *Ant. Jnl.* lii (1972).

Grimsby

[326] GILLETT, E., *A History of Grimsby* (London, 1970).

Ipswich

[327] MARTIN, G. H., 'The Borough and Merchant Community of Ipswich, 1317–1422' (unpublished D. Phil. thesis, Oxford, 1955).

[328] MARTIN, G. H., *The Early Court Rolls of Ipswich* (Leic. Univ. Dept. of Local Hist. Occasional Papers no. 5, 1954).

Kingston upon Hull

[329] *V.C.H. of Yorkshire: East Riding*, i, ed. K. J. Allison (1969).

Leicester

[330] MARTIN, G. H., 'Church Life in Medieval Leicester', in *The Growth of Leicester*, ed. A. E. Brown (Leicester, 1970).

[331] *The Records of the Borough of Leicester*, ed. M. Bateson, vol. i: *1103–1327* (London, 1899).

[332] *V. C. H. of Leicestershire*, iv, ed. R. A. McKinley (1958).

Lincoln

[333] HILL, J. W. F., *Medieval Lincoln* (Cambridge, 1948).

London

[334] BARRON, C. M., 'The Government of London and its Relations with the Crown, 1400–50' (unpublished London Ph.D. thesis, 1970).

[335] BARRON, C. M., *The Medieval Guildhall of London* (London, 1974).

[336] BARRON, C. M., 'Ralph Holland and the London Radicals, 1438–44', in *History of the North London Branch of the Historical Association*, ed. L. Snell (London, 1970).

[337] BARRON, C. M., 'Richard II and London, 1392–7' in *The Reign of Richard II*, ed. F. R. H. du Boulay and C. M. Barron (London, 1971).

[338] BARRON, C. M., 'Sir Richard Whittington', in *Studies in London History*, ed. A. E. J. Hollaender and W. Kellaway (London, 1969).

[339] BATESON, M., 'A London Municipal Collection of the Reign of John', *E.H.R.* xvii (1902).

[340] BIDDLE, M., HUDSON, D., and HEIGHWAY, C., *The Future of London's Past* (Worcester, 1973).

[341] BIRD, R., *The Turbulent London of Richard II* (London, 1949).

[342] BROOKE, C. N. L., KEIR, G., and REYNOLDS, S., 'Henry I's Charter for London', *Jnl. of Soc. of Archivists*, iv (1973).

[343] *Calendar of Early Mayor's Court Rolls of the City of London*, ed. A. H. Thomas (London, 1924).

[344] *Calendars of Letter Books of the City of London: A to L*, ed. R. R. Sharpe (11 vols., London, 1899–1912).

[345] *Calendars of the Plea and Memoranda Rolls of the City of London, 1323–1482*, ed. A. H. Thomas and others (6 vols., London, 1926–61).

[346] *Chronicles of the Reigns of Edward I and Edward II*, ed. W. Stubbs (2 vols., Rolls Series, 1882–3).

[347] *Croniques de London*, ed. G. J. Aungier (Camden Soc. 1st ser. xxviii, 1844).

[348] *De Antiquis Legibus Liber : Cronica Maiorum et Vicecomitum Londoniarum*, ed. T. Stapleton (Camden Soc. 1st ser. xxxiv, 1846).

[349] EKWALL, E., *Early London Personal Names* (Lund, 1947).

[350] EKWALL, E., *Studies on the Population of Medieval London* (Stockholm, 1956).

[351] EKWALL, E., *Street Names of the City of London* (Oxford, 1954).

[352] GRIMES, W. G., *The Excavation of Roman and Mediaeval London* (London, 1968).

[353] IMRAY, J. M., 'The Membership of the Mercers' Company', in *Studies in London History*, ed. A. E. J. Hollaender and W. Kellaway (London, 1969).

[354] LETHBRIDGE, T. C., 'Anglo-Saxon Settlement in Eastern England', in *Dark-Age Britain. Studies presented to E. T. Leeds*, ed. D. B. Harden (London, 1956).

[355] *London Assize of Nuisance, 1301–1431*, ed. H. M. Chew and W. Kellaway (London Rec. Soc. x, 1973).

[356] *The London Eyre of 1244*, ed. H. M. Chew and M. Weinbaum (London Rec. Soc. vi, 1970).

[357] *Munimenta Gildhallae Londoniensis*, ed. H. T. Riley (3 vols., Rolls Series, 1859–62).

[358] REYNOLDS, S., 'The Farm and Taxes of London', *Guildhall Studies in London History*, i (1975).

[359] REYNOLDS, S., 'The Rulers of London in the Twelfth Century', *History*, lvii (1972).

[360] SABINE, E. L., 'Butchering', 'Latrines and Cesspools', and 'City Cleaning in Mediaeval London', *Speculum*, viii, ix, xii (1933–7).

[361] STENTON, F. M., 'Norman London', in *Social Life in Early Eng.* ed. G. Barraclough (London, 1960: pub. as Hist. Assoc. pamphlet, 1934).

[362] STOW, J., *The Survey of London*, ed. C. L. Kingsford (2 vols., Oxford, 1908).

[363] THOMPSON, J. A. F., 'Tithe Disputes in Late Medieval London', *E.H.R.*, lxxviii (1963).

[364] THRUPP, S. L., *The Merchant Class of Medieval London* (Ann Arbor, 1948).

[365] *Two Early London Subsidy Rolls*, ed. E. Ekwall (Lund, 1951).

[366] UNWIN, G., *The Gilds and Companies of London* (London, 3rd edn. 1938).

[367] VEALE, E. M., 'Craftsmen and the Economy of London in the Fourteenth Century', in *Studies in London History*, ed. A. E. J. Hollaender and W. Kellaway (London, 1969).

[368] *V.C.H. of London*, i, ed. W. Page (1909): Ecclesiastical History.

[369] *Vitae Sancti Bonifatii*, ed. W. Levison (Mon. Germ. Hist., Scriptores Rerum Germ., 1905).

[370] WEINBAUM, M., *London unter Eduard I und II* (2 vols., Stuttgart, 1933).

[371] WHEELER, R. E. M., *London and the Saxons* (London Museum Catalogues, vi (1935)).

[372] WILLIAMS, G. A., 'London, 1216–1337' (unpublished Ph.D. thesis, London, 1960).

[373] WILLIAMS, G. A., *Medieval London: From Commune to Capital* (London, 1963).

[374] WRIGLEY, E. A., 'A Simple Model of London's Importance in Changing English Society and Economy, 1650–1750', *P. & P.* 37 (1967).

[375] *Year Book 1 & 2 Edward II* (Selden Soc. xvii, 1903).

Ludlow

[376] HOPE, W. H. St. J., 'The Ancient Topography of Ludlow', *Archaeologia*, lxi (1909).

[377] *V.C.H. of Shropshire*, ii, ed. A. T. Gaydon (1973): Ludlow Palmers' Guild.

Lynn, King's (formerly Bishop's)

[378] Historical MSS. Commission, *Eleventh Report* (1887), appendix 3.

[379] PARKER, V., *The Making of King's Lynn* (London, 1971).

Newcastle upon Tyne

[380] BLAKE, J. B., 'The Medieval Coal Trade of the North East', *Northern History*, ii (1967).

[381] FRASER, C. M., 'Medieval Trading Restrictions in the North East', *Archaeologia Aeliana*, 4th ser. xxxix (1961).

Northampton

[382] PEVSNER, N. and CHERRY, B., *The Buildings of England: Northamptonshire*, 2nd edn. (London, 1973).

[383] RICHARDSON, H. G., 'The Schools of Northampton', *E.H.R.* lvi (1941).

[384] *V.C.H. of Northamptonshire*, iii (1930): the Borough of Northampton, by H. M. Cam.

Norwich

[385] CAMPBELL, J., 'Norwich', in *The Atlas of Historic Towns*, ii, ed. M. D. Lobel and W. H. Johns (London, 1975).

[386] *Leet Jurisdiction in the City of Norwich*, ed. W. Hudson (Selden Soc. v (1892)).

[387] MYRES, J. N. L. and GREEN, B., *The Anglo-Saxon Cemeteries of Caistor by Norwich and Markshall* (London, 1973).

[388] POUND, J. F., 'The Social and Trade Structure of Norwich, 1525–75', *P. & P.* 34 (1966).

[389] *The Records of the City of Norwich*, ed. W. Hudson and J. C. Tingey (2 vols., Norwich, 1906–10).

TANNER, N. P., 'Popular Religion in Norwich': see above—[259].

Nottingham

[390] *The Records of the Borough of Nottingham*, ed. W. H. Stevenson, vol. i: *1155–1399* (London and Nottingham, 1882).

Oxford

[391] DAVIS, R. H. C., 'The Ford, the River, and the City', *Oxoniensia*, xxxviii (1974).

[392] DAVIS, R. H. C., 'An Oxford Charter of 1191', *Oxoniensia*, xxxiii (1968).

[393] JOPE, E. M., 'Saxon Oxford and its Region', in *Dark-Age Britain*, ed. D. B. Harden (London, 1956).

[394] LOBEL, M. D., 'Medieval Oxford', *Oxoniensia*, iii (1938).

[395] PANTIN, W. A., 'Before Wolsey', in *Historical Essays presented to Keith Feiling* (Oxford, 1964).

[396] PANTIN, W. A., *Oxford Life in Oxford Archives* (Oxford, 1972).

[397] *V.C.H. Oxfordshire*, iii, ed. H. E. Salter and M. D. Lobel (1954): The University of Oxford.

Pevensey

[398] DULLEY, A. J. F., 'Excavations at Pevensey, 1962–6', *Med. Arch.* xi (1967).

[399] DULLEY, A. J. F., 'The Level and Port of Pevensey in the Middle Ages', *Suss. Arch. Coll.* civ (1966).

Ravenserodd

[400] *Chronica Monasterii de Melsa*, ed. E. A. Bond (3 vols., Rolls Series, 1866–8).

Reading

[401] SLADE, C. F., 'Reading', in *Historic Towns*, i, ed. M. D. Lobel (London, 1969).

[402] *V.C.H. of Berkshire*, iii, ed. W. Page and P. H. Ditchfield (1923).

Romney

[403] BUTCHER, A. F., 'The Origins of Romney Freemen', *Ec.H.R.* 2nd ser. xxvii (1974).

St. Albans

[404] *V.C.H. of Hertfordshire*, ed. W. Page, ii (1908), iv (1914).

[405] WALSINGHAM, Thomas, *Gesta Abbatum Monasterii Sancti Albani*, ed. H. T. Riley (3 vols., Rolls Series, 1867–9).

St. Ives (Hunts.)

[406] *V.C.H. of Huntingdonshire*, ii, ed. W. Page and others (1932).

Salisbury

[407] ROGERS, K. H., 'Salisbury', in *Historic Towns*, i, ed. M. D. Lobel (London, 1969).

[408] *V.C.H. of Wiltshire*, ed. R. B. Pugh and E. Crittall, iii (1956): St. Nicholas' Hospital and De Vaux College, Salisbury; iv (1959): Roads.

Scarborough

[409] HEATH, P., 'North Sea Fishing in the Fifteenth Century: the Scarborough fleet', *Northern Hist.* iii (1968).

[410] *Three Yorkshire Assize Rolls*, ed. C. T. Clay (Yorks. Arch. Soc. Rec. Ser. xliv, 1911).

Southampton

[411] ADDYMAN, P. V., 'Anglo-Saxon Southampton', in *Vor- und Frühformen der europäischen Stadt im Mittelalter*, i, ed. H. Jankuhn and others (Abhandlungen der Akademie der Wissenschaften in Göttingen, 3rd ser. lxxxiii, 1973).

[412] ADDYMAN, P. V. and HILL, D. H., 'Saxon Southampton', *Proc. Hants. Field Club and Arch. Soc.* xxv, xxvi (1968–9).

[413] BURGESS, L. A., *The Origins of Southampton* (Univ. of Leic. Dept. of Eng. Local Hist. Occasional Papers no. 16, 1964).

[414] COLEMAN, O., 'Trade and Prosperity in the Fifteenth Century: Aspects of the Trade of Southampton', *Ec.H.R.* 2nd ser. xvi (1963–4).

[415] DOLLEY, R. H. M., 'The Location of the pre-Alfredian Mints of Wessex', *Proc. Hants. Field Club and Arch. Soc.* xxvii (1970).

[416] PLATT, C., *Medieval Southampton* (London, 1973).

[417] RUDDOCK, A., *Italian Merchants and Shipping in Southampton, 1270–1600* (Southampton Record Series, 1951).

[418] *Third Book of Remembrance of Southampton*, ed. A. L. Merson, i (Southampton Record Series, 1952).

Stamford

[419] ROGERS, A. ed., *The Making of Stamford* (Leicester, 1965).

[420] ROGERS, A., *The Medieval Buildings of Stamford* (Nottingham, 1970).

[421] *V.C.H. of Lincolnshire*, ii, ed. W. Page (1906): Religious Houses.

Stratford upon Avon

[422] CARUS-WILSON, E. M., 'The First Half Century of Stratford upon Avon', *Ec.H.R.* 2nd ser. xvii (1965).

Thame

[423] *V.C.H. of Oxfordshire*, vii, ed. M. D. Lobel (1962).

Thaxted

[424] NEWTON, K. C., *Thaxted in the Fourteenth Century* (Chelmsford, 1960).

Thetford

[425] DAVISON, B. K., 'The Late Saxon Town of Thetford: Interim Report on Excavations, 1964–6', *Med. Arch.* xi (1967).

Wallingford

[426] HERBERT, N. M., 'The Borough of Wallingford, 1155–1460' (unpublished Ph.D. thesis, Reading, 1971).

Wilton

[427] *V.C.H. Wiltshire*, vi, ed. E. Crittall (1962): the Borough of Wilton, by M. K. James.

Winchester

[428] BIDDLE, M., 'Excavations at Winchester': reports in *Arch. Jnl.* cxix (1962) and *Ant. Jnl.* xliv–(1964–).

[429] BIDDLE, M., 'Winchester: the Development of an Early Capital', in *Vor- und Frühformen der europäischen Stadt im Mittelalter*, i, ed. H. Jankuhn and others (Abhandlungen der Akademie der Wissenschaften in Göttingen, 3rd ser. lxxxiii, 1973).

[430] KEENE, D. J., 'Some Aspects of the History, Topography and Archaeology of the North-eastern Part of the City of Winchester with Special Reference to the Brooks Area' (unpublished D.Phil. thesis, Oxford, 1972).

[431] *V.C.H. of Hampshire*, i (1900): The Winchester Survey, by J. H. Round; v (1912): Winchester.

Windsor

[432] BOND, S., 'The Medieval Constitution of New Windsor', *Berks. Archaeol. Jnl.* lxv (1970).

Worcester

[433] BARKER, P., and others, 'The Origins of Worcester' *Trans. Worcs. Arch. Soc.* 3rd ser. ii, 1968–9).

[434] DYER, A. D., *The City of Worcester in the Sixteenth Century* (Leicester, 1973).

York

[435] ADDYMAN, P. V., 'Excavations in York, 1972–3: First Interim Report', *Ant. Jnl.* liv (1974).

[436] BARTLETT, J. N., 'The Expansion and Decline of York in the Later Middle Ages', *Ec.H.R.* 2nd ser. xii (1959–60).

[437] CRAMP, R., *Anglian and Viking York* (Borthwick Inst. of Hist. Research Paper no. 33, York, 1967).

[438] DOBSON, R. B., 'Admissions to the Freedom of the City of York in the Later Middle Ages', *Ec.H.R.* xxvi (1973).

[439] *The Historians of the Church of York and its Archbishops*, ed. J. Raine (3 vols., Rolls Series, 1879–94).

[440] JOHNSTON, A. F., 'The Plays of the Religious Guilds of York', *Speculum*, l (1975).

[441] RADLEY, J., 'Economic Aspects of Anglo-Danish York', *Med. Arch.* xv (1971).

[442] RAMM, H. G., 'A Case of Twelfth-Century Town Planning in York', *Yorks. Archaeol. Jnl.* xlii (1968).

[443] Royal Commission on Historical Monuments (England), *City of York*, iii, iv (1972–5).

[444] *V.C.H. of Yorkshire: The City of York*, i, ed. P. M. Tillott (1961): Medieval York, by E. Miller.

Index

Reynolds, Susan.

An introduction to
the history of
English medieval
towns

DATE			
Jan 07	again ——→2010		